KEY STAGE 2 / SCOTTISH LEVELS C–E

NON-FICTION
Writing Projects

SUE ELLIS, GILL FRIEL,
ELAINE WYLLIE, CATRIONA MACKENZIE,
JIM ALLAN & GILLIAN FLEMING

Published by Scholastic Ltd,
Villiers House,
Clarendon Avenue,
Leamington Spa,
Warwickshire CV32 5PR

2 3 4 5 6 7 8 9 0   9 0 1 2 3 4 5 6

Project Consultants
Sue Ellis and Gill Friel

Authors
Sue Ellis, Gill Friel, Elaine Wyllie, Catriona Mackenzie, Jim Allan and Gillian Fleming

Editor
Irene Goodacre

Series Designer
Joy White

Designer
Blade Communications Ltd

Illustrations
Caroline Ewen

Cover illustration
Joy White

Designed using Aldus Pagemaker

British Library Cataloguing-in-Publication Date
A catalogue record for this book
is available from the British Library.

ISBN 0-590-53475-0

Scholastic WORKSHOP

Contents

ACKNOWLEDGEMENTS

The publishers gratefully acknowledge permission to reproduce the following copyright material:

David Higham Associates for extracts from *Boy* by Roald Dahl © Roald Dahl (Puffin). **Peters Fraser and Dunlop** for the use of an extract from *Cider With Rosie* by Laurie Lee © 1970, Laurie Lee (1970, Penguin) and an extract from *I Can't Stay Long* © 1977, Laurie Lee (1977, Penguin). **Larousse Plc** for the use of an extract from *Scots School Dictionary,* edited by Iseabail MacLeod and Pauline Cairns © 1996, The Scottish Dictionary Association Ltd (1996, Chambers). Grateful thanks also go to Harper Collins for allowing use of a press release.

Every effort has been made to trace the copyright holders for the works reproduced in this book and the publishers apologise for any inadvertent omissions.

The authors would like to thank the children of Fintry Primary School, Fintry who helped in the development of these writing ideas.

Chapter One

INTRODUCTION

TEACHING NON-FICTION WRITING

This book has been produced to help teachers plan work that ensures that children:
- write effectively in a range of genres;
- write for a range of audiences and purposes, producing a variety of written products such as posters, letters, books, newspapers and reports;
- use writing as a tool for living, to plan, remember and articulate their ideas.

Writing for real

If children are to learn to write effectively and to use writing as a tool for thinking, they need opportunities to 'write for real'. If the learning context prompts genuine reasons for writing, children learn to regard writing as a natural tool to assist their thinking and as a powerful way to influence others. To achieve this, the context must ensure that children write for real people whom they know will read their work because they want, or need to, rather than to mark or correct it. When this sense of purpose and audience permeates the context, it drives the writing process. The children become emotionally involved in writing and care that it makes sense to the reader.

A sense of audience

Children's understanding of audience needs to be deeper than simply identifying potential readers and why they will read their work. They must realise that written messages can be interpreted differently by different readers and that this must be considered as they write.

Many children need to clarify the readers' likely previous knowledge and expectations and they need time to discuss the implications of this for what they say and how they will say it. They need to think about the readers' interpretations as they rehearse and plan, as they re-read and re-draft their work and as they watch others reading and evaluating their work. In this way children learn from observation of, and discussion with, their readers – and they learn to reflect on their writing and use this to inform future work.

The process approach and genre theory

A process approach to writing focuses on the child as a writer. The quality of the finished product and an analysis of its strengths and weaknesses can give some clues about what a writer needs to learn, but not the complete picture. The teacher needs to notice:
- how each child goes about his or her work;
- what the child wants to write about and express;
- aspects that come easily and others that prove more difficult;
- what the child finds satisfying and frustrating.

Once these have been identified the teaching can be targeted accurately.

The process approach highlights two important teaching elements. Firstly, that through the experience of writing, children learn specific techniques for different types of writing and develop skills in using language effectively. Secondly, that through the experience of writing children learn how writers go about their work. They need to be shown and encouraged to use a range of useful strategies to rehearse ideas, then to plan, draft, edit, publish and share their work.

The genre writing approach focuses on the nature of the written product. Writing can serve a multitude of purposes and each purpose employs distinct linguistic structures and vocabulary. Teachers need to know about these if they are to discuss with the children the strengths and weaknesses of their writing in a way that will move them forward in their understanding. Without such a framework it can be hard to know what to comment on in the children's work or to plan to ensure an appropriately balanced coverage. Young writers may benefit from being explicitly taught about the different genres and their typical characteristics.

This book introduces a wide range of genres within meaningful contexts, thus helping the teacher to ensure coverage in a way that works from and through the children's understandings and interests.

Context, content and process

Recent moves towards non-integrated curricula have raised questions about the relative importance of context, content and process. If content knowledge is only taught through decontextualised one-off activities, the children's learning may be superficial. Lack of opportunity to explore, re-frame, integrate and apply the content issues means that children do not learn how to use what they know and teachers are less likely to discover where ideas have only been half-understood.

Non-fiction writing: what children need to learn

Children clearly need to learn about the different purposes for writing and the typical characteristics of each. They also need to:

- communicate their ideas to real readers in a variety of appropriate contexts;
- learn to select genres that are appropriate for their purposes;
- use writing as a life skill so that they know how to take notes and make lists, charts and brainstorms;
- appreciate how writing can help them to clarify, remember and organise ideas or to recognise options and connections;
- understand the process of writing – the strategies writers use and how and when these may be helpful, as well as how to improve their writing by discussion, observation, reflection and evaluation of their own and others' work.

Each project has been designed to provide real and important reasons for writing and each integrates a variety of writing purposes, audiences and genres. Where appropriate, the projects involve incidental writing so that children learn to use writing as a tool for life, deciding when perfect presentation is, and is not, important. Feedback, evaluation and reflection are central to the learning process and to the projects; the children witness others reading and commenting on their work and are encouraged to read and discuss their own and others' writing in a variety of ways.

The subject matter: generic events, language and curricular topics

Non-fiction writing permeates the curriculum. The projects in this book incorporate three basic kinds of topic content:

- Generic events that happen in all schools such as parties, clean-up days and thank-you celebrations.
- Common curricular topics which can be implemented as they stand or serve as models giving ideas which can be adapted to any topic area.
- Language-focused topics which concentrate on literacy and knowledge about language.

In this way, the projects provide contexts that can dovetail with the school's current work without unduly overloading either children or teachers by demanding that large areas of the curriculum are covered in certain ways. The topic focus of each project is indicated on the chart on pages 8–9.

Title and focus	Star rating and Collaborative demands	Approximate length/ number of sessions	Recount	Report	Persuasive	Procedural	Explanatory	Writing as work/life skill	Publication formats	Evaluation and Celebration
Dinosaurs alive! Science	low	11 sessions 2 weeks		✔		✔	✔	structure and features of a reference book	book	book display worksheets with younger children
Planning a party Generic	low-medium	9 sessions 2 weeks	option	option	✔	✔	option	lists; brainstorms	lists; posters; invitations; Option: book; photo album	groups from class; adults invited to party
Children's holiday guide Environmental studies	low	7 sessions 1–2 weeks		✔	✔	✔		brainstorms	holiday brochures in presentation folder	class groups; local tourist officer
Sweet success Environmental studies	medium	12 sessions 2 weeks	✔		✔	✔	✔	brainstorms; lists	book; quest-ionnaires; rules; posters; instruction sheets	class book read by all in the class
Let's clean it up Environmental studies	medium	8 sessions 5 weeks	✔		✔	✔	✔	lists; questions	posters; question-naire; reports	peers, parents and staff of school
Autobiography Language	low-medium	16+ sessions 4–5 weeks	✔		✔		✔	notes; lists; brainstorms	padded book	written review by adult im-portant to child

Title and focus	Star rating and Collaborative demands	Approximate length/ number of sessions	Recount	Report	Persuasive	Procedural	Explanatory	Writing as work/life skill	Publication formats	Evaluation and Celebration
Making a class newspaper Language/ technology	medium-high	10 sessions 2 weeks	✔	✔	✔	✔	✔	lists	newspaper	readers in school and community
This is your life! Personal project	medium	11 sessions 3–4 weeks	✔		✔		✔	lists; notes; discussion prompts; brainstorms	'This is your life' presentation book	ceremony for subject
Dialect dictionary Language	low	12 sessions 3 weeks			✔		✔	structure and features of a dictionary; press release; notes	local dialect dictionary	peer review; local societies and community
Healthy bite Environmental studies	medium-high	12 sessions 3–4 weeks	✔		✔		✔	logos; lists; notes	business plan; adverts; letters; posters; minutes; forms; interview criteria	customers in school; community sponsors
Bullying Generic	high	8 sessions 3 weeks	✔		✔			lists; questions; notes	interactive bullying pack for other classes; assembly	peer comments
Sport Personal project	low	11+ sessions 2 weeks		✔		✔	✔	planning lists	project book	reflection on research strategies and review by self and peers

Involving the whole class: enthusiasm through collaborative and individual work

The projects involve children in writing alone, in pairs and in groups and each has a different pattern of collaboration; sometimes children work in pairs or groups to produce a joint piece of work, sometimes they work individually to bring a different element to a group product, sometimes the group work precedes, informs and inspires individual writing.

It is important that children experience working in a variety of groupings. Through this, they learn that writing is both a social and an individual activity. They learn when, and how, discussion with others can be helpful. Collaborative activities provide a nurturing environment for learning, allowing children to support each other, so that each produces a finished product better than either could produce alone. Collaboration can also make the projects exciting and real. Children learn that writing is not a lonely task, that it can be fun and can cement friendships. This promotes emotional involvement, while the discussion involved in collaboration helps children to grasp fully what they know, what they can do, and what they have still to learn.

The importance of thinking time

If children are to become emotionally involved in their writing they need time to live with a project, to care about it and become committed to writing it well. This type of commitment does not develop quickly. If children are being asked to make real decisions about their writing, they need time to turn ideas over in their minds and weigh up the alternatives. Once the seed of an idea is sown, it will grow not only in class, but at home, in the playground, walking to the shops, or waiting in the dinner queue.

Each of the writing projects has been structured to ensure thinking time for the project as a whole, and for individual pieces of writing. Ideas are often initiated in one lesson and carried through to the next. Children are sometimes encouraged to discuss issues at home with specific people, or to notice and draw on models in the environment outside school for their own writing. In this way, each lesson provides a springboard for the next and children are drawn in gradually. The perfectly successful project is one in which the children work enthusiastically during class time, but which also infuses their lives and thoughts, both in school and outside it.

THE NON-FICTION PROJECTS

This book aims to provide outlines for work that enable teachers to plan projects that are interesting, well sequenced, and pertinent to school life. Each project covers a range of types of writing and will help teachers to build on strengths, integrate and use previous teaching content and to identify weaknesses that may require further teaching input and development.

The introduction to each project provides a brief overview of what the children will do and highlights the range of genres covered. This information is also summarised in the chart on pages 8–9.

Each project thus ensures the children have a broad and balanced experience of writing. They also write in a variety of registers – from very personal to highly formal – and produce a range of written products including posters, letters, speeches, notes and booklets.

Where to start: selecting and planning a project

The children's previous writing experience, their skill in working collaboratively and their likely enthusiasm for the project content will all influence the teacher's choice of project, along with the time available and the particular curricular areas that the class are due to cover. Obviously, teachers will also want to ensure that over the course of a year, children write in a variety of genres and for different purposes and audiences. The chart on pages 8–9 indicates, for each project, the topic or subject focus, the approximate time-scale, the collaborative demands, the main genres and writing skills covered, and the different readers, written products and evaluation formats involved. This will help teachers to select a writing project which addresses the needs of the class and will interest the children.

Planning time for the projects

If the ideas are to be given time to develop continuity and momentum, the writing projects should be treated as concentrated 'blocks' of work. If too much time is allowed to elapse between writing sessions, the children become demotivated; they forget where they have got to, lose the enthusiasm built up in the previous session and feel that the end of the project is a long time coming. Flexible timetabling that allows children between three and five sessions per week for a project is ideal. Subjects which receive little attention during the project can be given additional time before and after it. Both teachers and children will appreciate that one, concentrated project in which children are keen to write is far more effective and enjoyable than several shorter activities when unwilling children are cajoled and pushed into producing something on paper.

Drafting, editing and publishing

All the projects assume that children are familiar with the processes of drafting, editing and publishing work. If children in the class have not met these key ideas before, it is a good idea to introduce drafting as a class lesson before starting work on a project. The concepts and skills of editing and publishing can be introduced as children reach these stages.

Explain re-drafting by telling the children that often, when writers first start a piece of work, their main concern is to get their thoughts down on paper. At this point, the writer is not too concerned about neatness, handwriting, spelling, punctuation or even sequence. Explain that the act of writing often highlights where ideas are unclear or only partially understood. The redrafting process can help clarify this. Show the children some writing you have re-drafted yourself – perhaps a report, a letter or a forecast of work. There is no need to allow time for a close scrutiny of the contents, but use it to illustrate the point that everyone (even teachers) produces rough drafts and that all writers develop their own code for inserting additional bits, changing the sequence or altering large and small sections.

Explain that writers often find they have to re-read a script regularly to collect their thoughts and keep the narrative flowing. As they read, they frequently make alterations, crossing out sections, or re-writing them using stars, arrows or numbers to indicate where the new passage should fit in. Show the children your own techniques and ask them which, if any, of these methods they have used in the past and which they may use in the project ahead.

CLASSROOM MANAGEMENT

Working with the whole class

For the teacher, working with the whole class simplifies many time-consuming aspects of planning and collecting or organising resources. Simpler class management and organisation free the teacher to focus on observing, teaching and working alongside the children. Whole-class projects also help the teacher to build excitement and enthusiasm, to the point where the work develops its own emotional momentum.

Projects which involve the whole class also provide opportunities for children to work with different partners and groupings. The children then benefit from seeing and responding to a wider range of ideas than would be generated within a single group.

Organising the projects with a class

Many of the projects ask the children to work with a writing partner or in a small group. Bear in mind that it takes time to establish working relationships and children need to be familiar with each other's work if they are to offer informed advice. It is therefore important that they stay in the same pair or group for all activities within a project unless specifically stated otherwise.

It is better to allow children to choose a friend, or someone they will feel comfortable working with, rather than assigning a partner, although obviously, the teacher must retain the right to veto some pairings!

Children should, however, be encouraged to be involved with different partners and groups for each new project since this ensures that they work with a range of people in the class and benefit from different working relationships as well as the varied viewpoints and feedback these generate.

Resourcing and organising the work

Schools will already have most of the resources required for the writing projects. It is often useful if children can be given:

- files in which they can keep loose pieces of writing for future reference;
- drafting notebooks in which they can record ideas, make notes and first drafts.

These two items ensure that no work gets lost, while the notebooks can often provide interesting evidence of changes that the child has made to initial drafts and ideas. Notebooks can also provide a good focus for discussion and review, during which the teacher will learn about the child and the child will learn about writing.

Children will also need a good supply of appropriate resources if they are to take pride in the presentation of their work. For most projects, they will need:

- good quality paper on which to write or mount their writing;
- coloured pens and pencils for illustrations;
- a variety of shapes and sizes of paper suitable for writing and for illustrations;
- scissors, PVA adhesive and spreaders.

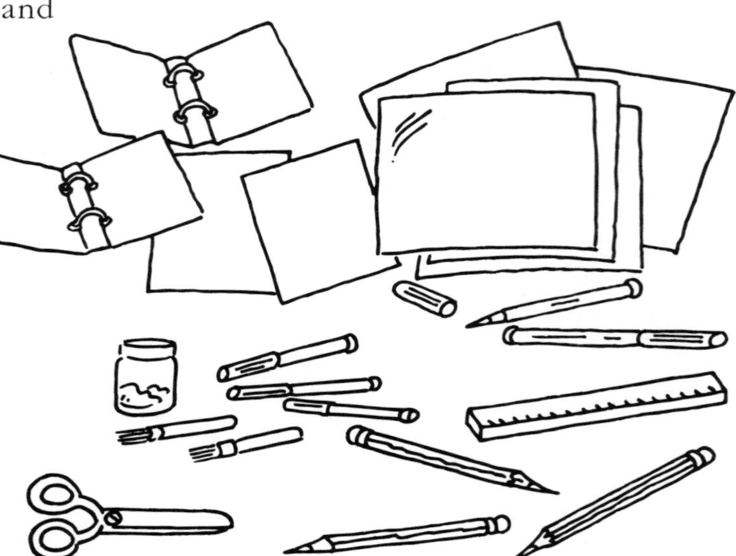

The project activities

The following information is given by icons at the start of each activity:

Class organisation details whether the children will be working individually, or in pairs, groups or as a class.

Time required gives an idea of how long each activity may take. Obviously this can only be a rough estimate and will be governed by individual teachers and classes.

Each activity has been structured under the following headings:

Teaching content explains the main teaching objectives of each activity.

What you need lists the resources required for the activity.

What to do explains exactly how to introduce and structure each lesson.

Scholastic WORKSHOP

Chapter Two

ASSESSMENT

ASSESSMENT

The non-fiction writing projects allow teachers to observe and work with children on their writing over a period of time and on different types of task. This allows them to form an assessment of each young writer that is informed by a rich variety of evidence.

Teachers who are interested in the children and knowledgeable about the process of writing and learning to write cannot help but notice different children's knowledge, skills or attitudes towards writing. These differences may be shown in the children's:

- confidence as writers;
- willingness to use writing as a tool for life; to help remember, organise or understand ideas;
- skill in note-taking, brainstorming, listing and so on;
- ability to select appropriate genres;
- confidence and skill in using particular genres;
- awareness of the power of writing to influence other people.

It is important that assessment and record-keeping should support teachers in analysing needs and providing appropriate teaching input and learning activities to develop each child's motivation, skills and understanding. It is, after all, this match that determines the speed at which children progress.

General assessment and record-keeping photocopiable pages

This chapter provides a number of generic assessment and record-keeping systems for use with the writing projects in this book. Teachers should use and adapt these to suit their own needs and the policies of the school.

Class/group project notes (page 16)

The class/group project notes are intended to provide an informal record of particular children who stood out during the writing project and why. Teachers should record their observations throughout the project.

The main genres are listed in the first box in the class notes. The teacher should refer to the chart on pages 8–9 and tick those genres that are covered in the particular writing project selected. There is also space to record the appropriate activity numbers as an additional reminder.

The second box provides space for teachers to comment on children's confidence, willingness and skill in using writing as a tool for thinking.

Individual project report (page 17)

The individual project report is intended to help teachers analyse work and identify appropriate support or challenges for the future. It targets three important areas:

- *The child as a writer.* This allows the teacher to comment on the general attitudes and confidence shown by an individual child during the writing project. Note any tasks for which the child showed enthusiasm or reluctance; her willingness and skill in using writing as a tool for life; when and why she needed help; achievements in collaborative and individual tasks and her understanding of purpose, audience and genres.

• *The quality of the written products.* This allows the teacher to use the genre framework to analyse the child's skill in selecting and using appropriate genres to communicate effectively.
• *Teacher-child discussion.* This allows the teacher to record and to comment on the child's ability to self-evaluate. It assumes the teacher has discussed as least some aspects of the writing project work with the child.
• *Next steps.* This allows the teacher to briefly note ideas for future teaching input in terms of whether the child would benefit from emphasis on aspects of context, content knowledge or process.

Teachers should choose when it is appropriate to do an individual project report. They should not feel the need to complete an individual report for every child in every project, although this may be useful if teacher and class are new to each other. Many teachers will choose to target particular groups of children for particular projects, planning to cover the whole class each term or half year.

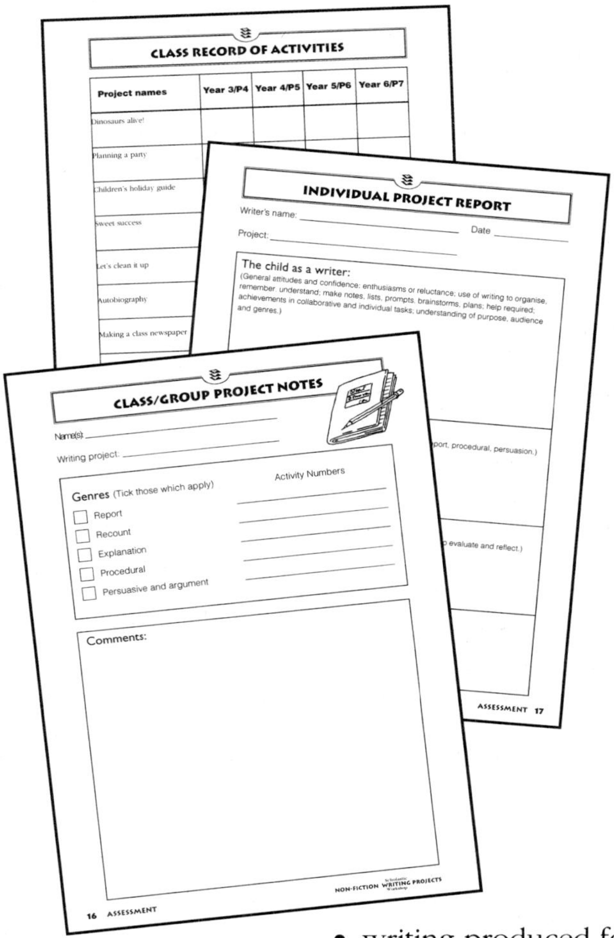

Class record of activities (page 18)

This provides a record of the writing projects covered each year and can be passed on to subsequent teachers of the class to help ensure continuity and balance.

Self-evaluation and peer evaluation

Each project contains an end-of-project opportunity for self-evaluation or peer evaluation. Some of these activities are collaborative, while others are individual.

Self-evaluation is, in fact, integral to each writing project as it encourages the children to become efficient and effective learners. It helps them to develop a framework to analyse their writing and monitor their own progress. It also helps to make them aware of what they know and what they can do. This allows them to gain control over their learning and develops their confidence, self-esteem and motivation.

Peer evaluation provides an equally powerful learning tool. Children often recognise strengths and weaknesses in the work of others before they see them in their own, and they are often more willing to analyse and comment on work that has been produced by someone they know rather than by professional authors. When they talk about each other's work, children have to offer and justify opinions; this encourages them to be analytical and to articulate and explain their ideas. This then, in turn, helps to broaden, clarify and consolidate their understanding and to link reading and writing, thus using their experience as readers to inform their writing.

Summative assessment

Many authorities recommend that teachers should try to keep an ongoing portfolio of the work of each child. This might contain:

• writing produced for the writing projects;
• evaluations and comments by the child;
• observations, evaluations and comments by the teacher, other readers, or people with whom the child worked;
• writing review forms completed by the child or teacher.

Teachers or schools need to devise their own policy to determine what is included in the writer's portfolio. There are several options:
• predetermine specific pieces of work to be included in all portfolios;
• determine set 'portfolio review times' when either the teacher or the children review the contents and balance of the portfolio, adding work as appropriate;
• encourage the children to select and add good examples of their writing as these are completed.

CLASS/GROUP PROJECT NOTES

Name(s): ______________________________

Writing project: ______________________________

Genres (Tick those which apply) — Activity Numbers

- [ ] Report ______________________________
- [ ] Recount ______________________________
- [ ] Explanation ______________________________
- [ ] Procedural ______________________________
- [ ] Persuasive and argument ______________________________

Comments:

INDIVIDUAL PROJECT REPORT

Writer's name: ______________________ Date ____________

Project: ______________________

The child as a writer:

(General attitudes and confidence: enthusiasms or reluctance; use of writing to organise, remember, understand; make notes, lists, prompts, brainstorms, plans; help required; achievements in collaborative and individual tasks; understanding of purpose, audience and genres.)

The quality of the written products

(Skill in selecting and using genres: explanation, recount, report, procedural, persuasion.)

Teacher - child discussion

(Notes on content of teacher–child discussion; the child's ability to evaluate and reflect.)

Next steps

(Aspects of context, content knowledge or process to target in future.)

CLASS RECORD OF ACTIVITIES

Project names	Year 3/P4	Year 4/P5	Year 5/P6	Year 6/P7
Dinosaurs alive!				
Planning a party				
Children's holiday guide				
Sweet success				
Let's clean it up				
Autobiography				
Making a class newspaper				
This is your life!				
Dialect dictionary				
Healthy bite				
Bullying				
Sport				

Scholastic WORKSHOP

Chapter Three

DINOSAURS ALIVE!

INTRODUCTION

Project description

In this project the children work individually, and in pairs, to produce reference books on dinosaurs. The conclusion of each activity becomes a page in the book. The project begins by asking the children to think of what they already know about dinosaurs and encouraging them to come up with some questions they would like answered. The children then choose questions to research and write up as a report. Other activities involve procedural and explanatory writing, with children using annotated diagrams to describe and explain the different types of dinosaur; considering the difference between fact and opinion, sequencing instructions and writing letters and quiz questions.

Although the project can stand alone, it works best as one part of a larger class project on dinosaurs. In this way the activities provide opportunities for children to revisit and re-use knowledge they have acquired.

Why this context?

Most children are fascinated by the amazing size and appearance of dinosaurs so will have a great deal of initial enthusiasm for the project. This motivation to learn more about these huge creatures, combined with the wide range of reference materials available, make this an ideal topic for children to develop researching and recording skills. The project provides opportunities for work in most areas of the curriculum, including mathematics (measurement and scale drawing), science (features of reptiles), history (finding evidence of the past) and so on.

Through writing their own reference books the children will become familiar with the content and style of report writing and the conventions of this type of book, such as contents pages and glossaries, and will be more skilful and confident when using reference books for researching future topics.

Project organisation

At the start of the project the teacher needs to decide whether the books are to be produced individually or by pairs of children working together. This will obviously depend on the needs of both the class and individuals within it. Before beginning the project, each child or pair should make up an A4- or A5-sized book (whichever is more appropriate), leaving the cover and title to be added at the end and the first page blank for a list of contents. This allows work to be stuck in place as it is completed so children can see their book 'grow'. Most of the activities involve the children working in pairs or as a class and some require practical work such as measuring.

Publication, celebration and review

The reference books which the children are to produce can be any shape (perhaps a dinosaur!) or size. The books should then be taken home, or to an infant class, along with a worksheet for the families, or infants, to complete.

Books the children may find useful

Dinamation's Dinosaurs (Campbell Books)
Dinosaurs – A Picture Dictionary (Derrydale)
Dinosaurs by Steve Pollock (BBC Factfinders)
Dinosaurs (Ladybird Books Ltd)
How Dinosaurs Lived (Piccolo Piper)
Spotters' Guide to Dinosaurs and other Prehistoric Animals by David Norman (Penguin Books)
Dinosaurs and their Relatives in Action by Gay Cassels (Intervisual Books Inc)
My First Pop Up Book of Dinosaurs by Roma Bishop (Brown, Wells and Jacob Ltd)

Teaching content

Generating questions to plan and structure a research topic and report.

What you need

Large paper, marker pens, writing materials.

What to do

Explain to the children that many people's understanding of dinosaurs comes from films, cartoons and stories. This means that their knowledge may be confused, inaccurate or incomplete. It also means that they may be left with many interesting questions about dinosaurs – about how they actually lived or how we know about them. They would probably like to have these questions answered.

Write the five key question words – what, where, why, when, how – on the board and explain that these will help the class to generate a great many questions about dinosaurs.

Take each word in turn and ask the class to think of questions beginning with this word. Encourage them to suggest any question at all about dinosaurs, no matter how wild and wonderful.

If children come up with a question that will clearly be impossible to answer, try to reword it or say that it is an interesting question, you do not know whether anyone knows the answer, but it would be interesting to think about. For example, if children are confused about life in pre-historic times they may ask, 'Did all the dinosaurs like eating people?' The teacher should then explain that people did not exist when the dinosaurs lived, but take the opportunity to help the children reframe the key idea into an answerable question, such as 'What did the dinosaurs eat?'

It is important to record all the questions on large sheets of paper so that the children have the opportunity to re-read them later in the project. As the children find out more about the topic, they will begin to see for themselves the problems in some of their initial questions. This is an important learning experience.

When you have a good list of questions, divide the children into working pairs. Tell them that they are going to make a book about dinosaurs and show the sample book to give them an idea of the size and format.

Explain that the book will include lots of different types of information and activities about dinosaurs and will take several sessions to write.

Suggest that it will be important to include a page or two at the beginning of their book explaining what dinosaurs were and answering some of the questions people may have about them.

Give each pair some paper. Ask them to read and discuss all the questions generated by the class and write the four or five that they think are most interesting on their sheet, spacing them at equal intervals down the page.

Allow about ten minutes for this, then ask some pairs to read out their choices. Discuss each set of questions with the class and discuss or model putting them into some kind of logical sequence, recording this by writing numbers in the box provided. Explain that, because there were many different kinds of dinosaur, they may want to research and write about just one type, or several types, picking those they find most interesting for each question.

Tell the children that they will start their real research in the next lesson but, in the meantime, they should begin to collect any information – books, posters, models – they have about dinosaurs and think of all the places they could go to find out more.

Ensure that both the class-generated questions and those selected by the pairs are stored in a safe place. Children will need them for the next lesson.

Teaching content

Using questions to plan and structure a report.

What you need

Reference books on dinosaurs, writing materials, sheets of selected questions from Activity 1.

What to do

If the class is large and the number of available reference books small, the children may need to work in shifts to find out factual answers to their questions.

Ensure that each pair has the sheet of questions they completed in the first activity. Tell the children that they may work together, taking each individual question in turn or reading the books and jotting down information relevant to any of their questions as they come across it.

Explain that they should use the space below each question to record relevant information that will help them to write short and interesting answers to that question. Tell them that this work is called research.

Revise with the class how to find the relevant part of an information book by using the index and contents page. Suggest that they look at the books together or separately, but that when they find a passage that deals with a question, one partner should read it aloud while the other writes the information, as briefly as possible, against the relevant question on the sheet. Explain that they do not need to write in complete sentences – note form will do. Point out that they should not copy reams from the books, but only write down the information relevant to their question. Emphasise that it is important they understand their notes as they will be using them to write the reports for their books. They should not copy words or phrases if they do not know their meaning.

Teaching content

Reports begin with general statements or a definition of the topic; reports contain factual information; illustrations, often with captions, can help the reader to understand an aspect of the report.

What you need

Lined paper of a suitable size to fit the book format, unlined drawing paper (pre-cut in a variety of suitable sizes and shapes), writing materials, written notes from Activity 2.

What to do

Introduce this session by congratulating the children on their research work. Take a few key questions and ask some of the pairs to read out the information they have recorded in their notes. Then tell the children that today they will be writing up the research they have completed.

Suggest that each report needs to begin with a short statement introducing the topic and explaining why it is interesting. The children could write this together, or the teacher might compose a good introduction with the whole class.

Now show the children how their questions can be used to form headings for the different sections of the report. Some questions may need to be re-framed slightly and, if so, this can be discussed with the class or individuals, as appropriate.

Ask the children to read the question and their research notes carefully, then write a short answer. Emphasise that the answer they write must make sense and should be written in complete sentences. No answer should begin with the words 'yes' or 'no'. Illustrate the report style by referring to examples from the information books that the children have been using. Point out that reports are written in an impersonal way that focuses on the topic without promoting the opinions of the writer.

Tell the children that it may be helpful in some cases for their answers to be illustrated with line drawings, photocopies of pictures from a book, or diagrams. Display some of the information books they have been using and point out how illustrations are positioned on the page and labelled with explanatory captions.

Give out paper and other writing materials and let the children get to work.

Teaching content

Requests for information, either by letter or telephone, should explain who wants the information and why.

What you need

Writing materials, headed notepaper.

What to do

Some children may choose to report on questions to which they cannot find answers in the reference books available. This situation provides a good opportunity for the teacher to highlight and model other forms of inquiry with the whole class.

Gather the class together and explain the question and the problem as it is. It is possible that other children in the class will have found some pertinent information in the course of their own inquiries.

If nobody has any help to offer, ask if the class has any suggestions about how, or where, this genuine problem could be investigated further. Explain that, although there are several things the children could do, the most direct would be to telephone or write to an expert on dinosaurs (or to someone who might know of an expert on dinosaurs). See if the children have any ideas about how they could find and contact such experts and list their ideas, along with your own, on the board. They may suggest, among other things:

- writing to the local museum;
- writing to a nationally famous museum;
- writing to the author of one of the reference books they have been using;
- writing to the publisher of one of the reference books they have been using;
- writing to an appropriate teacher in a secondary school or university;
- writing to a local historical society;
- writing to the question page of a newspaper or comic;
- writing to an appropriate television personality;
- asking parents, friends and knowledgeable acquaintances;
- using a CD-ROM, the Internet or other computer facilities.

Turn the individual question into a class problem and ask each pair of children to contact one specific person or organisation. Show them the various means of finding addresses such as Yellow Pages, Directory Inquiries and information and leaflets from local places. Authors may often be contacted through their publishers whose address is usually given at the front of the book. With larger organisations encourage the children to phone in advance to check the correct address and obtain the name of a person to whom they can address the letter.

Teach or revise with the children how to structure an appropriate letter. You may want to remind them of the following points:

- The person to whom they write will not know about them, the school or the project. They will have to explain this briefly.
- They will need to state precisely why they are writing. They should give the question that needs to be answered and explain exactly how the information will be used.
- They may also want to indicate why they thought this person or organisation would be able to help them.
- They should remember to include a stamped addressed envelope.
- They should end by thanking the person for taking time to read and (hopefully) reply to their letter.

If necessary, list these points on the board. Give out the draft writing paper and ask the children to work in pairs to compose a suitable letter to their allocated person or organisation. They should take turns to scribe and to prompt the writer by suggesting what could be said.

First drafts should be checked, then copied on to headed notepaper and, after a final check for errors, sent off to the appropriate address.

Teaching content

Information may be conveyed in the form of an annotated diagram.

What you need

Photocopiable pages 29 and 30, writing materials.

What to do

Give out the photocopiable sheets to each pair. Explain that these contain pictures and statements about various types of dinosaur.

Let each pair choose one dinosaur on which to focus. (It may be necessary to allocate dinosaurs if they all choose the same one.) Tell them to look carefully at the picture of their dinosaur and to draw arrows pointing to three or four of its most interesting features – perhaps the eyes, mouth, teeth, legs or skin. At the blunt end of each arrow they should write a few words describing this feature, such as:

The eyes are small and at the side of the head.
The back legs are huge and have claws.

Now tell the children to read the short statements written about their dinosaur and discuss how these link to the features they have highlighted in the drawings. Ask them to use their annotations and the statements to produce a short description of some key features, and an explanation of why each dinosaur is the way that it is. They may do this by re-writing the relevant statements, copying and combining them to make a logical sequence of sentences, many of which will take the form: 'The legs are... This is because...'.

Finally, explain that concrete examples often help a reader to appreciate some of the more amazing aspects of a description, such as the size of the dinosaurs. Ask the children to measure out the size of their dinosaur in the classroom or playground and give an example of how long it would be, for example:

The dinosaur is eleven metres long. If its head was at the classroom door, its tail would reach the netball post.

These can be used to 'round off' their description.

Once finished, ask each pair to share their work briefly with the rest of the class. Explain that the children will use their own work in their books, but that they may also photocopy the work of others to include information about three or four different types of dinosaur. A good way to organise this is to display all the work on the wall, with a blank sheet of paper under each. Ask the children to write their names on the blank sheet below any items they would like to photocopy. Remind them that each pair must use their own work and may copy, at most, information on three other dinosaurs.

Teaching content

Reports contain factual information. Unlike opinions they rarely contain the word 'I'.

What you need

Photocopiable page 31, unlined paper of a suitable size to fit the book format, adhesive, scissors.

What to do

Explain that most writing in information or reference books (the type of book the children are working on) gives factual information, rather than the writer's opinion.

Suggest that the people who read the dinosaur books may enjoy seeing how good they are at distinguishing fact from opinion and that it might be interesting to have this as a quiz section of the book.

Distribute the photocopiable sheet. Explain that it contains several statements, some of which are fact – the sort of statements one

might read in a report – and some opinion. Tell the children to read these, decide which are fact and which opinion, and then explain why.

After five minutes, call the class together and go through each statement in turn, hearing the decisions and explanations made by the children. Then show the children how to turn this into a lift-the-flap quiz section by cutting along the dotted lines, sticking the top strip of each question to the page-sized paper and writing whether it is *fact* or *opinion* on the paper under each question. Remind the children to leave enough space at the top of their paper for a suitable page heading.

Further development

Ask the children to write two more sentences giving factual information and two giving opinions to make four more quiz questions for this section.

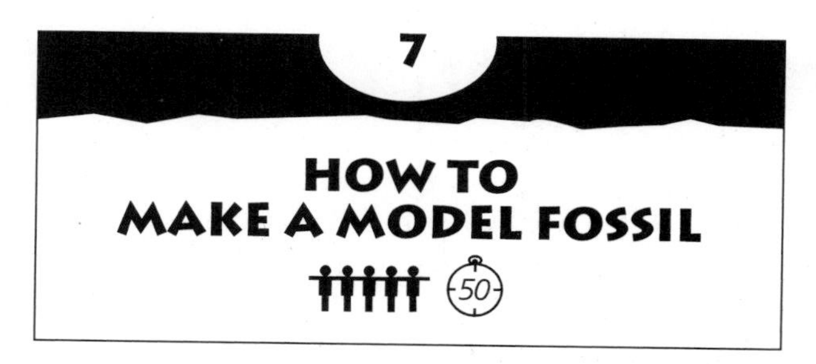

Teaching content

Sequencing instructions.

What you need

Photocopiable page 32, plaster of Paris, petroleum jelly, shells, Plasticine, yoghurt pots, adhesive, scissors, unlined paper of a suitable size to fit the book format.

What to do

Explain to the children that they are going to make a model fossil. Arrange the class in groups of five. Give each group:

- a shell;
- a piece of Plasticine;
- two yoghurt pots, one containing plaster of Paris powder, the other containing water;
- some petroleum jelly.

Give the following oral instructions as the groups make their plaster cast 'fossils'.

- Press the Plasticine *firmly* on to one side of the shell.
- Pull the shell away carefully, leaving a shell print in the Plasticine.
- Rub the shell print gently with petroleum jelly.
- Mix the plaster of Paris powder with water to a creamy consistency.
- Pour the plaster mix into the shell print in the Plasticine.
- When this has hardened, ease the 'model fossil' out of the Plasticine.

Allow time for tidying and handwashing.

Now give each child a copy of photocopiable page 32. Explain that the instructions on how to make a model fossil have been mixed up. Tell them to read through them and then decide, in their groups, what the order should be. Each person should then cut out and place (not stick) their set of instructions on the unlined paper in the agreed sequence. After ten minutes tell the groups to check they have the instructions in the right order by taking turns to read these out while a group member follows them, acting out making a 'fossil'. Go round checking the accuracy of these with the groups. When they are sure the sequence is correct they should stick them down, sketching in a rough drawing to illustrate each instruction. They can use this, or copy the instructions and pictures, to make a page for their dinosaur book.

Teaching content

Choosing information to be included in an author's biography. Formulating questions to elicit this information. Writing a short biography (recount genre).

What you need

Poster paper, writing materials, A4 paper.

What to do

Explain to the children that when people read a book, especially if they have enjoyed it, they often want to find out about the author. Therefore most books include a section that gives information about the person who wrote it. This is not written by authors themselves but by another person who has done research about them. Explain that this type of writing is called a biography. Tell the children that the books they are writing should each include a short biography of the author.

Write the following on the chalkboard.

Catherine Gifford was born in Crawley and has lived there for most of her life. She was educated at Hazelwick School and at Manchester University. During the Second World War she married and had three daughters, for whom many of her books were written. She qualified as a teacher and worked in a school for fourteen years before giving up to devote her time to writing.

Christopher Haslam lives in Ritewell. He is eight years old. His mother is an artist. His father works in the Castle Hotel in Ritewell. In his spare time Christopher enjoys water-skiing. He has also written: *All About Christopher*, *A Mother's Day Book* and *The Creature Inside the Egg*. Christopher studied birds of prey for three weeks before writing this book.

Arrange the class in groups of five. Tell them that these are examples of author biographies that have been included in books. Read each one through with the class. Establish that they can tell these biographies were not written by the authors themselves since they are written in the third person. Now tell each group to read over the biographies on the chalkboard again and decide the kind of information they learn about the authors from them. Appoint a scribe for each group to write these points on poster paper. Allow ten minutes, then ask for the posters to be pinned up on the wall. A spokesperson for each group can then give an example of the type of information listed. These suggestions will probably include:

- the author's family;
- where they live;
- their interests or hobbies;
- details of any other books or writing that they have done.

Tell the children that they are each going to write a similar style biography for a classmate. The first step to doing this will be to interview that person to find out the information they need. Remind them that they have already, in their groups, drawn up a list of the kind of information required. Give each child an A4 sheet of paper and tell them to draft three questions they could ask to elicit the required information. Demonstrate how they should set these out on their paper, leaving space to make a note of answers under each one.

After ten minutes pair each child with a 'biography partner'. Tell them to interview each other using their listed questions. Point out to the children that if they are asked about other writing they have done, they can mention work from previous classes, entries in class books or displays, individual poems, stories, diaries and so on.

Allow five minutes for each interview. Now tell the children to use their interview notes to write a short biography of their partner. These should begin with their partner's name, perhaps 'Ann Smith lives...'.

When the biographies are finished children should read what has been written about them to check that the information is correct. It can then be copied into the book. Try to include a small photograph if possible.

9

THE GLOSSARY PAGE

40

Teaching content

Explaining the purpose of a glossary. Establishing criteria to select words to include. Making a glossary page.

What you need

Paper cut to size, rulers, writing materials, a selection of books with glossaries.

What to do

Explain to the class that they are going to make a page which explains words in their dinosaur books which other readers might not understand. Tell them that this is rather like a mini-dictionary and is called a glossary. Arrange the children in groups to look at examples of the glossaries in the books provided. Through discussion of these the following points should emerge.

- The words selected for a glossary are generally words connected with the theme of the book that might not be understood by readers unfamiliar with its subject matter.
- The meanings of the words are written as succinctly as possible, in the same way as they would be in a dictionary.

• All the words listed in the glossary are arranged in alphabetical order.

Now tell each child or writing team to read through their dinosaur books and note five words they think should be included in their glossary. Remind them of the criteria for selecting words. Next, give out paper cut to page size and tell them to list the words they have thought of alphabetically down the left-hand side of their paper, leaving space beside each to write in the meaning.

Now arrange the class in pairs. Tell them to discuss each of the words on their respective lists, helping each other to explain the meanings as succinctly as they can. Tell the children that diagrams (humorous if they wish) can also be included as part of the explanation, so the word 'extinct' might be defined as 'died out', illustrated with a picture of a dinosaur on its back, with its legs in the air!

When these have been completed and checked, children may write up final drafts in their dinosaur books.

Teaching content

Explaining the layout of a contents page. Making a contents page for a book.

What you need

A book with contents page for each child, paper cut to page size, rulers, writing materials.

What to do

Tell the children that, now that their pages are written and numbered, they are ready to make the contents page for their books. Make sure that the children have their books open at the contents page. Discuss these with them to establish the following.

• The purpose of this page is to allow people using the book to find the information they want quickly and easily.

• Contents are listed in the order they appear in the book, not alphabetically as in an index.

• The page is usually set out in two columns, with subject headings on the left and page numbers on the right.

• The page number in the right-hand column is always the first page dealing with the subject.

Now give each child a sheet of paper the same size as their book page. Tell them that they are to plan out the contents page for their own book on this sheet. Before they begin they should count how many subject headings they will need and lightly rule pencil lines to make sure headings correspond accurately with page numbers.

When they have completed this first draft, tell them to swap it with a partner and check the accuracy of each other's work, using it to look up each subject heading in their books.

When the drafts have been checked they should be copied into the contents page of their dinosaur books.

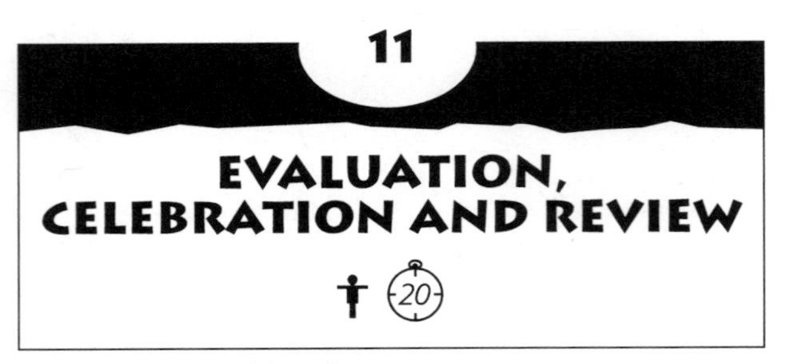

Teaching content

Reference books can be evaluated by watching real readers use them.

What you need

Books the children have written, writing materials.

What to do

The idea that the children are authors of *real* reference books should be reinforced by sharing their completed work with as wide an audience as possible.

Books could be displayed in the reference section of the school library while others could be loaned to a younger class.

To gain further evaluation, children could also be asked to make up a worksheet which could be used by children in younger classes when they read their dinosaur books. Suggest a suitable format, such as:

Turn to page... Was the stegosaurus a plant eater or a meat eater?

At some point, all books should be sent home, preferably with a worksheet (that the teacher has prepared) for the children's families to complete.

In this way they will get feedback on their work, as well as a chance to assess the effectiveness of the reference book.

TYPES OF DINOSAUR – 1

Triceratops

This dinosaur grew to be 9m long and was about the size of a small truck. It had a hooked beak – like a parrot – which it used to snap off the thick stems and leaves of tough plants. Then rows of sharp teeth helped to bite the leaves into smaller pieces.

It was huge and heavy and defended itself from larger meat-eating dinosaurs by charging at them, using its three large horns as weapons. The thick, bony frill ensured that its head looked twice as big and frightening when it lowered its head to charge, which helped to scare off predators. Male triceratops may also have used their horns to fight each other, just like male deer today.

Tyrannosaurus

This was the biggest, fiercest meat-eating dinosaur of all time. It was 14m long and 5m tall. Some of its teeth were 15cm long – the size of a human hand – and it could kill its prey with one bite. Its mouth was so big it could eat a child in one gulp.

It was not the fastest runner, although its long back legs helped it gallop as fast as a horse. The sharp claws on its back legs were used for fighting and killing other dinosaurs.

TYPES OF DINOSAUR – 2

Diplodocus

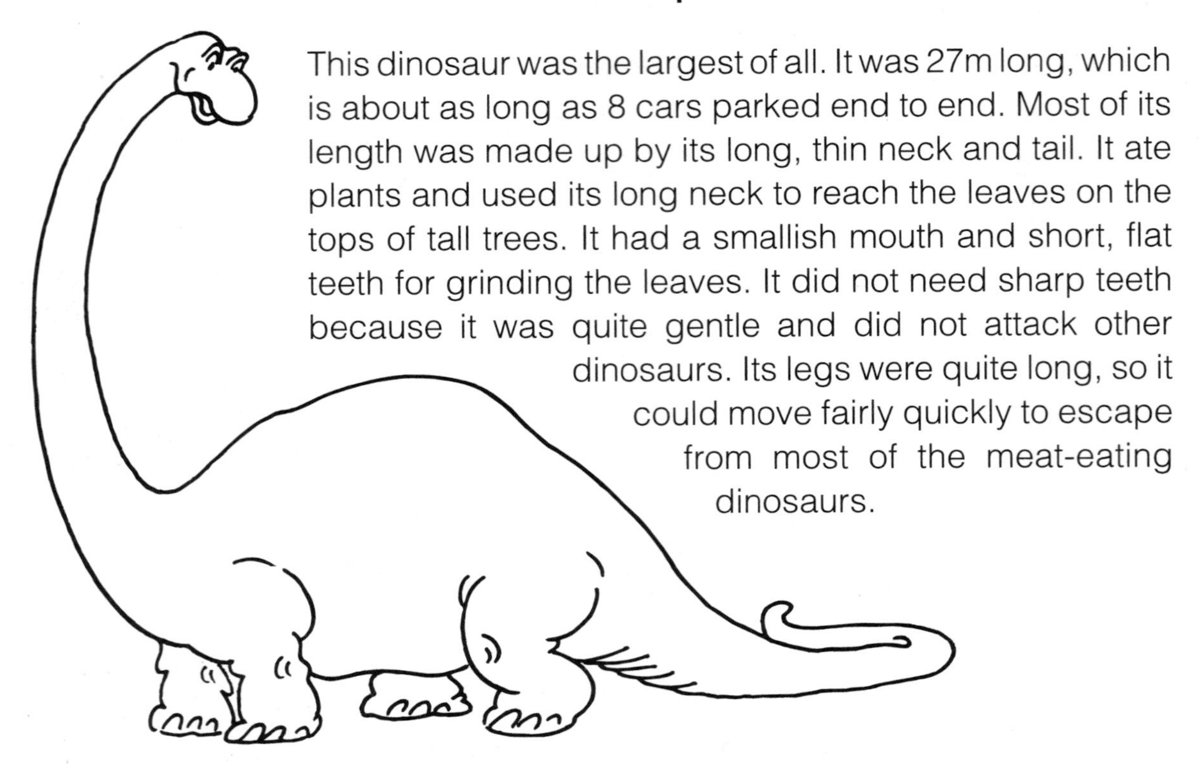

This dinosaur was the largest of all. It was 27m long, which is about as long as 8 cars parked end to end. Most of its length was made up by its long, thin neck and tail. It ate plants and used its long neck to reach the leaves on the tops of tall trees. It had a smallish mouth and short, flat teeth for grinding the leaves. It did not need sharp teeth because it was quite gentle and did not attack other dinosaurs. Its legs were quite long, so it could move fairly quickly to escape from most of the meat-eating dinosaurs.

Stegosaurus

This dinosaur was as tall as two men and was 7.75m long. The spines, or 'bony plates', on its back were attached to its skin (rather than its spine) and would probably have wobbled slightly as it walked. These plates helped it to control the temperature of its body. When the stegosaurus was too hot, they gave off heat and when it was cold they soaked up warmth from the sun.

The stegosaurus was a plant eater, but because it was big and heavy it needed to spend all day eating. It had a short neck and its front legs were shorter than its back legs, which tilted its head nearer to the ground so that it could eat low-growing plants. As its legs were quite short and its body was tilted, it didn't run fast and so it needed the sharp spikes on the end of its tail to defend itself against meat-eating dinosaurs.

In spite of its large body, its head was very small and its brain was the size of a walnut.

NAME

FACT OR OPINION: CAN YOU TELL?

Dinosaurs lived on Earth millions of years ago
I would not like to have lived on Earth millions of years ago because there were dinosaurs.
Meat-eating dinosaurs are more interesting to study.

Fossils are exciting to find because they can help us learn about the shape and size of dinosaurs.
Fossils have been found of dinosaurs, footprints and their bones. These give us information on their sizes and shapes.

I would like to find a fossil.
Some dinosaurs were meat eaters and others were plant eaters.
Meat-eating dinosaurs were more terrifying than plant eaters.

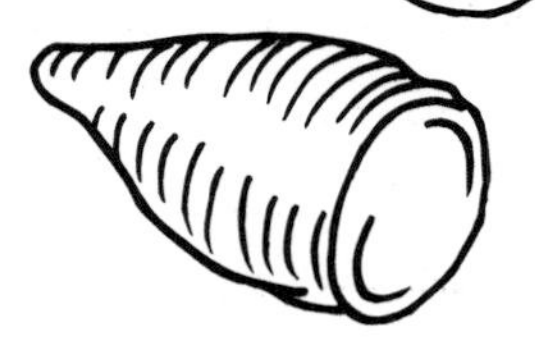

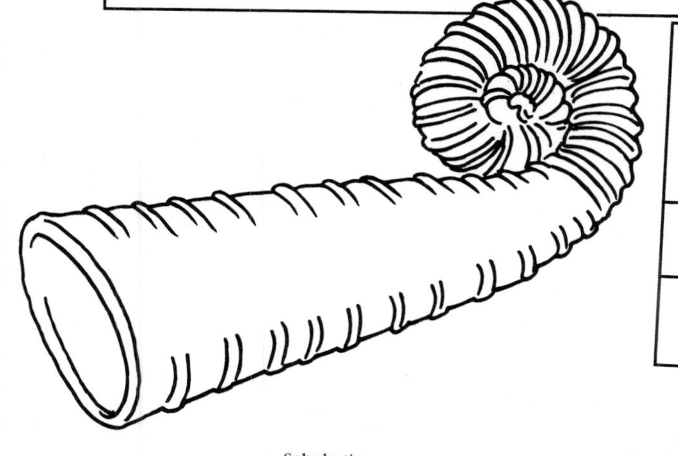

All dinosaurs needed to protect themselves from others, but they did this in different ways.
Not all dinosaurs were large.
There are no dinosaurs living today.

NAME

HOW TO MAKE A MODEL FOSSIL

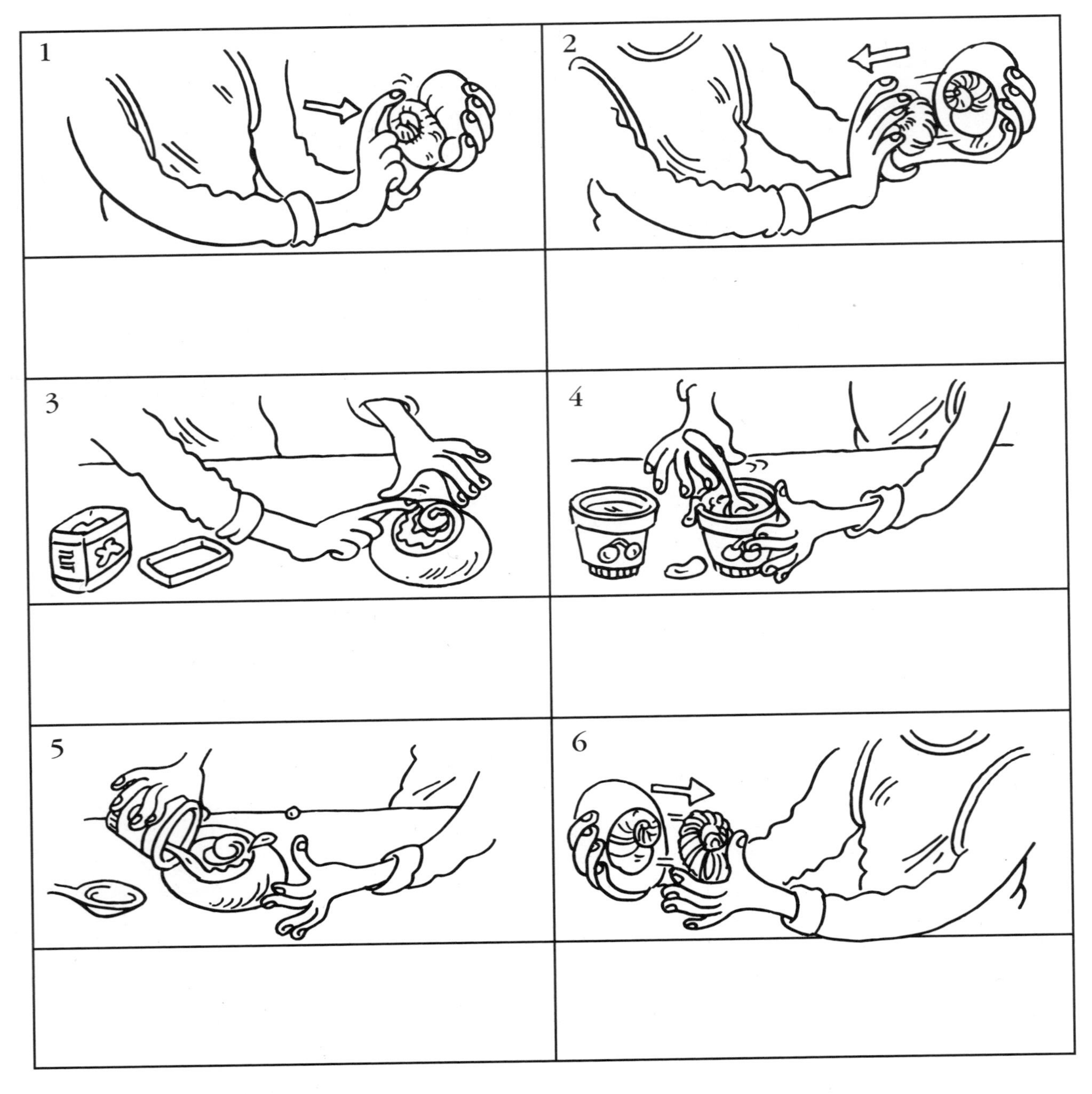

Mix the plaster of Paris powder with water.	Push the shell into the Plasticine.
Take the model fossil out of the Plasticine.	Take the shell out of the Plasticine.
Pour the plaster mix into the shell print.	Rub petroleum jelly on the shell print.

Scholastic WORKSHOP

Chapter Four

PLANNING A PARTY

INTRODUCTION

Project description

In this project, children plan and organise a party. They choose a theme, and draw up lists of what they have to do, allocating responsibilities and tasks fairly among themselves. They suggest designs for invitations and food names that fit with the party theme and individual groups then take responsibility for planning and organising a different aspect of the party such as food, games and music, decorations and invitations.

After the party, the children reflect on how the writing tasks helped them to organise their ideas, decision-making and actions. The teacher can also choose to ask them to write a recount of the party, an evaluative report or make a 'Do-it-yourself party book' about how to organise and run a party.

Why this context?

Parties are fun and are a familiar event in children's lives. Most children will have had experience of going to parties, and watching how they are organised. Through arranging their own party, children learn to use writing as a tool for organising their thoughts and actions in purposeful situations. Within the project, they write to persuade, inform, recount and instruct.

The project involves both individual and group work so the children learn about taking responsibility and the importance of being reliable. The strong motivation provided by the shared aim ensures that children work together in a variety of groups and, in the process, learn from each other.

The work is supported by a variety of means such as photocopiable sheets, ideas and plans written by children in previous activities, and direct teaching and modelling by the teacher.

Project organisation

The project involves both class and group discussion and decision making. The children are given opportunities to work in a variety of different groupings, and do not need to stay within the same group for all activities in the project. Some groups can be self-selecting, others involve quite complex tasks and decision-making processes. For these, the teacher may wish to allocate children to groups to ensure a productive spread of talents and personalities.

Publication, celebration and review

The project contains a number of different ways in which the children read and comment on their own and each other's work. Group plans of action are presented and discussed by the whole class. Suggestions for the layout and content of invitations, for party games, decorations and for appropriate and appealing names for the food are provided for groups working on these aspects. The final project evaluation involves discussion and assessment of the role that various types of writing played in helping the children plan, organise and prepare for the party.

The enjoyment of the party and the smooth organisation which underpinned its success provides, of course, an excellent celebration of the writing tasks. Arrange for someone to take photographs at the party to provide a lasting record.

Books the children may find useful

Usborne Party Fun by Claire Rosen (Usborne Publishing Ltd)
Birthday Fun by Ronne Randall (Kingfisher)
Usborne Hotshots Magic Tricks by Judy Tatchell (Usborne Publishing Ltd)
Children's Parties by Angela Wilkes (Dorling Kindersley)

Teaching content

An argument may be framed to appeal on the grounds of logical argument, or for emotional reasons. Different structures, imagery and language are used for each.

What you need

Photocopiable page 42, writing materials, scrap paper.

What to do

The impetus for this project may arise from the need to have a class party to celebrate a special occasion – a festival, seasonal celebration, end of year, term or project. Alternatively, it may arise from the need for the class to put on a party for another group in the community – the local nursery or old folks' home, for example.

Introduce the idea of the class (rather than the teacher) organising a party and explain who the party will be for, and why. Tell the children that choosing a theme can make their party fun, and help to generate ideas for games, clothes, decorations and food. Explain that each child will have the opportunity to put forward an idea for a theme for the party. They must also try to persuade the rest of the class by writing reasons why their chosen theme is particularly suitable. A class debate and vote will decide the final choice.

Ask the class to suggest party themes and record these on the chalkboard. Ideas may include: a disco; a pyjama or beach party; themes of monsters, animals, kings and queens; pirates or fairy tales.

Encourage the children to use their imagination and personal experience to come up with exciting and original themes. Remind them that when choosing a theme, they should remember the following:

- the reason for holding the party;
- who the party is for (age group, interests);
- when the party is being held (time of day or year).

Remind the children that these points may affect the suitability of the theme chosen, so a kings and queens theme might be suitable to round off a history project and a beach party would be more appropriate in the summer.

Distribute scrap paper. Ask each child to choose a theme and write it down. Then point out that to persuade the rest of the class, they will have to give reasons for their choice. They will need to think about how the theme might appeal to other children and why it would be suitable for the occasion and participants.

Tell the children to jot down at least three reasons why their suggestion would make a good party theme. Explain that they may present these reasons in the form of a logical argument, stating their opinion and the reasons for it. If they decide to adopt this approach, they would probably use an introductory sentence such as:

I think we should have a... party. This would be a good theme because...

Terms such as 'firstly', 'secondly' and 'finally' will help them to organise this type of argument.

Alternatively, they may present their choice and the reasons for it by appealing to the hopes and aspirations of their classmates. Explain that this type of persuasive argument is more likely to use emotive language and images. Read out some of the suggestions from the photocopiable sheet and ask the children to suggest others.

Give one copy of photocopiable page 42 to each child. Tell them to write their chosen party theme in the banner at the top and use the space below to convince others of this idea. Draw their attention to the suggestion boxes at the bottom of the photocopiable sheet. These contain ideas which they may find useful.

The finished pieces of work should be displayed in the classroom. Set a deadline by which they should have read all the submissions and be prepared to debate them. The children may vote either by a show of hands or by using the voting slip on the bottom of the photocopiable sheet.

When children are reading the work or discussing the vote, encourage them to comment on those arguments they find particularly well-presented and convincing, and why.

Teaching content

Writing helps us to generate, remember and organise ideas and actions.

What you need

Large sheets of paper, marker pens.

What to do

Arrange the children in groups of four or five. Explain that, before they have their party, they will need to make a checklist of things to do. Ask them to give reasons why writing a list is a good idea. They may suggest:

- to ensure they do not overlook or forget important things;
- to help them decide on the best order in which to do things;
- to know who is going to do what;
- to help keep a check on progress.

Ask the class to give some examples of things which will need to be organised before the event. They are likely to suggest ideas such as making decorations, sending invitations, choosing and making party food.

Give each group a large sheet of paper and a marker pen. Tell the children that they have ten minutes in which to brainstorm a list of decisions to be made and things to do for the party, recording their ideas on the paper. Then, tell them to try to put their list into chronological order. They may do this either by re-writing the list, or simply by putting numbers beside the different items.

Display all the lists on the classroom wall and give a spokesperson from each group a few minutes to explain their work. Then ask the class for general comments:

- Is there a big variation between the lists?
- Are all the lists realistic in terms of time, costs, space and so on?
- Do all the lists present a logical sequence of action?
- Which lists do the children think would provide a good basis from which to work. Why do they think this?

Having discussed the group lists and the children's ideas, work with the whole class to compile a list that is realistic and comprehensive. Try to ensure that there are at least four separate items which require organisation. (The ones covered in this project are games, food, decorations and invitations, but if these topics are inappropriate, the project activities can be adapted to suit other items which the children identify.)

Display the class list where it can be seen by everyone. This can be used for organisational purposes, for noting the names of children who are responsible for particular tasks and for keeping track of progress. Items on the list can be ticked off as they are dealt with.

Teaching content

Lists can help to organise action and provide a basis for discussion.

What you need

A3 paper, writing materials.

What to do

Arrange the children in groups of four or five. Explain that when people give parties, they write a list of the people they plan to invite, called a guest list. This helps them to organise the party as it gives a rough idea of numbers and ensures that nobody is overlooked.

If the party is to be for the class, explain that the list will obviously include all class members (who do not need to be listed at this point), but it may also include others who help the class, such as the caretaker, dinner ladies, cooks, the school secretary, parent helpers and so on. Explain that there may be a lot of people the class would like to invite, but that numbers have to be restricted because of the practical limitations of space, cost and time. Tell each group to consider carefully the reason for the party and discuss who they think should be invited, and why.

Distribute pens and paper and ask the children to begin writing lists of the guests they think should be invited.

Once finished, ask each group to share and explain their ideas. The whole class should then come to an agreement on the names of guests who should definitely be invited. These should be written on a class list.

4 INVITATIONS: COME TO OUR PARTY!

Teaching content
Sequencing items of information into a logical order.

What you need
A large sheet of paper and a marker pen for each group, scissors, scrap paper, pencils.

What to do
Explain to the children that if they would like guests to come to their party they will have to send out invitations. These will provide the guests with all the relevant information about the party and also give them time to prepare for it.

Organise the children into groups of three or four, appoint a scribe and a spokesperson for each one. Distribute a large sheet of paper and a marker pen to each group. Tell the children to write down all the information the guests will need to know about the party. Make sure they write the information in list form, with the items one below the other.

Ask the spokesperson from each group to read out their list, making sure the following items have been covered:

- an invitation to 'come to a party';
- who is holding the party;
- name of the guest being invited;
- where the party is being held;
- when the party is being held (time and date);
- what type of party it is (theme, does the guest need to dress up?);
- a request for a reply (called an RSVP).

At this point give the children an opportunity to make any changes or additions to their list. Hand out some A4 scrap paper to each group and ask them to design a layout and illustrations for their party invitations, referring to their list to ensure all information is included. Once the groups have finished, encourage them to share their work with the rest of the class, pointing out the similarities and differences in layout and the reasons for this, along with any good ideas for presentation. Tell the children that this information forms the basis of an invitation to guests and that all these draft invitations will be used as a basis for work later in the project.

5 BRAINSTORMING GAMES, FOOD AND DECORATIONS

Teaching content
Writing to generate and remember ideas.

What you need
Writing materials.

What to do
Organise the children into groups of four and distribute paper and pens to the groups. Ask the children to divide the paper into three sections, labelling these 'Games and music', 'Food' and 'Decorations'.

Remind the children of the theme of the party, its purpose and the people for whom it will be given. Ask each group to brainstorm as many ideas as possible for games, food and decorations, recording the ideas under the appropriate heading on their paper. They should draw a star by those ideas that they feel are particularly appropriate.

Once finished, display all brainstorms and briefly share them with the class. Explain that they will all be used in future activities.

6 FOOD NAMES

Teaching content

Choice of language and imagery can promote ideas in a powerful way.

What you need

Photocopiable page 43, writing materials.

What to do

Organise the children into groups of four. Remind them of the theme of the party and explain that the food, and its presentation, is an important part of any themed party. Point out that the food itself does not necessarily need to be unusual. Popular and familiar party food can be given new and exciting names that conjure up images associated with the theme of the party.

Distribute the photocopiable sheet. Explain that the top section details how common party food (crisps, juice, sandwiches, biscuits and jelly) was described for two parties, one of which had a pirate theme while the other used the theme of the circus.

Give each group between five and ten minutes to sort the food names into the two themes, and identify what each of the foods might be. Ask groups to report their results briefly to the rest of the class.

Now, ask the children to use the bottom part of the photocopiable sheet to generate ideas for food names for their own party theme. Emphasise that all suggestions should be recorded and that the writing must be legible. Collect these in for use by the 'food' group in Activity 7.

7 ACTION: GROUP PLANS

Teaching content

Writing an action plan helps the writer identify and sequence what has to be done.

What you need

Resources as listed for each group (refer to the boxes on page 39).

What to do

Much of the basic organisation and preparation for the party will be done in this session. The activity has been written for four groups, each of which will have responsibility for planning and implementing a different key element of the party:

- games and music;
- food and drink;
- invitations and looking after the guests;
- planning and making the decorations for walls and tables.

If your class has more key elements than this in its party plan, it may be necessary to have five or six groups, each taking responsibility for a different element. The groups will be fairly large, so it is important to allocate children to groups carefully to ensure a productive mix of personalities and talents in each one.

Divide the class into the appropriate number of groups and explain that each group will be responsible for planning and implementing a different aspect of the party. Ensure that the children understand that the group must take total responsibility for the element they are allocated. It is a good idea to appoint (or encourage each group to appoint) a chairperson who will ensure that everyone is involved in the decision making and does an equal share of the work.

Give each group their responsibility and explain that the group must:

- decide on the actual parts of the party that they must organise;
- identify what must be done or made before the party and produce a plan of action to achieve this;
- decide who will do each of the jobs identified on the action plan;
- list any jobs that will need to be done during the party and decide who will be responsible

for doing them.

Explain that each group has the resources listed in the boxes below. Distribute several copies of the photocopiable sheet (44, 45, 46 or 47 as appropriate) to each group (at least one per pair), and read it through with the children. Ensure that everyone understands what they have to do, and how they are to begin the task. You may wish to appoint a reader, who (along with the chairperson) will be responsible for reading the task to the group whenever it becomes necessary.

Invitations group

This group will design and make invitations for the guests.

This group will need:

- photocopiable page 44;
- the guest list;
- the class work from Activity 4 suggesting appropriate content and layouts for the invitations;
- good quality A4 or A5 paper, pencils, sequins, glitter, adhesive, collage materials and scissors.

Once finished, invitations should be photocopied and the copies placed in a class display booklet to provide ideas for future classes. The originals should be carefully stored until it is time for them to be sent.

Games and music group

This group will choose and plan the sequence of games, ensuring that props and equipment are available on the day and that everyone has a common understanding of the rules.

This group will need:

- photocopiable page 45;
- the section of class work from Activity 5 suggesting appropriate games and dances;
- several A3 sheets of paper, a marker pen and writing materials;
- access to art materials if required.

Once finished, this group's list of games should be displayed and a list showing the responsibilities of each child or pair should be given to the teacher. Each child or pair should list the equipment they must make or find for their game and write its rules clearly on an A3 sheet.

Food group

This group is responsible for choosing and preparing the food and ensuring menus and food labels are ready for use on the day.

This group will need:

- photocopiable page 46;
- the section of work from Activity 5 suggesting appropriate food;
- several A3 sheets of paper, a marker pen and writing materials;
- the work from Activity 6 suggesting appropriate names for food labels.

Once finished, the group should make menus and food labels. The shopping lists should also be written out clearly so that other class members can volunteer any items that they are prepared to provide. A timeline showing the plan of action should detail who will do what.

Wall and table decorations group

This group will plan and make wall and table decorations that fit with the party theme.

This group will need:

- photocopiable page 47;
- the section of work from Activity 5 suggesting appropriate wall and table decorations;
- several A3 sheets of paper, a marker pen and writing materials;
- access to art and craft materials if required.

Once finished, the group should work individually or in pairs to make specific decorations.

It may also be helpful to revisit and elaborate or modify the plan of action formed in Activity 2, writing specific names beside particular tasks to ensure that everyone is clear about what they have to do. If appropriate, this list can be turned into a timeline, setting deadlines by which each task must be completed.

Teaching content

Sequencing information in a logical order.

What you need

Writing materials, chalkboard, adhesive tape, camera.

What to do

Explain to the children that at many organised events a plan is written and attached to a wall. It contains a list of the order of activities and helps the guests and those organising the event to know what happens next. Tell the children that they are now going to organise the activities for their party and write a plan.

List the various party events on the chalkboard (arrival/departure of guests, games, tea...). Ask the children to suggest a suitable sequence. This will then become a plan for the party.

A number of children or groups could write up the plan on large sheets of paper. These could be decorated and displayed around the room at the party.

With all the hard work of planning and preparation behind you, hold the party. Take plenty of photos and have a really good time!

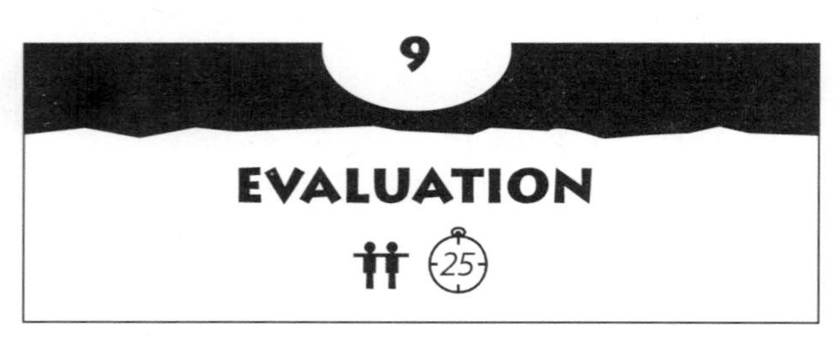

Teaching content

Writing helps the writer to plan and organise thoughts and actions.

What you need

Photocopiable page 48, writing materials.

What to do

After the party, talk to the children about what they enjoyed most and least about:

- being at the party;
- organising the party.

Distribute photocopiable page 48 and ask them to complete it in pairs. Explain that the first section focuses on organising and being at the party and the second section focuses on how the different writing tasks helped them to organise their thoughts and decisions.

Briefly revise the writing tasks listed to ensure that the children are all talking about the same task. Ask them to tick the appropriate box and write a short comment to explain why they ticked this box.

Once the photocopiable sheets have been completed, take each of the tasks in turn and encourage the class to share and discuss their decisions about whether the writing was essential, helpful or of no use. They should be able to justify their choices.

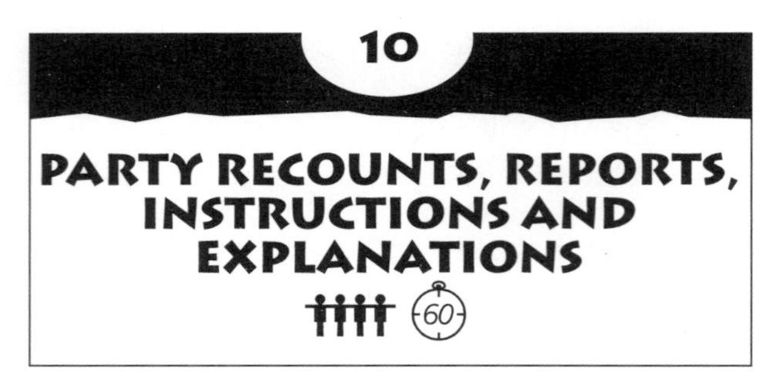

Teaching content

Recounts, reports and instructions all have different purposes and structures.

What you need

Writing materials, photographs taken at the party, paper cut to photograph size, chalkboard.

What to do

A short while after the party, some children may like to write a recount of what happened or an evaluative report of it.

Writing a recount: the party album

Show the photographs taken during the party to the children and discuss what is happening in them. Encourage the children to talk about their memories and recount their experiences.

Now organise the children into groups of about four and give each one a selection of photographs, ensuring that the photographs show different parts of the party, such as:

- the party preparations or guests arriving;
- early games and music;
- later games;
- the meal;
- games after the meal;
- guests leaving or the final tidy up.

Distribute a piece of writing paper approximately the same size as the photographs to each child. Ask the groups to decide on the chronological sequence in which the photographs were taken and number them accordingly. Ask each child in the group to take one photograph and write three or four sentences about it. Remind them to:

- write in the past tense;
- use chronological words (such as then, after, that). They may need to discuss which words are being used by others in their group to ensure continuity;
- describe and elaborate on the photograph, including their own memories, experiences or comments. Explain that this will make the account lively and interesting to read.

Suggest that a zigzag book would be a suitable format to display the recounts. Children should check their combined efforts for continuity and coherence before sticking their photographs and text into it in the appropriate sequence. Remind them to leave the first page blank so that they will be able to make and add a title and the names of the authors.

Writing an evaluative report

Remind the children of the various aspects of the party that needed to be planned and organised: games, food, decorations, invitations, and so on. List these on the board.

Organise the class into groups of about four or five and give each child some writing paper. Tell them that each person in the group must choose a different aspect from the list on the board and write a short report that details:

- why the aspect is important;
- the decisions they had to make;
- how well they feel this aspect was planned and organised, and why;
- any advice they could offer for next time;
- an appropriate illustration, labelled if necessary, to focus the reader's attention and highlight one aspect of the text.

Remind the children that they must each devise an appropriate heading for the aspect about which they are writing. They must make a group decision about how and where the headings should be written on the page, so that they all match. Then discuss whether headings should be:

- on the top line centre page, or on the left-hand side;
- capital letters or lower case;
- underlined or enclosed in a box;
- in a different colour or size of writing.

Once finished, distribute zigzag books or sheets of card or paper, large enough to display the work of the whole group. Tell the group to organise the report on the paper provided, leaving sufficient space for a border around each piece, an overall title and the names of the authors. Then ask them to mount the work and stick it into place.

Instructions and explanations

Arrange the children in groups of four or five. Explain that it would be a good idea to put all their experiences of the party to good use and write a 'Do-it-yourself party kit'. This could then be used by other children and adults who were organising a party. Brainstorm the different aspects that should be covered in such a kit, writing the children's ideas on the board.

Give each group a sheet of paper and ask them to copy the brainstorm list from the board and to add any additional ideas generated by the group members. Ask the groups to discuss and decide what they would each like to write about for their own party kit. They should then record who will take on each particular aspect of writing.

The children may need to be reminded of the structure and format of particular types of writing, and may need support when determining what they are going to write. If any children need further help to do particular kinds of writing, it may be more effective to make time for extra sessions and teach this to appropriate groups or to the class as a whole.

PARTY THEMES

If you decide to appeal to logic, you might use phrases such as:

I think we should have...

Firstly... Secondly... Finally...

If you decide to appeal to the emotions, you might use phrases such as:

The best parties...

Just imagine...

Parties need to be...

If we want to have fun...

If we want to provide a good time for others...

VOTING SLIP

Name ____________________

____

I have read the suggestions carefully.

The theme I wish to vote for is:

FOOD NAMES

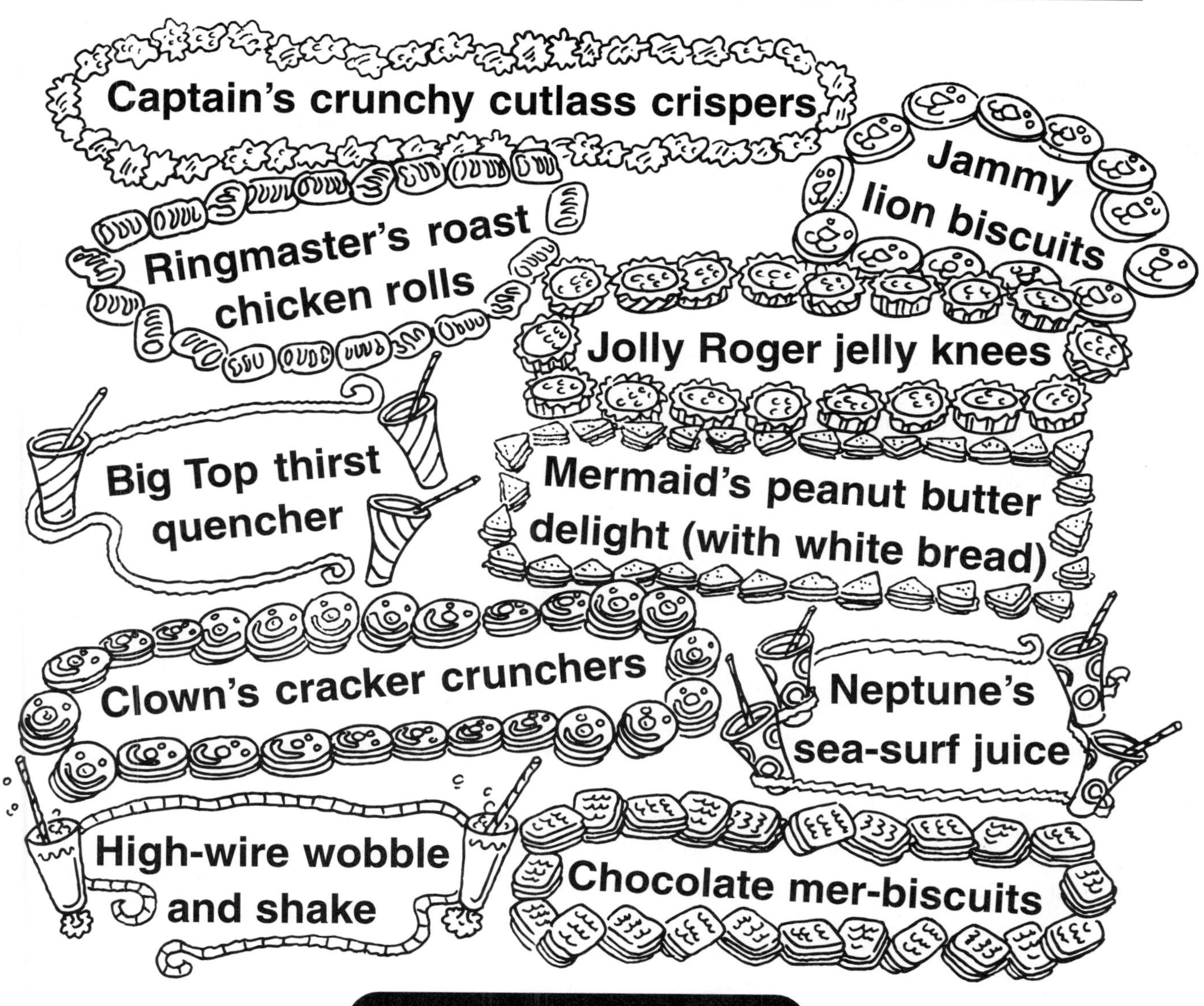

OUR FOOD IDEAS

Crisps

Biscuits

Jelly

Drinks

Sandwiches

INVITATION GROUP

You must design and make invitations for the guests.

You will need:

- the guest list;
- the class work from Activity 4 suggesting appropriate content and layouts for the invitations;
- good quality A4 or A5 paper, pencils, sequins, glitter, adhesive, collage materials and scissors.

Tasks

Display the class suggestions for invitations so that everyone in the group can read them. Discuss which ideas are best and why. Make sure that everyone takes part in the discussion and says what they think.

The chairperson must then give each person the name of a guest from the guest list.

Work on your own, or in pairs, to design and make exciting party invitations.
The invitations do not all need to be the same but *must* include all the important details about the party.

Read the advice at the bottom of this sheet to help you with particular techniques for making your invitation.

A border makes the invitation look attractive.
Use a ruler to make a border.

Decide on the key headings and how these will be positioned on the invitation.

Block out the lettering lightly in pencil first to ensure it will all fit into the space.

Decide before you start which words and letters will be done in capitals.

Look carefully at the materials provided for decorating your card and use them imaginatively.

You may want to decide to restrict your invitation to a few colours to make it look more striking.

Decide what illustrations you will have on your card, and where, before you start.

NAME

GAMES AND MUSIC GROUP

You must choose and plan the sequence of games, ensuring that props and equipment are available on the day and that everyone has a common understanding of the rules.

You will need:

- the class work from Activity 5 suggesting some appropriate games and dances;
- several A3 sheets of paper, a marker pen and writing materials;
- access to art materials if required.

Tasks

Display the suggestions for party games and music from the class so that everyone in the group can read them. Discuss which ideas are best and why. Make sure that everyone takes part in the discussion and says what they think.

As a group, choose the five games that would be the best for this party. Make sure you choose a suitable game:

- to start the party off;
- to play after the food;
- to play just before the food;
- to play at the end of the party.

Remember that the final list should have:

- a good variety of games – some that are quiet and some that are noisy or energetic;
- games that are appropriate for the party-goers and for the theme;
- games that most people are likely to know and enjoy;
- games that are appropriate to the space available.

Write the final list on the paper provided.

Now work in pairs. Allocate one game to each pair, who should discuss the rules and write them down. The following questions may help you do this:

- What equipment and music is needed for this game?
- What are the rules of this game?

How does it start?
What must the players do?
What happens in the end?
What happens to those who are out?
How do you know who is the final winner?

- Now list everything you need to do to prepare for this game.

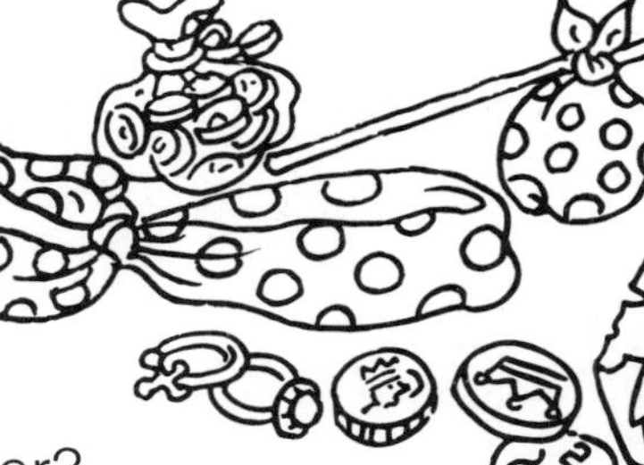

NAME

FOOD GROUP

You are responsible for choosing and preparing the food and ensuring that menus and food labels are ready for use on the day.

You will need:

- the class work from Activity 5 suggesting appropriate food;
- several A3 sheets of paper, a marker pen and writing materials;
- the class work from Activity 6 suggesting some appropriate names for the food;
- card, writing and colouring materials.

Crisps

Biscuits

Jelly

Drinks

Sandwiches

Tasks

Display the class suggestions for party food so that everyone in the group can read them. Discuss which ideas are best and why. Make sure that everyone takes part in the discussion and says what they think.

Try to agree on a list of party food and write this on a large sheet of paper.

Ensure that you have:

- some savoury and some sweet foods;
- some food that is suitable for vegetarians or people known to have special diets;
- food that is not too expensive and can be easily provided.

Put a * besides those foods that you think are essential.

Now discuss this list and agree it with the teacher.

NAME

WALL AND TABLE DECORATIONS GROUP

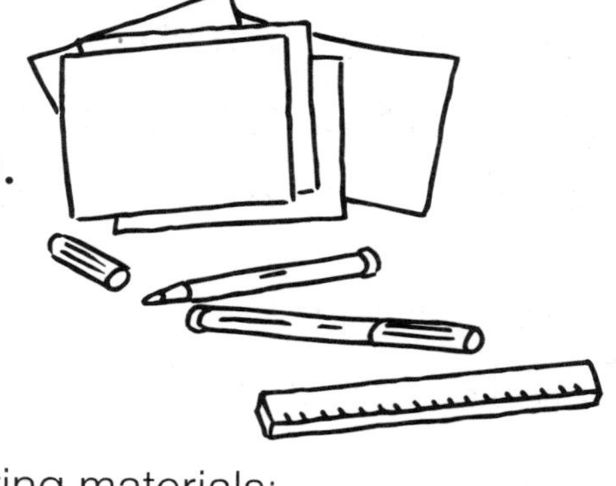

You must plan and make wall and table decorations that fit with the party theme.

You will need:

- the section of the work from Activity 5 suggesting some appropriate wall and table decorations;
- several A3 sheets of paper, a marker pen and writing materials;
- access to art and craft materials if required.

Tasks

Display the group brainstorms of wall and table decorations so that everyone in the group can read them. Discuss which ideas are best and why. Make sure that everyone takes part in the discussion and says what they think.

Agree a group list of wall and table decorations that fit with the party theme and write this on a large sheet of paper. Ensure that everyone in your group will plan and make some decorations for the party.

Divide your group into pairs.

Allocate at least one decoration to each pair, who should work together to write answers to the following questions in as much detail as possible.

List the materials and equipment you need to make and display this decoration.

List what you need to do to make this decoration.

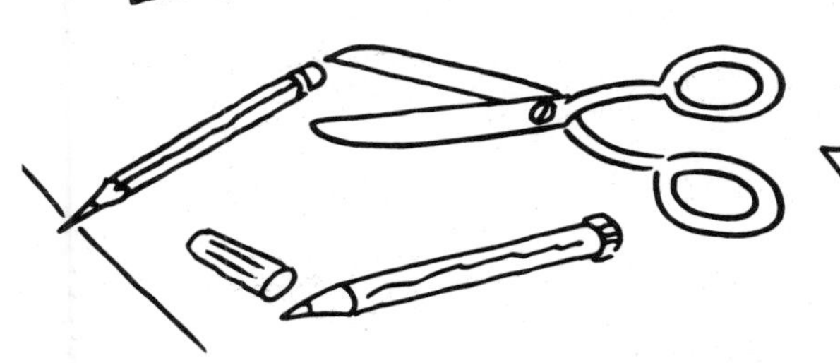

NAME

PARTY EVALUATION

The best part of this party was ______________________________

____

____

____

The best part of organising this party was ______________________

____

____

____

Here are some of the writing tasks that helped you to organise the party.

Think about each task and decide whether the writing was:

	essential	helpful	of no use	why
• Choosing a party theme.	☐	☐	☐	________
• Listing what has to be done.	☐	☐	☐	________
• Writing a guest list.	☐	☐	☐	________
• Writing invitations.	☐	☐	☐	________
• Writing action plans for food, decorations and games.	☐	☐	☐	________
• Writing to clarify the rules of games.	☐	☐	☐	________
• Writing interesting names for food.	☐	☐	☐	________

Scholastic
WORKSHOP

Chapter Five

CHILDREN'S HOLIDAY GUIDE

INTRODUCTION

Project description

Very few holiday leaflets target children in terms of the interests and activities they cover. In this project, the children work in groups of four to consider the tourist potential within their local area. Each group produces a series of leaflets aimed at children of their own age to advertise local places of interest and things to do or see.

Each group chooses six different topics for information leaflets. The first two leaflets are written by children working in pairs. After this each child works individually to write one further leaflet.

The work is presented as a set of six leaflets in a document wallet. The group designs a front cover that will appeal to children of their own age, ensuring that it gives all the information that their audience would expect and need. Finally, the finished work of each group is read by another group in the class.

Why this context?

Children will have had experience of seeing and using information leaflets and brochures for a variety of purposes. They may or may not have noticed that most of these publications are aimed at adults. Many children will find it fascinating to see how a brochure aimed at their own age group will differ from the adult version in both the topics covered and the language used.

Through this project, therefore, children learn about audience and purpose and about how these may determine language choices. They have opportunities to use report, instructional and persuasive writing and learn about the use of layout and presentation, headings and subheadings, diagrams, illustrations and maps.

Project organisation

Before the project, the children organise, discuss and assess a class collection of holiday brochures and leaflets.

They plan the overall project in groups of four but work initially in pairs and then individually. The paired work provides a supportive situation in which to make decisions about illustrations and layout. It also helps to ensure that each child has at least one other person in the class to whom they can turn for comment and support when crafting their first leaflets.

When each child works individually to produce one more leaflet, they are given opportunities to revisit and consolidate much that they have learned.

Publication, celebration and review

The work is published as a folder containing the six separate leaflets. The writers read and comment on their own work and the children then regroup to read and comment on one other brochure. Reflection and discussion are focused on both the chosen format and the content of the leaflets and are structured by using a photocopiable sheet.

If appropriate, a wider audience could be achieved by inviting a representative from the local tourist office, travel agency, council or the manager of a local amenity or resort to visit and comment on the display of work.

PRE-SESSION

Before this project, start a class collection of holiday leaflets and brochures. Make a space available for this on the wall, or provide a loose-leaf folder with plastic wallets into which the children can insert the items they bring. It is useful to divide the collection into two sections: one for local and one for non-local information.

Each child in the class should contribute at least one item to the collection. If they are not aware of any guides they have used, or do not have them at home, they should collect guides on the local area.

Where the children contribute leaflets, guides or brochures that they have actually used, encourage them to write a few sentences to indicate how useful these were. Where the children contribute local guides, they should be asked to comment on whether each leaflet would encourage them to go to the place mentioned. The comments slips on photocopiable page 56 may be used for this purpose.

The children should insert these written comments of the appropriate tourist guides in the plastic wallet.

Teaching content

Both informative and persuasive writing must consider the needs of the readers.

What you need

Photocopiable page 57, the collection of holiday guides (including some of the local area), marker pens, large sheets of paper.

What to do

If the children have not contributed many local guides and brochures to the class collection, ensure that you have a selection to discuss with the class.

Gather the children together and show them the collection of holiday guides and read any remarks written on the comments slips by individuals in the class. Discuss which the children thought were effective, which were not, and why. It is likely the children will comment on:

- the selection of places and the extent to which they interest children;
- how the places are described or portrayed.

Encourage the children to discuss both good and bad examples before asking them to turn their attention more specifically to those that deal with local facilities and places of interest. Ask the children whether they think:

- the available guides adequately highlight the possibilities of the local area for children;
- the descriptions appeal to children.

Suggest that the class could produce a better selection of guides to the local area than currently exist for children their own age. Suggest that the first thing to consider would be the selection of places and activities to be featured. These should be particularly appealing to their own age group.

Now organise the children into groups of four. Distribute the marker pens and large sheets of paper and ask each group to brainstorm the possibilities of their own locality for children visiting the area. Ensure that they understand that these may be official places (swimming pools, parks, leisure centres, cinemas) or unofficial places such as places to make camps, meet other children or simply 'hang out'.

Allow the groups about 15 minutes to jot down as many places as possible before asking each group to briefly present and explain their lists to the class. Then allow each group to add to their list any good ideas they have heard in the presentations. Next hand out photocopiable page 57 and encourage the children to classify their items under the headings listed on the sheet. They should try to add ideas to the categories under which they have few entries.

Teaching content

Careful selection of vocabulary, jokes and the use of devices such as alliteration can attract attention and appeal to particular readers.

What you need

Brainstormed lists from Activity 1, writing materials, photocopiable page 58, A3 paper, scissors, adhesive.

What to do

Give out the brainstormed lists from Activity 1. Remind the class that they are going to make a series of tourist leaflets specifically aimed at children of their own age visiting the locality.

Explain that each group will produce six leaflets. Ask the groups to read through their brainstorms and choose six items – one for each leaflet they will make. They should place a star or tick beside those they have selected.

Once these have been chosen, remind the class that it is important each leaflet has a suitable heading that will appeal to the age group it targets. Give out photocopiable page 58, one per group, along with the scissors, A3 paper and adhesive. Read through the headings on the sheet and ask the children to cut out each heading and then sequence them in order of priority, placing those that appeal most at the top. Headings that they find equally attractive or appealing should be placed beside each other. Allow the groups about five minutes to agree on a sequence and stick the headings on to the A3 paper in the agreed order.

Hold a brief discussion with the whole class about what made particular headings attractive. Do they think that their parents or grandparents would have chosen the same sequence? Why?

The children are likely to suggest that some of the following features made the headings appealing:

• the vocabulary used – kids, children's, flumes, challenge, cool...;
• the use of devices such as alliteration and imagery;
• the use of jokes and humour.

Now ask the groups to consider the six items for their own leaflets. Suggest they work together to write an appropriate heading for each item. These should be recorded on the back of the photocopiable sheet.

Explain that the first two leaflets will be produced by children working in pairs. Thereafter, each child will work alone to produce one further leaflet. Ask the children to determine the working pairs within each group and then decide which individual or pair will write about each item from the group list.

Teaching content

Directions and instructions must be clear and concise. Descriptions can be slanted to appeal to particular readers.

What you need

A3 sheets of headings from Activity 2, photocopiable page 59, scrap paper, writing materials.

What to do

Begin the lesson by reminding the children that they will be working in pairs to write about the item chosen in the previous activity. Each pair must try to produce the most effective leaflet possible.

Explain that any topic can be written about in a number of different ways. Distribute the photocopiable sheet which gives four different descriptions of the same place. Read it through with the class and ask the children which descriptions they find most or least appealing, and why.

Tell the children to bear this discussion in mind as they think carefully about how they will write about their chosen item. Suggest that it may help them to:

• identify the *most* appealing thing about this place or activity for children;
• consider other appealing aspects;
• note some key facts about this place or activity.

Tell the children to write a short description of the place or activity. This could be written from the viewpoint of an outsider looking in or in the form of the observations, feelings, noises or thoughts of someone inside the place or engaged in the activity. Explain that in either case the description should focus on the most appealing aspects and key facts.

Explain that the writers will also need to think about what information a stranger may need to find the place or activity, and any advice they may need on the best times or days to go. Such information should be clear and concise, making use of maps, diagrams and numbered points where appropriate.

The children can choose how to divide the work. They may wish to work together, taking turns to write, or one partner could write an inviting description while the other prepares the directions and advice.

Tell the children they will have about 35 minutes to produce a first draft. If they have chosen to work separately, suggest they meet shortly before the end of this time to read each other's work, suggest amendments or improvements and ensure that the two pieces of work read well together and cover all that needs to be said.

Teaching content

Headings and illustrations help to attract the reader. They also break the text into more manageable chunks.

What you need

Magazines with photographs that may be used in leaflets if required, drawing, writing and colouring materials, a selection of well-designed brochures and leaflets, A4 unlined paper, adhesive, scissors, unlined paper cut into a variety of shapes for writing and illustrations.

What to do

Ask the children to get back into their groups and allow time for each pair to read their work to the others.

Tell the children to look at the selection of leaflets and brochures provided and to note:

• the use of an overall heading and subheadings, such as 'When to go', 'How to find it', 'How to get there' or 'How much does it cost';

• the nature and position of any photographs and drawings.

Point out that the illustrations are provided to present an attractive image that complements the text – either showing people enjoying the activities or evoking an atmospheric setting. They may be of varying sizes and shapes and, like the subheadings, are positioned to break up the text into readable chunks.

Give out the A4 paper. Allow each pair to decide how their leaflet will be folded – in half, into three sections, or left as an A4 handout.

Suggest that each pair discusses and agrees the basic layout of the writing and how the headings and subheadings will be used along with the shape, size, content and location of pictures or diagrams. Tell the children that pictures may be hand-drawn or cut out from magazines. It may also be necessary to mention how diagrams, plans and maps are labelled.

Stress the importance of folding the A4 sheets accurately and neatly. Suggest that the main headings may be put straight on to the folded sheet, but that the subheadings, writing and illustrations are produced on separate pieces of paper and stuck into place. This allows the children to work separately and also means that a mistake by one child does not spoil the work of the pair. Explain that there may be further spaces left once the writing and illustrations are positioned and that the children should therefore be prepared to fill these with borders or additional pictures.

The children should now work in their pairs to produce their leaflets. Once finished, these should be shown and read to the other members of the group. If time allows, show the finished items to the class, commenting on *one* aspect of each that makes it effective. Store this work in a safe place until it is needed for Activity 7.

Teaching content

Persuasive descriptions should highlight the most appealing aspects of a place or activity. Directions and instructions should be clear and concise, using diagrams, maps and numbered points where appropriate.

What you need

Scrap paper, chalkboard, writing materials.

What to do

Point out that the children have now had the experience of writing and producing one entry or leaflet in pairs, so they will know exactly what they have to do when working individually to write and produce their next piece of work.

Remind each individual of the item they have yet to write about.

Remind the class of the main teaching points from Activity 3. These were that they may find it helpful to:

- identify the *most* appealing thing about this place or activity;
- consider other appealing aspects;
- note some key facts about this place or activity.

Remind them that they may write a short description, either from the viewpoint of an outsider looking in or in the form of the observations, feelings, noises or thoughts of someone inside the place or engaged in the activity.

They also had to think about the information a stranger might need to find the place and any advice they would want about the best times or days to visit. This information should be clearly signalled with an appropriate subheading. Diagrams, maps and numbered points may help to keep this clear and concise.

Before the children begin work, remind them that they may start their descriptions in a number of ways. The opening sentence may be:

- a question (Do you like to visit places that are quiet and still?);
- a statement (Simply the best place for having fun in... is...);
- a suggestion (Try a visit to... You may find it is the highlight of your trip...);
- a description (...is full of laughing kids, enjoying themselves doing...).

Write these on the chalkboard, then suggest the children spend ten minutes, in pairs, discussing each place that they will each write about. Then tell the whole class that they have 25 minutes to write (in silence) the first draft of their leaflets.

Once finished, tell the children to read their first drafts to their paired partner. Remind them to listen carefully and to make constructive suggestions. It may be helpful for them to identify:

- one thing that is particularly effective;
- one thing that is unclear or could be improved.

When doing this they should explain why they think so and suggest how it could be changed to make it better.

Once this discussion session is over, writers should reconsider their drafts, changing them if they wish.

Teaching content

Headings, illustrations and layout attract the reader and organise the text into workable chunks, making it easier to understand.

What you need

Magazines with photographs that can be cut up for illustrations, drawing, writing and colouring materials, a selection of well-designed brochures and leaflets, A4 unlined paper, adhesive, scissors, unlined paper cut into a variety of shapes for writing and illustrations.

What to do

Remind the children about how they worked in Activity 4. Explain that they may wish to fold the A4 sheet differently, or leave it unfolded this time. They should consider the overall layout carefully.

Construct with the class a list of things to remember and write the key points on the chalkboard:

- Headings and subheadings should attract the reader and divide the text into chunks.
- Illustrations may be drawn or cut from

magazines. They should complement the text by exemplifying activities or evoking atmosphere.

- Diagrams, maps and numbered points should be clearly labelled.
- Work should be prepared on separate pieces of paper, then stuck into position.

Give the children about 40 minutes to complete their finished product. Just before the end of the session, organise the children into groups and allow a short time for them to see the work done by others in their group. Then store all the work carefully ready to distribute in Activity 7.

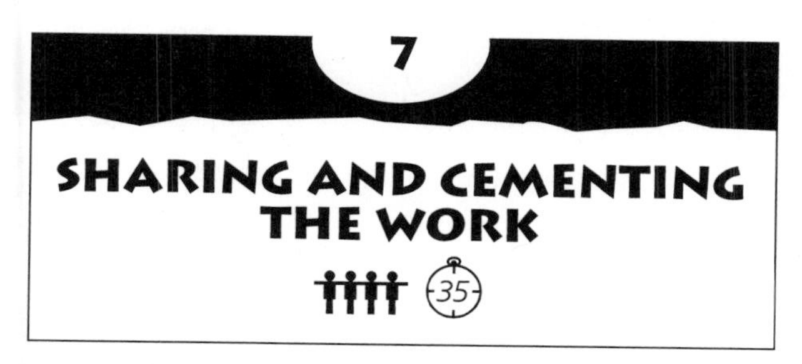

7 SHARING AND CEMENTING THE WORK

35

Teaching content

The title should reflect the content and attract the reader's attention.

What you need

Completed leaflets from Activities 4 and 6, writing and colouring materials, adhesive, card, document wallets, A4 map of area if required.

What to do

Distribute the completed leaflets and brochure entries from Activities 4 and 6, along with one document wallet per group.

Explain that the children should title and decorate a document wallet to hold all six leaflets. Remind the class that a title should reflect the content of the six leaflets and attract the readers. Suggest that the group discusses and agrees a title, then allocates one person to produce this while the others draw illustrations which can be glued on to the front face of the wallet. Obviously, they will need to agree appropriate sizes and subject matter to make sure the illustrations fit and do not duplicate each other. Show the children how to use thick lines to outline the edges of their wallet, making it look both distinctive and attractive.

Any groups with time remaining may like to indicate, on an enlarged local map of the area, the exact location of their featured places. The maps should be mounted on a larger sheet of card, with strips of paper and circular illustrations used to indicate the various locations.

8 CELEBRATING THE WORK

30

Teaching content

One can learn about effective writing, layout and use of illustrations by reading other people's work.

What you need

Work produced in Activity 7, photocopiable page 60, writing materials.

What to do

Ask the children to rearrange themselves so that they are standing at a different table from the one at which they usually sit. Explain that you would like no more than four children at each table, or each end of a table.

Now give out the completed work of each group, ensuring that no pupils are looking at their own work. Tell the children that you want them to look carefully at the leaflets or brochures and, as a group, to complete the questions and fill in their comments on a sheet which will be supplied to them.

Distribute a copy of photocopiable page 60 to each group and read it through with the class. Emphasise that the children must take this task seriously, and ensure that they spend about 20 minutes reading and discussing the work they have been given before completing the photocopiable sheet.

Once finished, display all the brochures and document wallets containing the leaflets on the wall, along with the completed photocopiable comments sheets.

If possible, invite officials from the local tourist board or council to view the display, give a short talk about how the organisation for which they work selects and makes advertising literature for the local area, and listen to the children's comments and ideas for producing advertising literature in the future.

NAME

MAKING A HOLIDAY GUIDE FOR CHILDREN

Name

Title of guide or brochure

Item featured

I have/have not* visited this place.

In my opinion, the entry in the guide does/does not* do this place justice.

It would/would not* encourage me to go because ______________

____

____

* delete that which does not apply

Name

Title of guide or brochure

Item featured

I have/have not* visited this place.

In my opinion, the entry in the guide does/does not* do this place justice.

It would/would not* encourage me to go because ______________

____

____

* delete that which does not apply

NAME

PLACES TO GO, THINGS TO SEE

Things to do

Places to go

People to meet

Ideas for when the weather is wet or fine

Things to do indoors or outdoors

Things children can do with other children

Things to do with the whole family

Things for kids to do alone

Quiet places or activities

Historical/active/social places

Places to eat/meet/shop/

Cheap places

Places for special occasions

Places for excitement or adventure

Places where you can learn or explore

NAME

INTRODUCING ...
THE FIRST CHILDREN'S HOLIDAY GUIDE

Swim and Keep Fit at Longbank Pool

VISIT OUR PARK

Meet the
CHALLENGE
of Longbank Adventure Park

Flumes & Rides
in Longbank Pool

NAME

DESCRIPTIONS OF THE SAME CASTLE

If you go along the winding lane to the north side of the village, you will find yourself at Roughan Castle. This was built in the 17th Century by Sir William Rant, who was a highly esteemed local landowner. The castle changed its name as a result of the peasants' revolts in 1895...

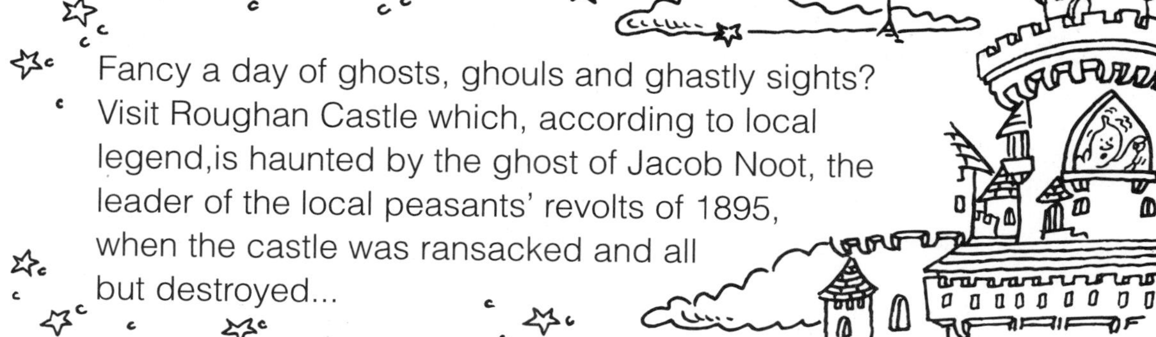

Fancy a day of ghosts, ghouls and ghastly sights? Visit Roughan Castle which, according to local legend,is haunted by the ghost of Jacob Noot, the leader of the local peasants' revolts of 1895, when the castle was ransacked and all but destroyed...

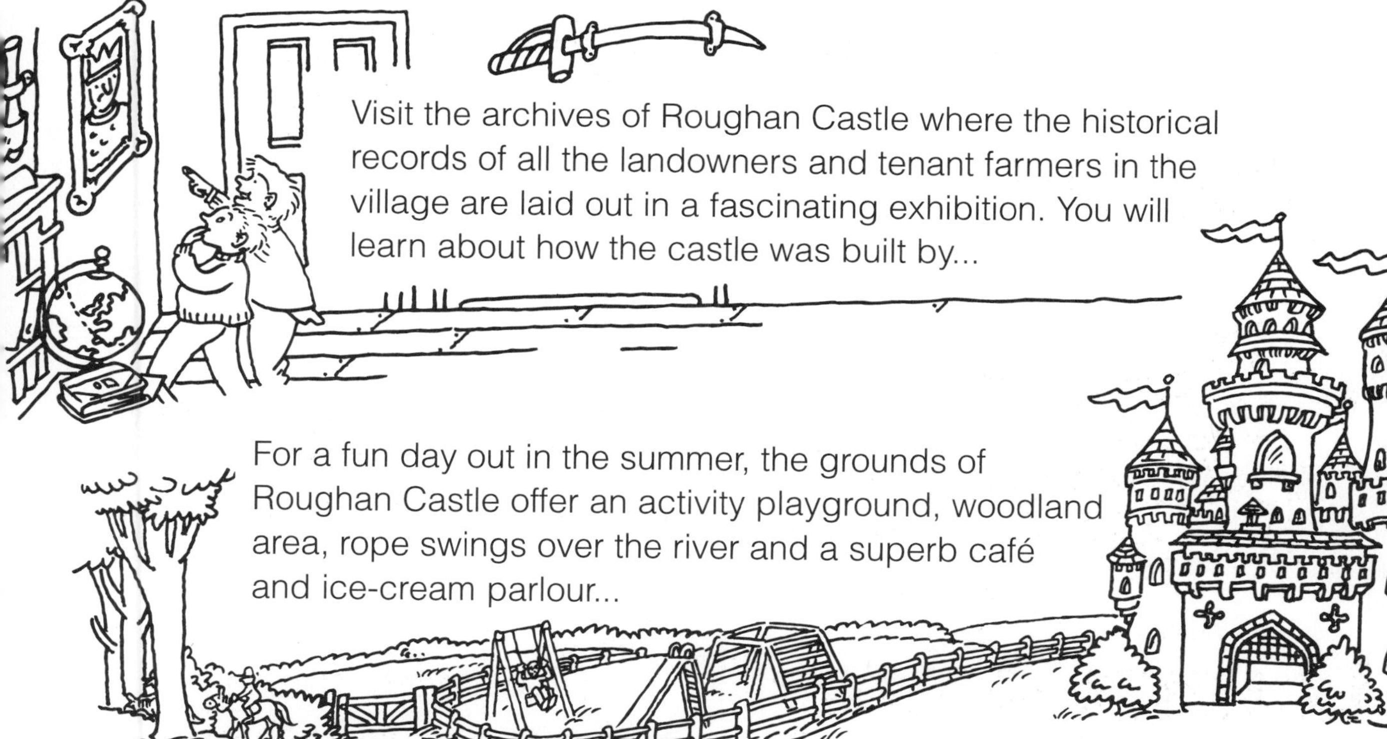

Visit the archives of Roughan Castle where the historical records of all the landowners and tenant farmers in the village are laid out in a fascinating exhibition. You will learn about how the castle was built by...

For a fun day out in the summer, the grounds of Roughan Castle offer an activity playground, woodland area, rope swings over the river and a superb café and ice-cream parlour...

NAME

CELEBRATING THE WORK

First thoughts on looking at the work:

1 ______________ because ______________

____

2 ______________ because ______________

____

3 ______________ because ______________

____

Examples of effective writing from this work are:

1 ______________

2 ______________

3 ______________

Examples of effective layout are:

1 ______________

2 ______________

Examples of effective use of illustration are:

1 ______________

2 ______________

This will be a good resource for children coming to this area because

____

Work by: ______________

Comments by: ______________

Scholastic
WORKSHOP

Chapter Six

SWEET SUCCESS

INTRODUCTION

Project description

The idea of sweet-making can be introduced to the class as their way of contributing to a forthcoming fundraising event. The children should be able to see how each activity in this project will contribute to the success of their sweet-making as, through them, they will make decisions about their sweets, such as which recipe to use, or what to call them. Presenting the children with this 'real' situation provides them with a strong motivation for their functional writing, as they will be able to see that it has a clearly-defined and practical purpose.

The form in which recipes are written introduces children to procedural writing, and gives them a formula for sequenced instructions that can be adapted for use in other situations. Opportunities for recounts and persuasive writing also arise. In addition to the language activities the project will also generate opportunities to introduce:

- mathematics, through money and weight.
- science, by exploring how changes occur in materials when they are mixed, heated and so on.
- health education, by considering hygiene connected with food. The project could be developed to include healthy eating.

Why this context?

From the outset the children will feel that they are working together to make a success of their sweet-making, and also to benefit a worthwhile cause. This collaboration will not be limited to the class but will involve:

- staff and pupils from other classes;
- family members;
- the local community, who may display posters in their shops or buy the sweets.

In this way children will be provided with many opportunities to communicate and interact with both adults and children.

The context allows feedback from all those involved, giving the class a chance to evaluate their work from the sales of their sweets and the opinions expressed on them. There is also the added bonus for the children that they can evaluate the most important product – the sweets – by tasting them!

Project organisation

Before starting the project the teacher will need to check all the practical aspects involved:

- availability of funds to finance the sweet-making;
- cooking facilities in the school;
- possibilities of help from parents – responding to the children's questionnaires, helping with cooking and so on;
- establishing the date and location of the fundraising event for which the sweets are to be made.

Children will approach the project more easily if they have become accustomed to the form in which recipes are written and the vocabulary associated with them. A classroom collection of cookery books, baking equipment and so on would provide this opportunity.

The project activities require the children to work in groups, varying in number from four to six. Some of these result in a collaborative outcome while others expect a piece of work to be produced individually, following a group task.

Publication, celebration and review

The possible publication formats are many and varied. These include:

- questionnaire forms;
- illustrated baking rules;
- instruction sheets;
- advertising posters and notices.

Each of these should be presented to a wider audience by making a class book, giving examples of the activities involved at each stage. So the 'Getting started' section would include a copy of the questionnaire sent out, and the information gained from it.

Children could also compile a class recipe book of favourite sweet recipes contributed by parents and staff. This idea could be developed to include recipes from different cultures, or healthy recipes.

Teaching content

How to structure a questionnaire. Persuasive wording will elicit relevant responses.

What you need

A range of brand name sweets (different flavours and textures), chalkboard, writing materials.

What to do

Explain to the children that they are going to make sweets to sell at a fundraising venture. Tell them that before they decide which sweets to make it would be helpful to find out what kind of sweets their prospective customers (the pupils, parents and staff of the school) prefer. In order to do this they are going to compile a questionnaire to send out to these prospective customers.

Show the children a selection of familiar brand-name sweets. Using these as examples, brainstorm with the class the attributes of particular sweets that make them favourites. Look for responses such as:

'I like these white ones because they're really minty.'
'Toffees are my favourite because they're chewy and last a long time.'

In this way establish the reasons people have for preferring one sweet to another based on *flavour* and *texture.* On the board make up a list of the words suggested by the children under these two headings. Now organise the class into groups of five before writing the following questionnaire format on the board.

Class ______________ will be making sweets to raise funds for ________________. Before deciding on the kind of sweet to make, they want to find out which would be the most popular.
Please tick one box only.
1 Which type of sweets do you prefer?
2 Which flavour do you prefer?
Please return this questionnaire to school by
______________________________.
Thank you for completing it.

Read over the first part to check that children understand that the purpose of this section is to explain to people why they are being asked to fill it in.

Next, read over the second part to explain that this will give them the information they want about the kind of sweets their customers would buy. In their groups they should decide how to word this section of their own questionnaire, making sure that the options they offer are clear, for example a choice between 'soft or crunchy' but not 'hard or crunchy'. The choice of flavour is also important – mint, chocolate, coconut and so on. Remind them to refer to the list on the board.

After 15 minutes ask a spokesperson from each group to read out their choices. Discuss and compare results to reach a conclusion on the wording to be used in the final draft of the questionnaire. The final draft can then be handwritten or produced on a word processor by a group from the class. Make sure they include the date on which the questionnaire should be returned.

Since the children will be collating the results, only send out a manageable number of questionnaires.

Teaching content

How to collate information from a questionnaire. Prioritising criteria.

What you need

Questionnaires from Activity 1, writing materials.

What to do

Explain to the class that they are now going to check the information filled in on their questionnaires. They will do this in groups of five, with each group taking a turn to check the results. Appoint a scribe for each group and ask them to list all the choices offered on their questionnaire. They should then count how many people chose each texture and flavour and record this information on their sheet.

Ensure that the children have chosen an appropriate method to use when collating the information, such as sorting, counting then recording, dealing with one part at a time. Tell them that when this is done they should read over the results and write down what they have learned about the kind of sweets preferred by their prospective customers.

When all the sheets have been completed ask a spokesperson for each group to read out their conclusions. Establish that most people said they prefer sweets that have a __________ texture and are __________ flavoured. Tell the children this information will now be used to help choose the sweet recipe.

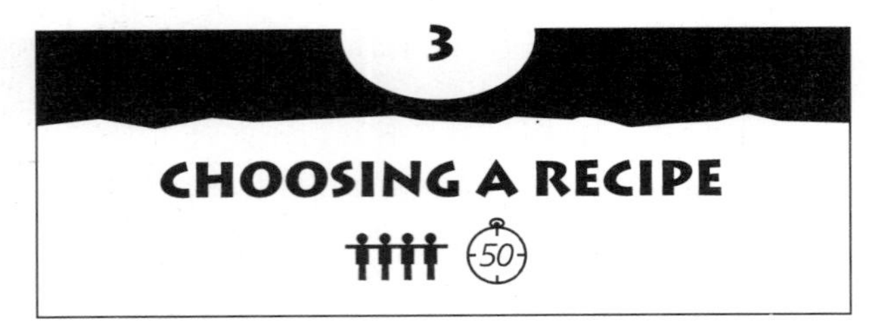

Teaching content

Arguments can be structured by listing points for and against; they must be supported with evidence and often end with a conclusion or recommendation.

What you need

Sets of recipes chosen from photocopiable pages 71 and 72, A4 paper, chalkboard, writing materials.

What to do

Before the lesson choose some or all of the recipes from photocopiable pages 71 and 72. Ensure that your choices enable the children to put forward arguments for and against their suitability, based on the results of their questionnaire and the cooking facilities available in the school. If you do not choose to use all five recipes, copy your selected ones on to one sheet.

Explain to the children that they are going to choose one recipe for their sweet-making from a selection that you will give them. Arrange the class in groups of four and give each group copies of the recipes you have selected. Tell the children that these are the recipes from which they will choose, and point out that they should bear in mind the following:

- Would it be popular with most of the prospective customers?

(Refer to the results of their sweet survey.)

- Is it a suitable one to make in school?

(This will depend on the cooking facilities available, for example it may need to be a no-cook recipe.)

Write each of these questions on the board so the children can refer to them.

Read over one of the recipes from the photocopiable sheets with the children to make sure they understand the way a recipe is set out. Establish which part of the recipe relates to each question on the board, for example the list of ingredients will indicate the flavour of the sweets. Ask each group to appoint a scribe before handing out A4 paper. Demonstrate how this is to be completed by asking the children to help fill in the frame for Recipe 1 on the chalkboard.

Recipe 1

For:	Against:
• It is hard.	• It is not a popular flavour.

Now tell the children to repeat this procedure with the other recipes.

After 15 minutes ask a spokesperson from one group to report which recipe their group thinks is best and the reasons for their choice. Ask which other groups have chosen that recipe, and find out if their reasons for selecting it are the same as those of the first group. Repeat this procedure until all groups have reported, keeping a record of the choices on the board.

Finally, use this record to see which recipe or recipes most groups selected. If there is no obvious choice then discuss the arguments put forward for each one to reach a conclusion with the class about which recipe to select. It may be necessary to encourage compromise!

4

RULES FOR SWEET SUCCESS

Teaching content

Rules should be framed in a positive way to persuade people to obey them. Rules need to address the reader directly.

What you need

Wallchart entitled 'Handy Hints for Cooking', folded lengthways into three sections, with subheadings: *Before cooking, During cooking* and *After cooking*, A4 and A3 paper.

What to do

Explain to the children that they are going to produce a set of simple rules for the day they make their sweets that will result in happy, healthy and safe cooking. Show them the wallchart and tell them that their rules (handy hints) will be divided into three sections. Point out the three subheadings on the chart.

Talk about what they need to do if they are to cook successfully. Areas to cover include:

- good hygiene;
- ingredients, equipment and procedures;
- tidiness;
- safety.

List these on the board for children to refer to when making up their 'Handy hints'.

Arrange the children in groups of four. Give out blank A4 paper and appoint a scribe for each group. Tell them that each group is now to think of rules that will remind people what to do before they start baking. The scribes should write these down.

After ten minutes ask a spokesperson from each group to read out their rules for *Before cooking*. Discuss these suggestions and choose the two that the class consider most important. Write these in the relevant section on the chart.

Repeat this procedure for the other two stages. Some of the following will probably be suggested:

Before cooking:
Wash your hands
Wear an apron
Read the recipe
During cooking:
Measure carefully
Mop up spills
Be careful with knives

After cooking:
Wash equipment
Wipe tables
Taste the results!

When the rules have been chosen and filled in on the wallchart, ask the children to write out and illustrate individual copies of 'Handy hints for cooking'. These might be given to other classes to use when they cook; a copy can be included at the beginning of a class recipe book and, of course, the children will refer to them when making their sweets.

5

SWEET-MAKING

Teaching content

Following a procedure. Helpful instructions tell the reader what to do but also give advice about how to do it. Reflecting on the procedure to identify areas of difficulty.

What you need

Ingredients and equipment for each group, recipe cards with an extra heading 'Cook's tip', copies of 'Handy hints' from Activity 4, writing materials, extra adult helpers if possible.

What to do

Before the lesson starts, prepare a table for each group, laying out their equipment and copies of the chosen recipe. Ingredients can be set out separately on a labelled table. A weighing area can also be set up if there are not enough scales for each group to have a set.

Arrange the class in groups of six at the prepared tables. Explain to them that they are going to make their sweets following the recipe cards provided. Remind the children of the reason for their sweet-making and tell them that they want to be proud of their product!

Discuss the way a recipe is set out, listing the ingredients then giving sequenced instructions. Read through the list of ingredients with the class and make sure they know what each one is by asking volunteers to find them on the ingredients table. Tell them to check with an adult when they are weighing ingredients.

Now read over the method, making sure the children understand cooking terms which may be unfamiliar, such as 'sieve' or 'beat'.

Remind the children of the 'Handy hints' for cooking (devised in Activity 4). Suggest that they check they are following these at each stage of their cooking. Tell each group to appoint a 'reader' whose job is to read each instruction aloud to his or her group. Now set them to work making the sweets.

When the sweet-making is finished tell them to discuss, in their groups, which part of the recipe they found trickiest, something that it would be useful to know about before starting the recipe – perhaps that the sweets get very sticky when you roll them so you must remember to put icing sugar on your hands. Tell them this is their 'Cook's tip' – a piece of advice for someone who has never used this recipe. Appoint a scribe for each group to add this advice to their recipe sheet. Allow ten minutes for this, then let each group share their 'tip' with the rest of the class.

Further development

A collection of families' favourite sweet recipes could be made. Ask those who contribute them to add their own 'Cook's tip'. These could then be made into a class recipe book; copies could even be sold at the fundraising event.

Teaching content

Effective sweet names use persuasive language and imagery. Techniques such as alliteration and rhyme ensure they are easily remembered.

What you need

Selection of well-known and well-named sweets, sample of the class sweet per child, ballot box, slips of paper, poster paper, A4 paper, chalkboard, pencils and felt-tipped pens.

What to do

Explain to the children that they are going to choose a name for the sweets they have made. Arrange the class in groups of four and ask them to brainstorm names of sweets that they think are effective. Encourage them to name types of sweets rather than brand names, for example dolly mixtures, jelly babies, chocolate

buttons and so on. Appoint a scribe for each group to write these suggestions on poster paper, then ask reporters to read aloud the names their group likes best. Point out to the children that the names they have written down are obviously easy to remember, otherwise they wouldn't have been able to draw up lists. Discuss the reasons why memorability is so important when sweets are being named.

Now give each group some samples of a well-known sweet. Tell them to examine and taste these in their groups and decide the reasons why they think that particular sweet was given its name. After five minutes of discussion ask a spokesperson from each group to tell the others what their sweet was and why it got its name. Expect responses such as:

'We think our sweet is called a chocolate button because it is a button shape and is made of chocolate.'

When each group has contributed, point out that sweet names need to suit a characteristic of the product. Make a list on the board of those mentioned. These should include: taste or flavour, shape and colour.

Remind the children also of the 'memorability' factor. This is generally aided by literary devices such as alliteration.

Next give each child one sample of the sweets they made. Tell the groups that they are to write a list of appropriate names for this delicacy, remembering to refer to the criteria on the board. After ten minutes ask each group to select the name they like best from their list. The chosen names should now be written in large writing on individual pieces of A4 paper and pinned on the wall. Explain that the class will be given the chance to vote for the sweet name they like best. (Point out, however, that groups are not allowed to vote for their own sweet name.) A spokesperson from each group should be allowed to explain why they think their group's name is most fitting!

Now give each child a slip of paper and ask them to copy the suggested sweet names on to it. Explain that this is a ballot paper and they should mark with an 'X' the name they think suits their sweet best. Ballot papers should be posted in a ballot box, possibly made from a shoebox. The class teacher, or a group of children, should then empty the box and, once the votes have been counted, announce the winning name.

7 PACKAGING THE SWEETS

Teaching content

Instructions are procedural writing; instructions should be sequenced in chronological order and start with an imperative.

What you need

Cardboard cut to size to hold six sweets, six class sweets, small plastic food bags, sweet name labels and adhesive tape – one set per group, plus another set per child.

What to do

Explain to the children that they now need to learn how to package their sweets. Arrange the class in groups of four, checking that they have all washed their hands. Give each group a piece of card, a bag, six sweets, sweet name labels and a roll of adhesive tape. The packaging is to be carried out as follows:

- Put the card into the bag.
- Arrange the sweets neatly on the card.
- Fold the top of the bag and tape it down.
- Tape a name label on top.

When every group has completed this successfully, write

You will need:
This is what you do:

on the chalkboard and ask them, individually, to use it to write out an instruction sheet of how to package their sweets.

Read over the sheet to make sure they understand what to do. Tell them to bear in mind the following when writing instructions.

- Number each instruction.
- Start each with a 'command', for example: *put* the card..., *fold* the bag and so on.
- Make sure they are in the correct sequence.

Allow 20 minutes, then ask the children to form pairs. Tell them to wash their hands again, swap instruction sheets with their partner and package another six sweets, following their partner's instructions *exactly* as they are written. After ten minutes let the children check how accurate and clear their instructions were. They can then try to rectify any problems. The class can now continue packaging the rest of the sweets for their sale

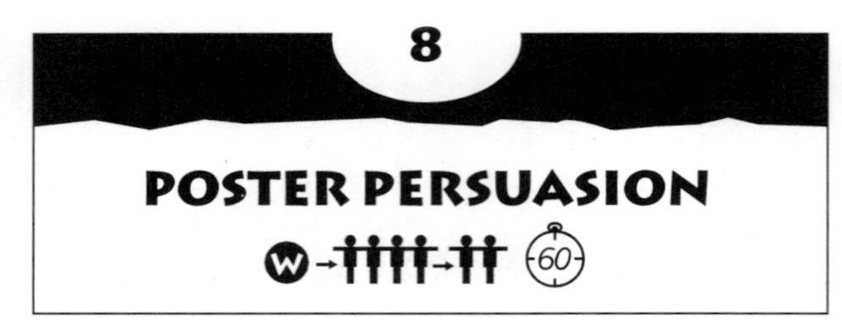

Teaching content

Effective advertising is persuasive. It states what the product is and describes it in a way that will be attractive to the reader. Different readers may find different aspects attractive.

What you need

'Sample' posters – commercially produced or made for previous events in school, A3 and A4 paper, rulers, pencils and felt-tipped pens, wallchart with the following information – name and price of sweets, date, time and venue of fundraising event, chalkboard.

What to do

Explain to the class that they are going to spread the word about their sweets by making posters to advertise them. Tell them that posters are one of the most popular forms of advertising. They encourage us to do everything from buying a fizzy drink to putting litter in bins! Now arrange the class in groups of five. Give each a 'sample' poster, before copying the following questions on to the chalkboard.

1 **What is the purpose of this poster?**
2 **How do you know?**
3 **Who is the poster aimed at?**
4 **Is there any way you think it could be improved?**
5 **Where would be the best place to display it?**

Read through the questions with them, making sure they understand the activity. Tell them to look carefully at their poster and discuss each question within the group before writing their answers on a sheet of A4 paper.

Allow 20 minutes for this, then ask each group to pin their posters up for the rest of the class to see, while a reporter reads out their answers. Discuss these, concluding that to make an effective poster we must:

- state clearly what the 'product' is;
- make it eye-catching – a simple slogan combined with an appropriate illustration;
- know our 'target' audience;
- display the poster where the 'target' audience will see it, for example an anti-litter poster in a holiday resort or a jumble sale poster in a local shop.

Write this checklist on the board, then arrange the class in pairs to make their own posters. Make some A3-size and others A4 – shops may prefer to display the smaller size. Tell them to remember the first three points on the checklist on the board when they are designing their poster, and to check the relevant information on the wall chart (which should be displayed prominently).

Before they begin they must decide the following:

- What is the product they are advertising?
- What information about it do they need to include?
- Can they think of a catchy slogan or an eye-catching (mouthwatering) picture that will appeal to the 'target' audience (pupils, school staff and parents) and encourage them to buy?

Tell the children to sketch out a first draft, planning their drawing and writing. Once these have been checked by the teacher they can go on to make their posters.

Finally, decide with the class where the posters should be displayed.

Teaching content

Instructions about directions, prices and products need to be short, clear and eye-catching.

What you need

Poster paper, cardboard, felt-tipped pens, rulers.

What to do

Explain to the children that they are to make the written notices that will be displayed on the day of their sale. Brainstorm a list of formats for the notices – perhaps name banners for the stall, notices telling the price of the sweets or signs giving directions to the stall.

Assign one of the listed formats to each group and give them appropriate paper and writing materials.

Give them the following guidelines before they start:

- Decide what information needs to be included.
- Draw light pencil lines to guide lettering.
- Print letters as large as possible.

• Sketch everything out in pencil to make sure it fits before using colouring materials.

Further development

Preparation for the event should also include role-play activities (customers and sellers) to give children the chance to practise greeting customers, giving change and so on.

Teaching content

A recount tells what happened in chronological sequence. It should both inform and entertain the reader. Notes can help the writer to structure the writing.

What you need

A4 paper, cardboard, writing materials.

What to do

Explain to the children that they are going to share their 'sweet success' by making books telling the story of their sweet-making.

Arrange the class in groups of four. Tell the children that each writing team will work together to make a book. Each person in the group will write a recount of *one* step in the sweet-making. These will be:

• Introduction – why did we decide to make the sweets? (This will be the easiest of the recounts to write.)
• Preparation – telling how we went about choosing the kind of sweets to make.
• The story of sweet-making.
• Selling the sweets – obviously this recount should be written by children who were involved in the sale.

Assign one of these to each child, bearing in mind the level of difficulty and checking that they were involved in the activity about which they have been asked to write. Now tell the children to form new groups with all other pupils who are writing about the same step. Tell them, in these groups, to discuss what happened, making notes of points they think should be included in their recounts. While they are doing this, go round each group joining in their discussions and 'jogging their memories' if important points are being omitted.

After ten minutes ask the children to use their notes to write their own recounts. Remind them that the purpose of their book is to entertain, as well as tell what they did, so their writing should include their own impressions of what happened, for example 'It was really funny when...', 'We were nervous waiting for our first customer'.

When the recounts have been written and checked, final drafts should be made. Encourage each writing team to arrange them chronologically to make the pages of the book. The cover of the book can be made by cutting a piece of cardboard into the shape of the sweet, decorating it and writing on the title 'Sweet success' and the names of the authors.

Include a copy of the recipe in a pocket inside the front cover.

Teaching content

An introduction must state purpose clearly. A friendly writing style is more likely to persuade people to reply. Open-ended questions allow people to say what they think.

What you need

Photocopiable page 73, A4 paper, writing materials.

What to do

Congratulate the class on the effort they put into making their sweet-making venture a success. Suggest that it would be interesting to find out what customers who bought the sweets thought of them. Arrange the class into groups of five, and give out copies of photocopiable page 73 (one per group). Explain that this is an evaluation form devised by children in another school to gather opinions about jam they had made. Read it through with the children and suggest the class devise a similar form to elicit feedback on their sweets.

Ask each group to brainstorm feedback they have had about their sweets from friends and family. Appoint a scribe to write down these remarks. After ten minutes ask a reporter to read out the comments from each group, which will hopefully reflect views such as:

• thought they were delicious;

• liked the name;
• wished there were more in the packet.

Tell the children that their evaluation form must be filled in by a representative group of their customers, such as parents, pupils or school staff. Suggest that their first task is to decide which aspects of their sweets they wish to have opinions on. They may, for example, like to ask about appearance, texture, taste, name, packaging or cost. Take one of these as an example to show the children how to form an open-ended sentence, such as 'The sweets tasted...'

Now give them ten minutes to write out some questions for the final section on the sheet under the heading 'What did you think of our sweets?' Point out that the first section is the introduction to the form. Remind them of the questionnaire they made at the beginning of the project, and check they remember that they must explain clearly:

• who is sending out the form;
• why it is being sent out.

Use the introduction from photocopiable page 73 to illustrate that the writing style needs to be friendly and positive. An introduction that is unclear, or that is written in a cold and impersonal style, is unlikely to elicit a high response rate.

Finally, explain that near the top of the sheet they will need to write instructions for filling in the form.

After 15 minutes ask a reporter from each group to read out all three sections, reaching a class decision on the best wording for the final draft of the evaluation form. This can then be made up by a small group of children.

Further development

The results can be collated using the method in Activity 2. Make a wallchart of the results and display the comments.

Teaching content

Establishing criteria to define the success of a project. Self-assessment of their work based on these criteria.

What you need

Photocopiable page 74, chalkboard, writing paper, writing materials.

What to do

Explain to the children that they are going to write a letter to the people who helped them, thanking them for their help and telling them of the success of the sweet-making. Ask the children to suggest what sort of information on the project most adults would be interested to hear, and write this on the board. They will probably suggest some or all of the following:

• how much money was raised;
• who the money was donated to, and why;
• what the children enjoyed about the project;
• what the children learned from doing the project;
• what other people said about the sweets.

Check the children understand that there are several possible answers, and that when describing what they learned, they should state specific skills – 'I have learned to weigh' rather than 'I learned to make sweets'.

Distribute photocopiable page 74 (one between two). Explain that this contains jumbled starter sentences which may help them to write their letters. Explain that they do not have to use all the starter sentences and that these are mixed up and not in any particular order.

Ask the children to identify the starter sentence which might provide a suitable opening for their letter. Suggest they start with this. Explain that they should use any other starter sentences that they think would make their letter interesting and informative for their parents or other people who helped.

Give out writing paper and ask the children to work individually on their letters. When completed, check each letter individually to ensure that they make sense and do not contain major or silly errors.

The photocopied letters can be used to make an interesting end-of-project display.

NAME

CHOOSING A RECIPE

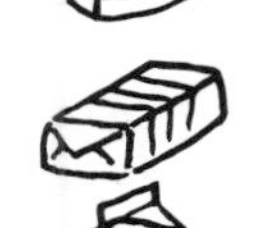

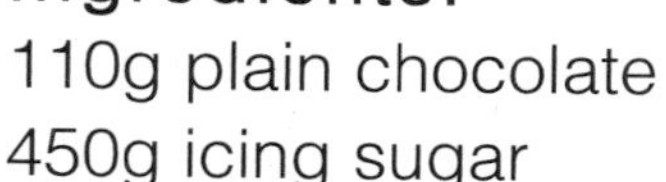

Ingredients:

110g plain chocolate
450g icing sugar
50g margarine
2 tbsp milk
1 tsp vanilla essence

What to do:

Put the margarine and chocolate into a pan.
Melt them over a gentle heat.
When they have melted, take the pan off the heat and stir in milk and vanilla essence. Gradually beat in icing sugar to make a smooth mixture. Pour this into a lightly-greased tin.
Leave until cold then cut into squares.

Ingredients:

125g margarine
2 tbsp icing sugar
6 tbsp drinking chocolate powder
2 tbsp cocoa powder

What to do:

Melt the margarine, icing sugar and drinking chocolate powder in a bowl. Stir it well to make a ball. Break off small pieces and roll into little balls. Coat each of these with cocoa powder. Store them in the fridge.

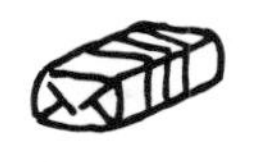

Ingredients:

450g icing sugar
peppermint flavouring
evaporated milk
1/4 tsp cream of tartar
green food colouring
melted chocolate

What to do:

Sieve the icing sugar and cream of tartar into a bowl. Add the peppermint flavouring and green colouring. Mix with enough evaporated milk to form a stiff paste. Dust hands with icing sugar and roll small pieces of mixture into little balls. Place each in a small paper case. Brush the top of each sweet with melted chocolate.

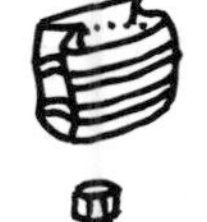

NAME

CHOOSING A RECIPE

4

Ingredients:

a small can of condensed milk
17g desiccated coconut
red food colouring
250g icing sugar
1 tsp vanilla essence

What to do:

Sieve the icing sugar into the bowl.
Add the condensed milk, vanilla essence and desiccated coconut.
Stir this mixture with a wooden spoon until it becomes stiff.
Divide the mixture in half and put one half in a second bowl.
Add a few drops of red colouring to one bowl and stir until the mixture becomes pale pink. Spread the white mixture in the bottom of a Swiss-roll tin, then spread the pink mixture on top. Put it into the fridge to harden, then cut into squares.

5

Ingredients:

225g icing sugar
pinch of cream of tartar
raspberry flavouring
chocolate drops
110g desiccated coconut
evaporated milk
red food colouring

What to do:

Sieve the icing sugar and cream of tartar into a bowl.
Add the flavouring, colouring, coconut and enough evaporated milk to form a stiff paste.
Dust hands with icing sugar and roll small amounts of mixture into balls.
Place each in a small paper case and decorate with a chocolate drop.

- Other flavours and colourings can replace the raspberry if wished.

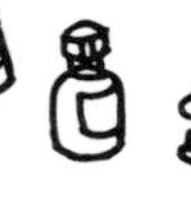

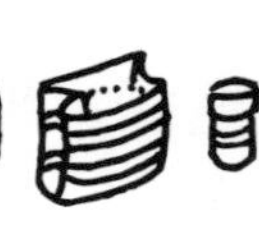

NAME

NEWTOWN PRIMARY SCHOOL JAM

Last weekend a national newspaper gave a report on good jams. Sadly, the testers had not tasted Newtown Primary Jam.

We would like to have your opinion on this delectable, delicious delight. Please colour the correct face and return the form to school.

If wished, the top of each sweet can be brushed with melted chocolate.

1 The look of this jam is   

2 The colour of this jam is   

3 The thickness of this jam is   

4 The taste of this jam is   

Comment

Signed ______________________________

brilliant!

good

bad

Thank you!

NAME

THANK YOU LETTER

Thank you for . .

You will be pleased to know we raised . .

We decided to give the money to .... because . .

Before I did this project I knew . .

Through doing this project I have learned . .

People said our sweets were . .

My favourite part of the project was . .

You may remember we wrote to you . .

Chapter Seven

LET'S CLEAN IT UP

INTRODUCTION

Project description

The writing outcomes are not the only main objectives in this anti-litter campaign. If the pupils can become more environmentally aware, and clean up the school, then the project has been a success, while at the same time their writing abilities will be greatly improved by working through this topic. In organising the information they gather and in communicating it to various audiences they will also be learning through the process of writing.

In this project children set up an anti-litter campaign, so playing an active part in:
- identifying the scale of the problem;
- surveying the attitudes of pupils, teachers, parents and other school personnel towards the problems;
- communicating their findings to others;
- mounting a campaign to raise awareness and change behaviour;
- measuring the effectiveness of their campaign.

The project focuses on litter in the immediate environment but it would be possible to broaden the scope to look at waste on a wider scale, taking in waste disposal, recycling, what constitutes waste, how waste is defined differently in different cultures and how technology can offer solutions to some of these problems.

Why this context?

In this project, children are required to conduct a survey of the litter problem in and around school, and to plan a campaign to improve the situation. Many schools will already be involved in environmental projects and wish to promote positive attitudes towards caring for the environment. Children are often more interested in things that affect them directly so work on the immediate area is a good starting point.

This topic will provide the children with many opportunities for active and investigative experiences and will develop their skills in collecting and handling information. Recording information systematically is also an important part of information handling and prepares the children for the discipline required to write non-fiction texts effectively.

Project organisation

The activities in this project afford many opportunities to write in a variety of non-fiction genres. Advice for teachers is mainly concerned with providing structures and support to help children select appropriate formats and registers for their writing. In the course of the project they will be involved in writing in the following genres:
- explanations of the purpose of a questionnaire;
- a recount of their investigations and findings;
- procedural writing in the form of instructions on how to conduct a survey;
- persuasive posters, to be compared with posters which give information.

In this project the emphasis is on investigation, and children should be aware that data-collecting activities can be time-consuming. To support the idea of a campaign, one activity leads to another, sometimes supplying data to be used in a later writing task.

The entire anti-litter campaign is likely to last for about six weeks. One possible timescale would be:

Week 1 – The teacher negotiates with the headteacher the aims and purpose of the project and the ways in which the headteacher might be involved in supporting the children's efforts. The teacher then arranges with the caretaker or cleaning staff for litter to be collected from an agreed location within the school.

Week 2 – Children construct questionnaires and conduct their surveys of opinions.

Week 3 – Children collate and analyse the results of the survey to identify possible courses of action.

Week 4 – Children prepare anti-litter materials to help them communicate information to others and to encourage other children in the school to join their campaign.

A few weeks later – The children monitor the results of their campaign and evaluate its effectiveness.

Should you choose to extend the project to include more elements of design and technology (such as designing 'environmentally-friendly' packaging or multi-purpose litter collectors or dustbins) more time could be allocated. This would also provide additional opportunities for procedural and explanatory writing activities.

The writing opportunities of the project could also be extended by encouraging the children to apply for specific jobs in the litter-reducing enterprise.

Teaching content

An inquiry must start with a clear definition of the problem and attendant questions. Questions may be framed in an open or closed way and each will yield different information. A questionnaire must have a clear purpose to guide the selection and sequence of questions.

What you need

Large sheets of paper, two bags of litter (see 'What to do'), writing materials.

What to do

One week before you start this activity ask the person who cleans your classroom to gather up any litter left lying on the classroom floor at the end of each day. Ask the caretaker also to collect a bag of playground litter.

Begin the lesson by showing the children the contents of the classroom litter bag and asking them where they think all this litter came from. It is important to make clear that you are not really interested in apportioning blame for this (and even admitting that you may have contributed to it yourself!). Explain that you want them to help you solve the problem of how to keep the classroom cleaner and tidier. Next, show them the contents of the playground litter bag to help them understand that the problem extends beyond the classroom so the solution you work out will need to address this problem too.

Discuss with the class:

- How serious do they think the problem is?
- Who else might be concerned? (Caretaker, cleaners, other teachers, other pupils, parents.)
- How can they find out how others feel?

Suggest that they might be able to design a questionnaire to help find out how others feel. Will one questionnaire be suitable for everyone?

Explain that you want to begin by thinking of the most important questions that will help to find out how aware people are of the litter problem and how they feel about improving the situation. Explain that you might also be able to incorporate other people's suggestions on how to improve things in your campaign so it would make sense to ask for these now. Remind the children of the 'Who? What? Where? When? Why? How?' categories of questions, such as:

- Who drops litter?
- What kind of litter presents the biggest problem?
- Where are the untidiest areas?
- When does most litter accumulate?
- Why would you like to see the litter problem improved?
- How can things be improved?

Ask the children to form groups of four. Give each group a large sheet of paper and a pen and encourage them to make a list of questions to include in the questionnaire.

Allow 15 minutes for the groups to write out their questions, then cut the sheet into strips with one question on each strip. An effective way to unite the class ideas is to ask the first group to pin their first question on the wall and invite other groups to pin any similar questions beneath it. This will provide an opportunity to examine the wording of the questions and to find a form of words that might be suitable for all groups likely to be included in the survey sample.

This is also the time to decide which questions should be open and which ones closed. Remind the children that closed questions are those that require a yes/no response or one selected from a number of multiple choices. Open questions allow the respondent to make a more extended statement of their views. Discuss with the children the advantages and disadvantages of each type. Encourage them to see that it is easier to collate the responses from closed questions (for example adding up the number of yes and no responses) but this does not yield a great deal of information. Open questions usually provide more information, but take more time to record and collate.

The balance of open and closed questions will need to be appropriate for the children's ability in handling information. As a class, work on the questions they have generated. Decide on the best form of words for each and the order in which they should appear. This will produce the main body of the questionnaire.

Teaching content

An explanation must clearly state the problem and the specific purpose of what is to follow. Giving reasons will encourage people to respond.

What you need

Large sheets of paper, chalkboard, writing materials.

What to do

Begin by reviewing the purpose for your questionnaire and the list of questions drawn up in Activity 1.

Explain to the children that when you ask people to complete a questionnaire you have to tell them why you want to interview them. This is much easier if you provide the explanation as an introduction. If this has been written very clearly it will also give the option of leaving the questionnaire with the respondent to complete alone. The children could decide at this point on the people who should be interviewed and those who might be asked to complete it independently, so teachers and senior pupils might fill in the questionnaire on their own while younger pupils would be interviewed by members of the class.

Point out that, in considering how to structure an introduction, children are being given an opportunity to explain to the respondents the purpose of the questionnaire. In groups of four they should write an introduction which will include a statement of the problem and their reasons for conducting the survey.

The following frame could be written on the chalkboard to help some of the children structure their explanation:

Class 5 has been looking at the amount of litter dropped in our school and...
As a result of this we have decided to conduct a survey because...

Once the children (with the teacher's help) have decided on the most suitable explanation (which might come from one group or be an amalgam of various contributions) a final word-processed draft could be printed and photocopied.

Before actually conducting the survey, other decisions, such as the size of your sample population, the various categories within the sample and a time schedule for the survey, should be made. Discuss with the children the number of people to be included in each category and give individual pupils responsibility for delivering and collecting questionnaires and interviewing where appropriate. The following table drawn on the chalkboard and completed with the children should help to organise this:

Category of person
Pupils (classes)
Teachers (names)
Other staff (names)
Parents and others (how many)
Number to be surveyed
Interview or self-completion
Date to be completed by
Pupils responsible

Teaching content

A report describes and analyses information. Key questions or headings can help a writer structure a report. The conclusion of a report can recommend action.

What you need

Large sheets of paper, chalkboard, writing materials, completed questionnaires.

What to do

You will want to collate the results for each of the categories separately in the first instance and then combine them. Different groups can be given responsibility for collating information gained from parents, teachers, pupils and other school staff. A table of information will help the children collate the data systematically but its precise format will depend on the types of question asked in the questionnaire.

Closed questions, to which the respondents gave yes/no answers, for example:

Do you think we have a litter problem in our school?

or where multiple choices were offered, for example:

When do you think the playground looks most littered? First thing in the morning? At lunchtime? At hometime?

will provide data which is easier to handle. For questions such as these a table of the following type is suitable:

	Question 1	Question 2	Question 3	Question 4
Response 1				
Response 2				
Response 3				

The children can then record the results as tally scores.

Open-ended questions are more difficult to handle and the most efficient way of doing so is to list comments or suggestions. So if respondents have been asked to give ideas on how to improve the litter situation these could be listed by each group and a combined list could then be made by using the same 'pinning' technique described in Activity 1.

Ask each group to write their main findings on a large sheet of paper. They should then report the views of the category whose responses they are collating to the class.

Help the children to reach conclusions by analysing each set of responses and asking questions that will help them to summarise and extrapolate from the information. The sample list provided in Activity 1 will provide a good starting point.

- Who drops litter?
- What kind of litter presents the biggest problem?
- Where are the untidiest areas?
- When does most litter accumulate?
- Why would you like to see the litter problem improved?
- How can things be improved?

The other questions generated by the children will provide additional information, and this should be added to the summary conclusions listed on the chalkboard. Now ask the question, 'How can we mount a Let's Clean It Up campaign?' and organise a class brainstorm to produce practical suggestions gleaned from the children's own ideas and from the questionnaires.

Try to group these with the children into:

- people to communicate with and how best to do it;
- further areas to investigate, for example are there really litter 'black spots'?

4 PLANNING THE CAMPAIGN

90

Teaching content

Identifying strategies to improve the litter situation. Persuasive writing can exert a powerful influence over the actions of others. Persuasive writing must appeal to the reader and portray a clear and succinct message. Writers need to think carefully about the readers if they are to persuade them.

What you need

Writing materials.

What to do

Explain to the children that you would like them to work in groups (with half the class working on classroom litter and half on playground litter) on the following tasks:

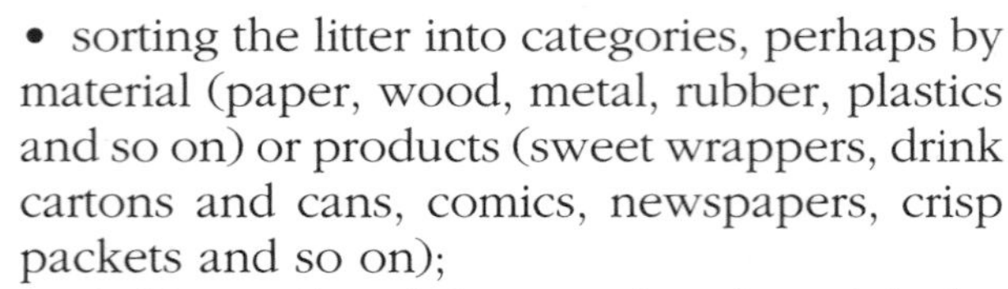

- sorting the litter into categories, perhaps by material (paper, wood, metal, rubber, plastics and so on) or products (sweet wrappers, drink cartons and cans, comics, newspapers, crisp packets and so on);
- making a list of the people who might be responsible for dropping the litter.

Explain that this will help them to identify their target audiences for any communications. Ask each group to design a table on which they can record the results of the sorting exercise. The previous activity offers a model of a table which could easily be adapted to show different types of litter and possible culprits. The children should themselves decide on the precise headings that they will use to categorise this information.

When the groups have completed this sorting and analysing task, ask them to suggest different media through which you could communicate

anti-litter messages. The range suggested will depend on the experiences of your pupils but given the extensive exposure most children have to advertising this should elicit a list that will include many of the following: posters, badges, leaflets, 'environmentally-friendly packaging', letters, teletext messages, advertisements for your school or class newspapers, radio broadcasts or a script for a short video presentation.

Next involve the children in a discussion of the various media (suggested above) that could be used to put the anti-litter message across. With the class decide on the most suitable methods. Obviously, the range that you employ will depend on your pupils' familiarity with persuasive print and the resources which you have available.

Point out that campaigns usually have a logo that appears on all communications and acts as a quickly identifiable reminder of the campaign and its aims. A logo should be simple, eye-catching and may or may not include a short motto or slogan. Challenge them now to:

produce a logo, in black and white only (to allow for reproduction) which will fit on to a badge 6cm x 6cm and include a symbol of 'cleaning up' and no more than three words (if any).

Ask the children to work in pairs, pinning up their finished designs on an allocated display area. When all are completed, give a number to each logo and ask the children, individually, to vote for the most effective, reminding them of the specified criteria. The winning badge should be produced for the class to launch the campaign. Additional badges should be reproduced to distribute to others as and when the campaign is extended to a wider audience.

Teaching content

A recount is structured chronologically. A recount enables the writer to evaluate actions and progress so far.

What you need

Photocopiable page 84, chalkboard, writing materials.

What to do

Writing to the headteacher will provide an opportunity for you and the children to take stock of your investigations so far and to set out your action plans in a systematic way.
In preparation for this you should have alerted the headteacher to the proposed campaign and negotiated support in the following areas:
- back-up support through mention at school assemblies;
- resourcing the provision of additional litter bins;
- linking 'anti-litter consciousness' to existing positive behaviour award schemes, perhaps naming a particular class as 'Litter heroes of the week'.
- featuring the class efforts in reports to school boards or in communications to local press to extend publicity.

Discuss with the children the different ways in which they could communicate findings to the headteacher, explaining that he or she might be able to help 'spread the word'. Ask for suggestions on how to pass on the information and list these on the chalkboard:
- inviting him or her to come and hear about their efforts;
- sending a delegation to explain what they have been doing;
- writing a formal letter explaining their findings.

Explain that when campaign organisers are trying to enlist support their usual first line of approach is a letter, because that provides an accurate written record of the information sent and gives the recipient time to think about the issue before responding.

Ask the children 'What does the headteacher need to know?' This will encourage them to reflect on what they have been doing and to organise the information in a logical and sequential fashion. Ask also what outcomes they are seeking from their letter. Do they only want to inform or are they actively seeking assistance? Photocopiable page 84 provides a suitable frame for children to tell in sequence what has happened so far and to state their aspirations.

Ask the children to work in pairs to make notes on what is important for the letter. Provide each pair with a copy of the photocopiable sheet to help them structure this first draft of the letter. Pairs should briefly form sixes to compare these notes before embarking on subsequent drafts.

Finally compose a class letter based on suggestions from all the children.

Teaching content

Words to indicate sequence help the reader to understand instances. Readers bring different knowledge to their reading and make different interpretations.

What you need

Photocopiable page 85, writing materials.

What to do

Set up this activity as a problem-solving challenge for groups. So far, the children have collected data by using a questionnaire. The next stage of the survey is to identify the worst litter trouble spots in the school grounds. To do this the children will have to observe carefully and devise a means to record their findings. The additional dimension in this activity is for the children, in groups, to write instructions for another group, suggesting how to approach the survey of trouble spots. Give out one copy of photocopiable page 85 to each group and read over the introductory information with the children, encouraging them to suggest how to:

- collect evidence easily;
- record and display results;
- identify the trouble spots on a plan.

Set time frames for this activity, suggesting that their observations will have to take place at certain times (decided upon in advance) and that all the observations must be completed by a specified date.

Ask the children, individually, to note down their ideas of the two worst litter spots in the school. They should then confer, in groups of four, to identify the three or four common spots identified by the group. Remind them that they will have to test their hypothesis and that this is the purpose of the survey.

Now explain that each group is going to design a survey and write instructions as to how it will be carried out. Remind them that groups are to exchange sets of instructions and carry out a survey designed by another group and that the second part of the photocopiable sheet is to help them write clear instructions.

First they will have to decide on the nature of the evidence to be collected (perhaps counting the amount of litter on the ground or watching the behaviour of people at these litter spots). They will also have to decide on when, and how often, this is to be done – you may wish to remind them of the time frames that have been set for this.

When groups have completed their instructions these should be passed to the group who will carry them out. Each group should be given the opportunity to comment on the clarity of the instructions they have received and to ask questions.

There will be two sets of outcomes from this activity. The first will be the results of the survey itself, which should be communicated to the caretaker and the headteacher. This might be for information only or it might be accompanied by suggestions on the redistribution of existing waste bins or the provision of additional ones.

As a second outcome, the activity will provide opportunities for children to review how effective their written instructions really are. Encourage each group to use one colour to highlight the parts of the instructions that were clear and another colour for the parts that could be improved.

Organise the children into new groups of four, made up of two of the writers and two who followed the instructions. These groups should now work to provide a final draft which could be displayed, along with the survey results, at a place close to the litter trouble spots.

Teaching content

Posters may be used to give information and to persuade others to a particular viewpoint.

What you need

A3 paper, felt-tipped pens.

What to do

Session 1

By now the children should have collected evidence of the nature and extent of the school's litter problem. They now need to disseminate this information as effectively as possible. Suggest that they present their findings in a series of meetings that might include any of the following:

- other classes of children;
- school governors or boards;
- a meeting of the PTA;
- the local community council.

Once you have chosen meetings explain that these will have to be publicised by means of posters. Brainstorm the kind of information that should be included.

- Where the meeting will be held.
- When it will be held.
- What it is about.
- Who will be speaking.
- Who is eligible to come.

Ask the children to prioritise the information indicating how it should be sequenced and the size of print that should be used for different points. These aspects, as well as colour, overall impact and clarity, can be considered when the posters are evaluated.

Session 2

Remind the children that the first set of posters they worked on gave information about a particular event. Explain that campaigners often make use of posters to put their message across by using eye-catching images and persuasive slogans that are easily remembered and remind the public of the campaigners' aims. Give the children the following examples:

'Watch out – there's a thief about!'
'Clunk-click every trip.'
'Say No to drugs.'

Take the opportunity to show how rhyme, alliteration and personification can be used to good effect. Remind the children of the purpose of the logo devised at an earlier stage in the project and suggest that the poster slogans might also be used to produce some new badges. These would help to keep the campaign fresh in everyone's mind.

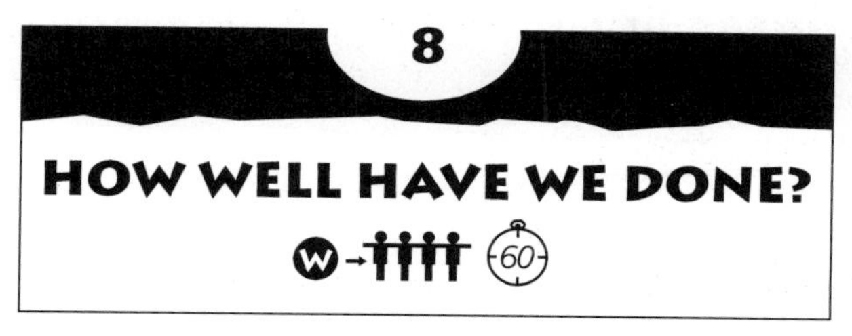

Teaching content

Reviewing the effectiveness of the campaign.

What you need

Photocopiable page 86, writing materials.

What to do

This activity should be conducted after the campaign has been running for two or three weeks. All of the strategies employed will have played a part in raising awareness of the problem and should have encouraged a change in people's behaviour.

Explain to the class that campaigners always like to know whether or not they are getting their message across to their intended audience. Distribute photocopiable page 86 and use it to structure a discussion on what can be evaluated and how this might be done.

Ask the children which techniques they have used so far to find information. List these as a reminder:

- asking questions of others;
- observing and recording how people behave;
- quantifying amounts of litter in particular locations.

Then suggest that these will be useful again as they collect evidence for their evaluation.

Allocate each group one of the six categories listed on the sheet and ask them to discuss how they would go about carrying out an evaluation. After about 15 minutes ask them to report back to the class. Decide together when each part of the evaluation should be conducted and how the results should be communicated to the whole school to congratulate them on their efforts.

Campaign 'Clean-up' could be rounded off with a celebration at assembly and the award of certificates to all classes participating.

NAME

DEAR HEADTEACHER

◆ Before you write to the headteacher list all of the important facts and ideas that you think should go into your letter. Look at the letter outline below to help you do this.

Dear ______________________________

Class __________ has been looking at ______________

____

We decided to find out what people thought about the litter problem and we ______________________________

____

We found out that ______________________________

____

____

Now we would like to make things better so we have decided to ______________________________

____

____

We hope that ______________________________

____

____

Yours sincerely,

NAME

LITTER TROUBLE SPOTS

◆ You are going to plan a survey of litter blackspots in your school for **another** group to carry out. Your instructions will have to be very clear so that they will be able to:

- collect evidence easily;
- record and display their results;
- identify the 'trouble spots' on a plan of the school playground.

Set out your instructions in the box below.

Title of survey ______________________

What you are to find out ______________________

____

Evidence to be collected ______________________

____

What to do

First you ______________________

____

Next you ______________________

____

After that ______________________

____

____

____

____

NAME

HAS CAMPAIGN 'CLEAN-UP' WORKED?

We need to find out if all our hard work has improved the litter situation in our school.

Work with your group to suggest how we can find out about each of the following:

What we did	Purpose	How to evaluate
Questionnaire	To find out whether people felt there was a litter problem and to raise awareness.	
Trouble spots	To find out which areas in the school had most litter and to improve these.	
Letter to the head	To keep the headteacher informed and ask for support.	
Meetings	To tell others what we had found out and raise awareness.	
Badges	To make everyone feel involved and take part in keeping the school tidier.	
Posters	To inform and persuade others to 'sign up' to the campaign.	

Chapter Eight

AUTOBIOGRAPHY

INTRODUCTION

Project description

In this project, children consider the nature and craft of autobiographical writing. Extracts from famous autobiographies provide inspirational models and are used to teach the necessary recall and writing techniques. Children consider why autobiographies are written, and identify important turning points and memories around which they can plan their own writing. Class lessons teach some key research and writing techniques drawing on the common experiences of pre-school years, first days at school, family folklore, experiences of illness, sweets and great loves and hates. Thereafter, the techniques can be applied to the children's individual turning points and memories identified at the beginning of the project. Alternative topics for further writing might include pets, moving house, happy memories, special people, key triumphs or presents given and received.

The school work may be only the beginning of an ongoing autobiography. Blank pages at the end of the publication allow the project to continue to flourish once the work in class has ended. Each child's work is celebrated and reviewed by a relative or other adult who knows the child well.

Why this context?

Autobiography is a vitally important genre within non-fiction. There is an ease in writing about events that have happened, as the sequence is obvious. The skill likes in selecting and focusing the storyline. Children learn that recount writing often works best when it has a sharp focus and that tiny events thus have significance. They are also shown how writers combine and rework short pieces of writing into one longer piece, drawing on different rehearsal and planning strategies. Most importantly, the project encourages continued autobiographical writing.

In addition, there are obvious opportunities for personal development and a growing understanding of self. The project highlights the relevance of individual tiny happenings in people's lives and provides opportunities for parents to become involved in their children's school work.

Project organisation

The project involves children working individually, in pairs, groups and as a class. Discussion from paired and group work prompts and supports both the recall and the writing process. The class lessons allow the teacher to build enthusiasm and teach the key research, planning and writing techniques. They also ensure the project gathers sufficient momentum for the children to want to continue writing about their own individual life events and memories.

At the beginning of the project, each child needs a large, unlined exercise book (preferably A4) so that written work and illustrations can be stuck in place as they are finished, and an envelope folder in which to keep their lists of ideas, planning sheets and short written pieces which may be combined or reworked.

Publication, celebration and review

The work is presented in an unlined exercise book which may be decorated with a padded cover. Ribbons may be attached and then tied to close the book.

Completed autobiographies are reviewed by a parent or other important adult and a photocopiable sheet prompts written reviews which can then be attached to the final pages. Extracts may also be read to younger children and peers.

Teaching content

Reasons why people write biographies and autobiographies. Personal reasons for writing.

What you need

Photocopiable page 101, large marker pens, large sheets of paper.

What to do

Establish that children know that a biography is the account of somebody's life, written about them by another person, while an autobiography is an account of a person's life written by the person herself. Give the children an example, such as the biography of Helen Keller, and ask them to supply reasons why authors might choose to write a biography. They will probably suggest some of the following:

- The author admires the person and wishes to share this admiration.
- The person about whom the book is written is notorious and readers want to know more. The author sees this as an opportunity to sell a lot of books!
- The subject of the biography is a famous, yet very private person and therefore other people are curious. The author is lucky enough to be given exclusive interview.
- The subject of the book has had an astonishing experience that will be of interest to others and has sought the help of a professional writer to record this.
- The author recognises that knowing about the personal qualities and experiences of this individual will help others to live their lives with more meaning.

Having discussed the purposes for writing biography, organise children into groups of four and ask them to brainstorm, on the large sheets of paper, the reasons why a person might want to write an autobiography. The initial discussion of biography should help with ideas, as some autobiographies, though not all, are written for similar reasons.

Allow five minutes for this activity, then ask a spokesperson from every group to give one reason for writing an autobiography. Display the completed sheets in a prominent place.

Distribute photocopiable page 101 to each group. This gives a number of reasons for writing an autobiography. Read through the sheet with the class, comparing the reasons listed with those generated by the group discussion. Point out that people who decide to write about their lives may have different reasons for wanting to do so.

Tell the children that, in the next few weeks, they are going to write the first part of their autobiographies. It is therefore important that they begin to think about their own personal reasons for wanting to write an autobiography because this will help them recognise interesting material and select an appropriate writing style. Point out that this will be only the beginning of an exciting personal publication, but that subsequent episodes may be written later in life, without teacher guidance!

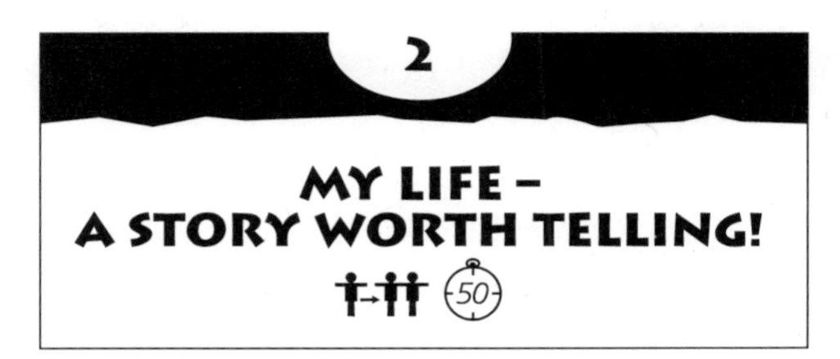

Teaching content

Explanations need orientation sentences at the beginning. Autobiographies generally begin with a section in which the author explains the reasons for writing.

What you need

Photocopiable page 101 and completed sheets from Activity 1, chalkboard, writing materials, blank books.

What to do

Ask the children to consider the reasons for writing an autobiography discussed in the last activity, listed on photocopiable page 101 and their completed sheets. Tell them to write a list of personal reasons, in order of priority, as to why they would like to write such a book.

Allow ten to fifteen minutes for this and then explain that most autobiographies begin with an explanation of why the writer has decided to commit memories and thoughts about life to paper. This sometimes forms the first chapter or can be presented as an introductory 'Author's note'. Sometimes the explanation is given as part of the acknowledgements for those who have helped in the writing of the book, or in the dedication. Tell the children that they will write their explanations in an introduction that will come before the first chapter. Remind the children that an explanation needs a few sentences at the beginning to orientate the reader. Model this on the chalkboard with sentences such as:

I have decided to write my autobiography because I have some interesting stories to tell about childhood in Britain at the end of the twentieth century. Another reason is...

Learning about how people grow up in different countries in the world is always interesting. Hearing about this from the people themselves is even more interesting, and this is one of the reasons why I have decided to write my autobiography. Another reason is that...

My family came to Britain from another country so I can tell people what it is like to move to a new country and culture. Another reason why I want to write my autobiography is that...

Tell the class to write their own first sentences or choose a model from the chalkboard. Allow five minutes for this, then ask each child to choose a writing partner. They should now use their first orientation sentences, and their lists of reasons, to try out their introduction on their partner. This will help them to consolidate their ideas before they start writing. Children should be encouraged to ask questions, and make suggestions, if they can think of other reasons that should be added to their partner's lists. When they are satisfied with their work, the children should write out the introductions to their autobiographies as a paragraph of continuous prose and stick them in place on the first page of the autobiography book.

3 SIGNIFICANT STOPS

Teaching content
Recounts are told in chronological order. Planning a menu of choices for writing.

What you need
Poster-sized paper, writing materials, folders.

What to do
Tell the children that an autobiography is an extended recount. It tells of the relationships, loves, hates, fears, aspirations and beliefs of a person as they develop through the events that affect that person's life. It is usual for the autobiography to be recounted in chronological order, but only the most significant events are recorded, as these are the areas of life that are interesting to read or write about. Reassure the children that every person who has lived to the age of nine or ten already has important points of development, change and drama to record. Some people have astonishing adventures to write about by this age, experiences that are quite different from most people's. But even if we have not led exciting lives we will all have significant turning points in our lives that we can share with others – one good example of this is starting school.

Organise the children into groups of six and ask them to brainstorm ideas about major experiences that most people will have shared, perhaps an accident, moving house, learning how to skate, swim or ride a bike. One scribe from each group should write the ideas on a poster and, after ten minutes, ideas should be shared with the class. Posters should then be displayed and discussed. The children will probably mention most of the following experiences: birth, accidents, birthdays, holidays, festivals, illness, gifts (given and received), people loved, interesting people, religion, talents, hobbies, starting school, nursery, friends, moving house, moving country, changing school, favourite and least favourite music, first step, first word, my house, my secret place, favourite room, best subject, favourite books, favourite TV programmes, pets, favourite games, jobs done in the house, riding a bike, fears, favourite time of year, sports, clubs, learning to swim, big trouble, greatest surprise (given and received), a big shock, arguments, disappointments, a happy day, a sad day, brothers and sisters, travelling, favourite sweets, best treasures, hopes for the future, wishes for the world, favourite clothes, the job I'd like to do when I grow up, the subject I look forward to studying at secondary school.

Next ask the children, individually, to draw up a random menu of significant life events that might be included in their own autobiography. Once this has been done they should organise their random lists in chronological order. Explain to them that they will probably not include all of these events in their autobiographies but the longer the list, the greater choice they will have.

Over the coming days, ask the children to add to their lists any events they remember while discussing ideas for their autobiography with other family members. Sometimes relatives can fill in the gaps of half-remembered highlights in a young life and these should be included. Children should also begin to collect memorabilia to make their autobiographies come alive (such as photographs, letters, cards, tickets, programmes and hospital tags). Give the children folders in which to keep precious memorabilia and ongoing writing, including the list, or menu, of ideas written in this activity, planning sheets, brainstorming sheets and rough drafts. It is a good idea to photocopy photographs and as much of the memorabilia as possible and send originals home immediately.

BIRTH AND EARLY YEARS

Teaching content

How to research for information for a personal recount. Inserting quotations to enliven a recount.

What you need

Photocopiable page 102, chalkboard, writing materials, autobiography books, writing folders.

What to do

Tell the children that most autobiographies begin with an account of the birth of the writer and some information about their early years. This information must be found by interviewing parents or other people involved in these events, as nobody can remember their own birth or the first few years of life.

Tell the children that they will now have to do some research about their birth and early years. Distribute a copy of photocopiable page 102 to each child. Read through this together and encourage the children to write the names of people they intend to ask for information next to the questions they will be asked. Stress the fact that comments from people must be recorded exactly, on a separate sheet of paper as some of these will be quoted.

Give a strict time-limit of a set number of days for this task to be carried out and then have a reporting-back session, during which all the children should be given the opportunity to offer one piece of information they have discovered about themselves when they were babies or toddlers.

Now ask the children to write their first chapter, including all the information they have gathered, relating what other people said about the writer as an infant and occasionally quoting the actual words that were spoken by the people interviewed. Model this on the chalkboard by taking an example of what one child's relatives said about her:

I began to walk when I was eleven months old. My Mum said that I was the earliest walker in our family and Aunty Mary said, 'I remember being in the supermarket and you were making a terrible fuss because you wanted to walk and didn't want to sit in the trolley. In the end I let you out and you tottered and fell all the way round the shelves. It was a good idea because then you slept all the way home in the car because you were exhausted.'

Remind children that if they are reporting what other people have said, but not using their *exact* words, then speech marks should not be used. It is only when the actual words spoken by a person are written down that speech marks are appropriate. Point out how clearly we can hear a person speaking when their actual words are recorded. It seems almost as if the person is speaking directly to us. This is why quotation of actual words is called *direct speech*. Suggest that a few examples of direct speech will talk straight to the reader and give a clear insight into the life of the child.

The questions on the photocopiable sheet are organised chronologically to provide an ordered sequence, although sentences will have to be inserted to ensure that the information provided makes sense and reads like a story.

When the rough draft is completed, writing partners should read each other's recounts and point out places where the writing does not flow in a clear sequence of ideas or the information does not make sense. They should also check the writing and provide help with spelling mistakes and punctuation. At this point, an interesting title that relates to the personal events may be chosen for the first chapter. Children should now make a final copy of this chapter and attach it in place in their book. Rough drafts and the planning sheets should be clipped together and stored in their writing folder.

Teaching content

Personal recount writing is sharpest when informed by vivid memory. Brainstorming a long list of ideas for later writing selection.

What you need

Photocopiable page 103, scrap paper, writing materials, writing folder.

What to do

Remind children that in Activity 3 they created a menu of significant events in their lives. Many items on this list will have been drawn from information family members have given them about their lives and some will be genuine memories. Others will be a mix of family legend and remembered facts. Tell the children that the most inspired autobiographical writing generally springs from events that are clearly remembered by the writer.

Distribute photocopiable page 103, one between two, and read the first two extracts with the children. Discuss the way in which both writers talk about memories. Laurie Lee seems to have had to dig deep to remember details of his very early life but Roald Dahl has stories that he can't wait to share with an audience. Stress to the children that some will remember events in their lives more easily than others and when they come to list their memories, they must constantly remember the final sentence in the passage by Roald Dahl, 'All are true'.

Next read through the earliest memory of Anne Scott, which appears very trivial and unconnected to any interesting story. When writing her list of memories, Anne gave this the title 'Shoes on a windowsill. Age three years'. It is often the case that the clearest memories we have are of seemingly trivial moments in our young lives. When looking back to our earliest memories, we have cameo visions that seem relatively unimportant, but somehow images, smells and sounds come with startling clarity out of nowhere.

Before making a start on writing their autobiographies, tell the children that they are going to write a list of any clear memory flashpoints that they have, going back as far as possible. Some of these may coincide with the items on the lists written in the last activity, but some of these memories may have seemed too trivial to be included on that list.

Distribute scrap paper and ask the children to think of their most vivid memories, writing a heading or title for each. Tell them that they are not to actually write about their memories at the moment, merely to supply a heading. Next to each they should write the approximate age they would have been at the time of the event. Tell them that they will not be including all of these memories in their autobiography but will select the most interesting or clearly-remembered to enrich and enliven their writing.

Ask the children now to do what most writers do – sleep on their ideas. Later give time in class for them to add to and reorganise their memory lists. This 'Memory list' should be stored in the writing folder and will be used alongside the 'Main life events list', when they come to choose the chapters that they will use in their autobiographies.

6 EARLIEST MEMORIES

Teaching content

Ordinary events can be made interesting by detailed, clearly-remembered description. A recount is written in chronological order.

What you need

Photocopiable page 104, writing materials, clear Memory lists.

What to do

Ask the children to take their lists of memories from their writing folders and select the earliest two memories. Tell them that these are the memories about which they will be writing in the next chapter of their autobiographies.

Distribute copies of photocopiable page 104, one between two, and ask the children to look again at the seemingly unimportant first memory of Anne Scott. Ask them to comment on the writing, looking first at the factual information about the life of the writer that is conveyed in this memory.

The passage, in fact, is filled with detail about Anne's life. Some of it is factual – she lived in a flat, the windows were of the 'sash' variety and she had a Mum who, although never described in detail, the memory implies was loving and caring.

Anne's description triggers the pungent smell of white spirit cleaner for any reader who has ever used this to clean shoes. The piece of writing conjures up an image of two still figures standing in the sunshine waiting quietly for shoes to dry on the windowsill. The memory is beautiful and speaks to us of an era when mums and children had time to wait for shoes to dry in the sunshine!

Having extracted all the information possible from this piece of writing, stress the fact that no memory is worthless, even though it may seem trivial at first glance. Ask the children to take each of their first two memories and write about them, including as much detail as possible. Write the following points on the chalkboard to act as memory joggers, but stress that this is not a definitive list and that many children will remember details beyond those referred to on the list:

- place (with as much description as possible);
- people present (with as much description as possible);
- time of day (how could this be indicated in the writing?);
- colours;
- smells;
- feelings;
- sounds.

Having used the above list to make notes, the children should reorganise all the information to compose two paragraphs of continuous prose. When they have completed both paragraphs, they should take the writing home and read it to a parent, asking them to fill in any gaps in information about where and when the incidents occurred.

Tell the children that Anne's mother was able to tell her that the memory came from the flat in Teesdale Street, where Anne had lived for the first four years of her life. So, when she finally wrote about her memory, Anne was able to write:

For the first four years of my life I lived in Teesdale Street and I have a clear memory of one thing that happened to me when I was there. I was in the small kitchen/dining room of our flat...

Give the children time in which to gather further information surrounding their memories, then ask them to write about these in a chapter entitled 'Earliest memories'.

7 EARLY SCHOOLDAYS

Teaching content
Planning for recount writing.

What you need
Photocopiable page 104, writing materials, lists of memories and life events, writing folders.

What to do
Ask the children to look at their lists of significant life events, compiled in Activity 3 and indicate if they have included any incidents that happened in school. Explain that school plays a central part in our early lives so no autobiography would be complete without a chapter on the subject. Ask the children to check if they have included any early school memories on their memory lists.

Remind them that it is the convention for recount writing to start at the beginning of a time period and work through it in sequence. This may be difficult in this instance as most of us forget our first school days and remember infant schooling only in patches. Suggest that it is also the case that when several people get together and discuss shared experience, memories may be triggered about incidents that have been long forgotten.

Organise the class into groups of five or six and ask the children to look at photocopiable page 104, which structures a discussion about first days at school. Children should not complete the section called, 'An embarrassing or humiliating misunderstanding', as this will be done in the next activity. Encourage them to use their memory lists during this activity.

Children who started school elsewhere should be spread throughout the groups and asked to make first comments on each discussion point. Ensure that the rest of the group listen to them by pointing out how interesting it is to hear from people with different experiences. It is also amazing to recognise the similarities that exist in the experiences people have in quite different schools.

Remind the children that you don't expect them to remember their first day at school (though some may) but you want them to think back as far as possible through infant classes.

Once they have discussed their early infant days, most children will remember events and scenes they had long ago forgotten. They should now read the questions on the photocopiable sheet and write their answers on a separate sheet of paper, working individually. Remind them that the section at the bottom of the sheet is not to be completed at this stage and that the sheet should be carefully stored in the writing folder as it will be required for the next writing session.

8 LEARNING FROM GOOD AUTHORS

Teaching content
By reading good writers, we can model our own work on the best. Note-taking for one piece of writing may take several sessions.

What you need
Photocopiable page 104 and 105, chalkboard, writing materials.

What to do
Remind the children of the way in which discussion of early schooldays triggered long-forgotten memories. In the same way, the autobiographies of people who went to school in very different circumstances from ours and

in different countries, may also trigger our memories because we discover that some authors have shared similar feelings and emotions to our own. Reading pieces written by good authors always helps us to look more critically at our own writing. Distribute photocopiable page 105, one between two, and read through the two vivid descriptions of the authors' first days at school.

The actual details of the events and feelings of the two writers are completely different, but there *are* ways in which both experiences were similar. In pairs, ask the children to list these similarities. If they have difficulty getting started, then model a few ideas on the chalkboard, perhaps that both had a misunderstanding that caused them pain but caused hilarity for others! Allow about 12 minutes for this activity and then ask for feedback. Children will find this difficult unless they read the texts very carefully. Even if each pair only finds one similarity this is still a good effort. Between all the children in the class the list may include points such as that both authors:

- hated the crowds;
- felt dizzy when encircled by bigger children;
- became bad-tempered;
- were confused;
- were laughed at by other children.

Tell the children that, during infant years, it is probable that all school pupils will experience the sort of emotions and experience listed above. Growing up is all about learning to cope with these situations and feelings. Ask the children to think of an embarrassing incident or misunderstanding that occurred when they were infants. Allow approximately five minutes for pairs to tell one another about their experiences as this will allow the memory to be firmed into a clear recount. Partners should ask questions about any parts of the story that are muddled. Children should now write this experience in the box at the bottom of photocopiable page 104. The planning sheet must then be stored carefully, ready for the next activity.

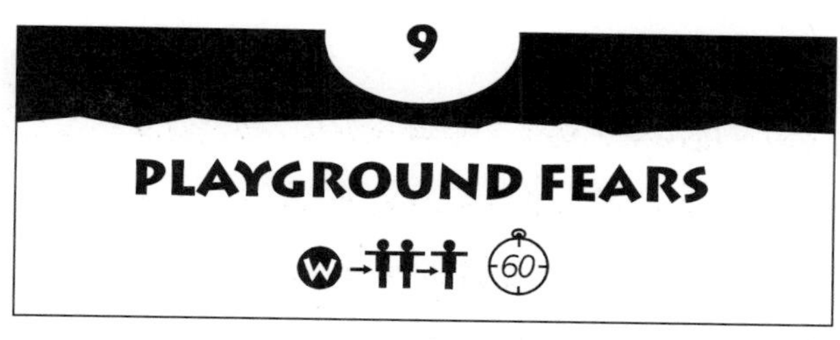

Teaching content

Studying the work of great authors can help us to improve our writing. Punctuation can be used to speed up or slow down the pace of writing. Careful selection of vocabulary is essential to good writing.

What you need

Photocopiable page 105, writing materials.

What to do

Distribute photocopiable page 105 and ask the children to look again at Laurie Lee's passage from the words 'The playground roared...' to '...stole my potato'. Explain to the children that the feeling of speed and vitality that threatens the small child is created in the passage by the use of punctuation and language. Laurie Lee claims that he rewrote this book several times before it pleased him and that every punctuation mark and every single word and group of words were chosen with great care. Tell the children that they are going to look closely at two aspects of language in this passage to observe how cleverly it has been written. They will then be able to model a piece of writing on the work of a great author – a wonderful way to learn.

First, ask the children which punctuation mark Laurie Lee has used to build up a threatening, headlong feeling of speed. It is the lists, punctuated with commas, that pitch the reader headlong into the passage.

Organise the children into pairs and ask them to write a list of the verbs that are used in the passage. If necessary, remind them that a verb is a 'doing' word. Allow five minutes for this, then ask each group to suggest one verb and write these on the chalkboard. The list should include the following: 'roared, burned, skating, skidding, closed, flew, prod, plucked, spun, screwed, stole'.

Discuss the speed, noise and violence of these words and suggest that when the children write, they too must attempt to convey meaning through carefully chosen vocabulary.

Explain that it would be possible to look at many other features of vocabulary, language and figures of speech chosen by the writer as he crafted this short passage. Give the children the opportunity to comment on any other features they can observe. They may notice the use of adjectives or perhaps the use of simile and metaphor.

Gather in the photocopiable sheets but leave the list of verbs on the chalkboard. Distribute writing paper and ask the children to write a short piece about being tiny in the busy playground using images and words that convey the sense of noise and violent movement. Allow them to use some of Laurie Lee's vocabulary from the list on the chalkboard. Remind the children that lists punctuated with commas can lend a sense of headlong speed to a piece of writing.

Teaching content

Organising different pieces of writing into one recount.

What you need

All the planning sheets and pieces of writing from previous activities.

What to do

Tell the children that they are now going to write their third autobiography chapter about their early school days. Ask them to take out and read through their photocopiable planning sheet of 'earliest school memories' from Activity 7. Explain that this provides a rough chronological sequence for writing about infant school days. They may choose not to cover some points or to cover them in a different order, but at some point they should include their writing about an embarrassing misunderstanding and the writing about the playground. Ask the children to number the ideas on the memories sheet in the order in which they want to write about them, including these two pieces of writing in the numbered sequence. Tell the children that professional writers often have several pieces of writing, completed at different times, which they fit together to create the finished piece of work.

Children should now write their third chapter, choosing a suitable heading for this. Tell them that if they want to include chapters about later schooldays they will be able to choose to do this at a later stage.

Teaching content

Recount writing follows a time sequence. Recounts require an introduction to present the main idea to be developed in the piece of writing.

What you need

Letter for parents (see page 97), chalkboard writing materials.

What to do

Most autobiographies give background information on the writer's family.

Tell the children that they are going to record something of the history of their families, but rather than giving a very general background, they are going to write about a well-known family story that has become part of family folklore! This type of story will have been told so often, and become embellished in the re-telling, until no one knows what is truth and what is fiction. Explain that the story will probably be about the brave or funny deeds of one well-known family member. Point out to the children that family stories can tell outsiders a great deal about what a family is like, because stories are only told about the things that people take a pride in.

Some children will immediately come up with a story to tell, but for those who don't, explain that the story may be about an incident in the lives of one of their parents or grandparents. It may be about something as big as a car crash or climbing Mount Everest, or as small as a holiday at the seaside, or a school experience. As long as it happened to a family member, then it is part of their family folklore! Prepare a letter to parents, such as:

School name and address

Dear Parents
Thank you for the help and support you have already given your children in writing their autobiographies. I'm sure you will be delighted when you read their interesting work. The completed publication will be sent home for you to read and enjoy, but in the meantime I wonder if you could help your child with one more activity?

Most autobiographies include a section on family history and, for this chapter, children are being asked to write a well-known family story. Most families have stories which could become part of family folklore. These are generally about the brave or funny deeds of one particular family member. Sometimes the stories are of epic proportions, such as war experiences or accounts of moving to a new country. Sometimes they retell smaller events and the best stories can be about the childhood adventures of a grandparent or great-grandparent. If your family has no such stories, could you please choose any family member and pay tribute to this person in a brief account of his or her life? Please tell your chosen family story to your child, so that an interesting piece of family history will become a central part of the autobiography.

Would you please think about this and tell the story by (date) __________.

Thank you for your help with this work.
Yours faithfully

Send your completed letter home to parents, or other adults with whom the children live. Allow them a few days to find a good tale by asking around in the family. If they are having difficulty, advise them to ask if their great-grandparents were involved in any wars and, if so, what stories they tell or told about this experience.

Some parents or grandparents may have come to Britain from other countries, so advise children to ask if they have stories to tell about this experience. Stress throughout that good stories don't have to be about grand events. Encourage children to ask relatives about childhood accidents, special days out and family parties.

Next, under the chapter heading of 'A family story', ask the children to write the recounts of their stories. Remind them that a recount is generally told in a logical time sequence of events, with a clear beginning that introduces the subject of the recount. Model three beginnings on the chalkboard to illustrate appropriate starting points:

There are many stories told about my family and the one I like best is about...
In my family people like to tell stories and I like the one about...
Family stories are very important. They tell you a lot about what a family thinks is important. That is why I like my family's story about...

Allow the children to copy one of these if it helps them to get started on writing. Children who think up their own starting points should be encouraged to use them.

12

SWEET TRUTH!

Teaching content
Closely observed detail can add truth and vitality to descriptive writing.

What you need
Photocopiable page 106, art and writing materials, magnifying glasses if possible, children's favourite two types of sweets.

What to do
Give the children a few days advance warning that they should bring in two different types of favourite sweet. (Be sensitive to any children who are not allowed to eat sweets.) Tell them that you will store these in envelopes with their names on to make sure they do not eat them before the lesson.

First, ask them to observe the two sweets closely then draw a sketch of each. If possible, provide magnifying glasses so that the finest detail may be recorded. Encourage children to capture their colour as exactly as possible.

Ask the children to read through the steps at the bottom of the photocopiable sheet and to use these to help them write one paragraph of continuous prose about each sweet. Finally, they should organise this into a chapter for their autobiographies in which writing is illustrated using closely observed drawings.

Explain to the children that adults often forget a great deal about their young lives but they rarely forget their favourite sweets. Sadly, however, adults find it difficult to recapture, completely, the rapture of a well-loved sweet. Reading a well-written description might help adults to see, feel the texture and taste the wonders of a favourite sweet once again. Tell the children that if they write about their favourite sweets, their vivid writing will act as a memory jogger for adults today and will also remind themselves in the future of the joys of particular favourites.

Distribute a copy of photocopiable page 106 to each child and read through the extract from *Boy* with the children. Some of Roald Dahl's favourite sweets may be equally well loved by members of the class.

Ask the children if they can spot the technique he uses to enable us to taste the very essence of these sweets. It is, of course, his close scrutiny of every aspect of the sweet. He gives a detailed and closely-observed description of the appearance of the sweet, before writing in several different ways of its taste and texture on his tongue. Now return the children's envelopes containing their two favourite sweets and provide a plentiful supply of paper.

13

THE LONGEST NIGHT

W → 1 → 2 → 1 (60) +

Teaching content

Intense personal memories produce evocative writing. An opening orientation sentence is a feature of recount writing. Recounts follow a chronological order.

What you need

Photocopiable page 107, chalkboard, writing materials.

What to do

Tell the children that by the time they reach the age of eight or nine years old most people have been ill, even if only for a couple of days. Sickness is an experience that all human beings talk about. Discussing and sharing the horrible details of illness helps us to come to terms with trauma in our lives. It is easier to write about illness than many other subjects because we remember the details clearly. This may be because we have time to reflect upon our experience when lying in bed.

Establish the fact that every child has had the experience of being ill, and remind them that although an upset stomach or a very sore throat may not appear to be as dramatic as chicken pox or whooping cough they can make you feel just as ill. Accidents resulting in injury also cause pain and illness and should therefore be included.

Distribute a copy of photocopiable page 107 to each child. Read through this together, then ask them to answer the questions in the first section, individually, in note form, on a separate sheet of paper. Allow ten minutes for this, then ask several children to read out a few of their responses.

Next, discuss the disturbing night-time experience of being ill. Tell the children that some of the most deep and sharp emotions that we ever feel in our lives are associated with night-time illness and it is therapeutic, as well as important for our personal records, to write these down.

Ask the children to write notes on the questions asked in the second part of the photocopiable sheet. Allow several minutes for this before asking the children to go through their answers with a writing partner. This discussion will help to firm the ideas they already have and the sharing may trigger more vivid responses.

Ask the children to write a paragraph based upon this initial planning. It may help if a few paragraph starters are modelled on the chalkboard:

One of the worst times during my illness was at night. I remember...

At night-time I used to hope the morning would come soon. During the dark hours I...

Children should now write their chapter about being ill. Remind them that they should insert their night-time paragraph at an appropriate point to keep the chronology of their recounts in the correct sequence.

Teaching content

Writing explanations is made easier if they are talked through first. Explanations are generally written as a sequence of ideas.

What you need

A hated or loved object brought to school by each child, chalkboard, writing materials.

What to do

Tell the children that the possessions we value most or truly detest, or give clear clues to the sort of people we are. Explain that in future years it would be fascinating for them to read about and remember the possessions that were of greatest value to them and also read of the possessions that they hated most when they were nine or ten years old!

Tell them that there is a game played on television in which guest celebrities are all allowed to choose their three worst possessions and lock them away for ever. Tell the children to imagine that they have been asked to take part in this game. They are going to write explanations as to why they have selected these three objects.

Begin by asking the children to identify their three most hated possessions. Brainstorm on the chalkboard any ideas they have. There will probably be suggestions of items of clothing, bought for them by other people who don't know their personal taste and have no fashion sense. There may be horribly sensible items of furniture in their bedrooms, toys that they don't want to play with and school bags that are definitely not cool. Ask the children to write down their three chosen items and then, in note form, up to four reasons why each one should never be seen again.

In order to balance this list of most hated possessions, encourage the children to suggest things they really love. Again, brainstorm a list on the chalkboard (allow children to include pets). Ask the children to select their three most precious possessions and then write a few reasons why these objects or animals are so well cherished.

Ask every child to bring one of the favourite or rejected items into school and allow each to explain his or her choice. Remind the children that explanations must begin with a sentence introducing the subject and then proceed with an orderly list of reasons. In this case they will begin with one of the following starter lines:

This is one of my favourite possessions because...
The reasons why I detest this possession and would be glad to see it locked away...

Having practised giving an explanation, children will next write about their six choices in six paragraphs of explanatory writing. This will make up the next chapter of the autobiography and should be given an appropriate title.

15 WRITING MORE

Teaching content

Generating, selecting, presenting and sequencing ideas for recount writing.

What you need

Memory lists from Activities 3 and 5, writing materials.

What to do

Many children may now be keen to write about individual turning points or memory flashbacks that they identified in Activities 3 and 5, but may require further support, either to keep on task or to help identify and plan the writing content.

Topics you may wish to consider include:

- pets;
- moving house;
- a happy moment frozen in time;
- key triumphs achieved for the first time;
- the best present ever given or received.

The teacher may select topics and set an agenda for individuals, groups or even the whole class, or the children might be allowed to choose topics for themselves. There will always be children for whom a particular topic is inappropriate, so any class or group approach must be sensitive and flexible.

Encourage the children to discuss their memories and ideas for the writing content with family and friends, and to sleep on their decisions. Illustrations in the form of photographs and drawings should ideally be collected before the writing begins.

16 PUBLICATION, CELEBRATION AND REVIEW

Teaching content

Celebration and review of writing.

What you need

Photocopiable page 108, autobiography books, cardboard from cardboard boxes (cut to the cover size of the book), tissues or foam for padding, covering material, ribbon, scissors, adhesive and adhesive tape.

What to do

Show the children how to make attractive padded covers for their books by covering them with stiff card, scored down the spine to allow it to fold. This can be padded by taping on tissues or foam and then covering it with a piece of material. The padded cover can then be stuck onto the original cover of the exercise book. Lengths of ribbon attached midway along the edges of the front and back covers can be used to tie the book closed.

Give out copies of photocopiable page 108 and read it through with the class. Tell the children to ask an adult at home to read their finished book and answer the photocopiable review sheet questions, writing in the box provided and then continuing on the back of the sheet if necessary.

If this causes problems for some children in the class, non-teaching adults on the school staff may be willing to help with this celebration and review process. Once completed, the writing generated by the sheets should be stuck onto the final page of the book, which should be headed 'Reviews'.

The photocopiable sheet can also be used within the class. Organise the children into pairs and tell them to read and review their partner's books, recommending one chapter in particular. Authors could also undertake to read one chapter to an infant pupil. All reviews should be stuck into the 'Review' section at the back of the book.

Finally, children should be reminded that this is not the end, but the beginning of keeping autobiographical records of their individual (and therefore interesting and unusual) lives!

NAME

REASONS FOR WRITING AUTOBIOGRAPHIES

People with interesting lives wish to leave a record.

Those who have known famous celebrities want to tell other people about their meetings and relationships.

People like to feel that their lives are worthwhile and interesting to others.

People who have lived in different countries want to share this important experience.

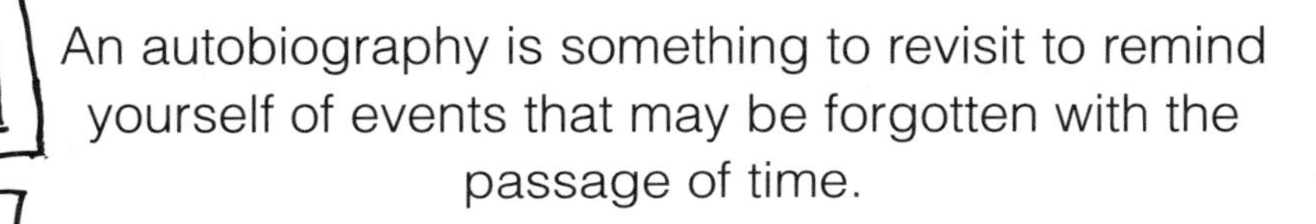

An autobiography is something to revisit to remind yourself of events that may be forgotten with the passage of time.

Writing about events helps people to make sense of, and come to terms with, upsetting experiences.

Some people feel that their experiences will help others.

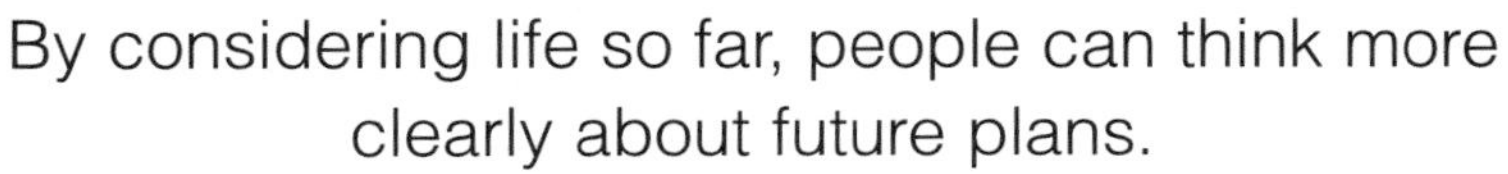

By considering life so far, people can think more clearly about future plans.

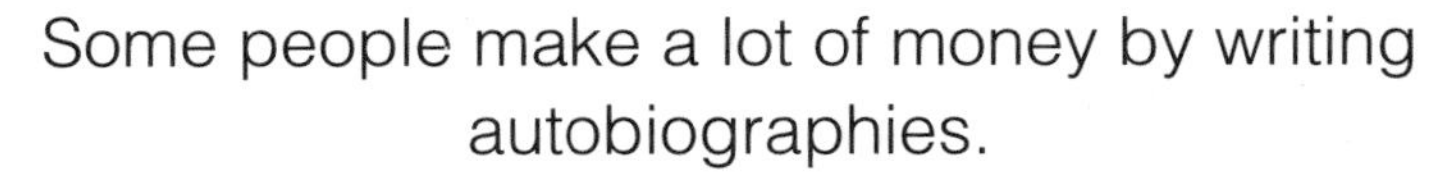

Some people make a lot of money by writing autobiographies.

A person who seems to have an ordinary life can often make ordinary experiences seem extraordinary for other people to read about.

NAME

RESEARCHING EARLY YEARS

Where was I born?

Are there any funny or dramatic stories surrounding my birth?

What names did you consider calling me?

Were there arguments about my name?

How was my name finally decided?

Tell me all about the naming ceremony or celebration for my birth.

Did I sleep well at night or keep everyone awake?

Was I bad- or good-tempered as a baby and did I like other people?

At what age did I cut my first tooth?

At what age did I take my first step?

At what age did I speak and can you remember what I said?

Was I ever seriously ill when I was a baby?

When I started to eat solid food, what did I like most?

What was my favourite toy?

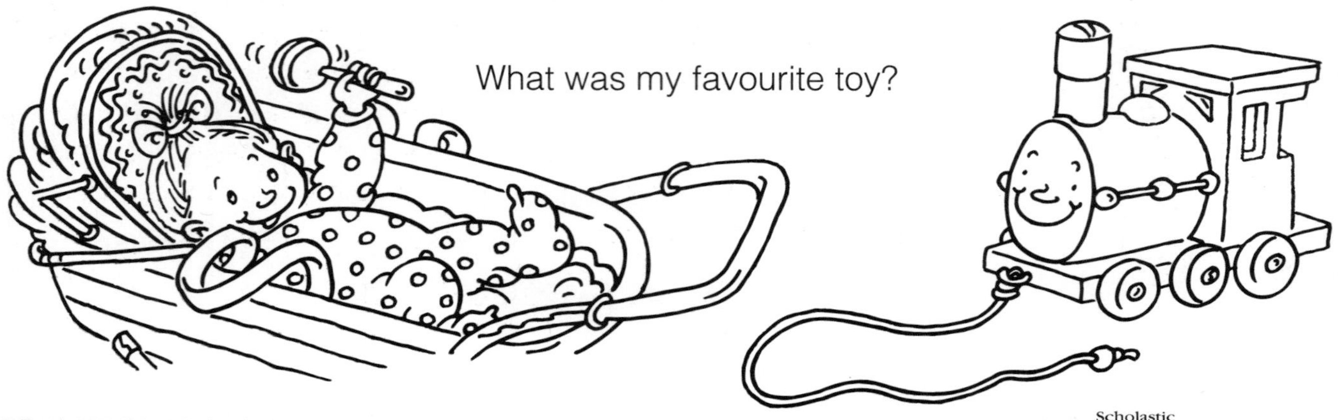

NAME

MEMORY FLASHES

'...throughout my young days at school and just afterwards a number of things happened to me that I have never forgotten.

None of these things is important, but each of them made such a tremendous impression on me that I have never been able to get them out of my mind. Each of them, even after a lapse of fifty and sometimes sixty years, has remained seared on my memory.

I didn't have to search for any of them. All I had to do was skim them off the top of my consciousness and write them down.

Some are funny. Some are painful. Some are unpleasant. I suppose that is why I have always remembered them so vividly. All are true.'

From *Boy* by Roald Dahl (Puffin)

'...It was only gradually that memory began to stir, setting off flash-points like summer lightning, which illuminated for a moment some field or landmark, some ancient totem or neighbour's face.

Seizing these flares and flashes became a way of writing, episodic and momentarily revealing, to be used as small beacons to mark the peaks of the story and to accentuate the darkness of what was left out. So I began my tale where this light sparked brightest, close-up, at the age of three, when I was no taller than grass, and was an intimate of insects and knew the details of stones and chair-legs.'

From *I Can't Stay Long* by Laurie Lee (Penguin)

'After the age of four I have many memories that form into stories about small episodes in my life. Before that I have one sharp memory of being in the small kitchen/living room of our flat. There are two pairs of shoes on the sill outside the sash window. One is a pair of women's court shoes and the other a pair of tiny sandals. Both shine brightly white in the sun. They have been coated with a spirit cleaner and the smell is clean and clear in the air. My mother is a warm and large presence standing beside me as we wait for the shoes to dry.'

by Anne Scott (unpublished)

NAME

EARLIEST SCHOOL MEMORIES

- Do you remember anything at all about your first day at school?

(Most people remember nothing. Don't invent stories.

This is a non-fiction recount.)

- Did you want to come to school every morning?
- What do you remember wearing for school?
- Describe what you remember about the classroom.

(Remember to include its size and decor, furniture, seating arrangements, temperature, smells,sounds and your main feelings.)

- Who was the first teacher you remember?
- Did you like being in the playground? Why?
- Do you remember liking another child in the class?
- Name one book you remember learning from.
- Did you like this book? Why?
- What two things did you like doing best in class? Why?
- Describe one thing you did not like about school.
- Which part of the day did you look forward to?

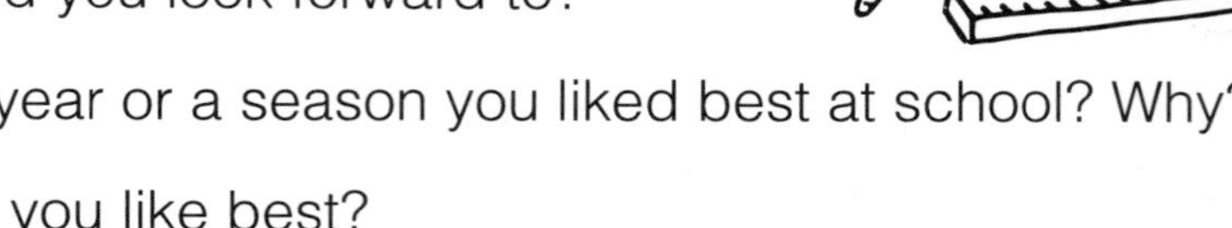

- Was there a time of the year or a season you liked best at school? Why?
- What school games did you like best?

An embarrassing or humiliating misunderstanding

NAME

EARLY SCHOOL EXPERIENCES

'...I arrived at the school just three feet tall and fatly wrapped in my scarves. The playground roared like a rodeo, and the potato burned through my thigh. Old boots, ragged stockings, torn trousers and skirts, went skating and skidding around me. The rabble closed in; I was encircled; grit flew in my face like shrapnel. Tall girls with frizzled hair, and huge boys with sharp elbows, began to prod me with hideous interest. They plucked at my scarves, spun me round like a top, screwed my nose, and stole my potato.

I was rescued at last by a gracious lady – the sixteen-year-old junior-teacher – who boxed a few ears and dried my face and led me off to The Infants. I spent that first day picking holes in paper, then went home in a smouldering temper.

'What's the matter, Loll? Didn't he like it at school, then?'

'They never gave me the present!'

'Present? What present?'

'They said they'd give me a present.'

'Well, now, I'm sure they didn't.'

'They did! They said: 'You're Laurie Lee, ain't you? Well, just you sit there for the present.' I sat there all day but I never got it. I ain't going back there again!'

From *Cider with Rosie* by Laurie Lee (Penguin)

'...I wasn't used to crowds, for as a small boy I hadn't gone out much, but used to play near home. I began to feel so dizzy that my sister, who was now blushing had to come and hold me up. The other pupils were laughing and I started blushing because I was angry. I thought they were stupid and inconsiderate.

Since it was January, the beginning of a new year in school, the chairs were on the tables. The teacher told us to sit anywhere on any chair. I was still a little confused and without thinking I climbed onto the table and onto the chair sitting on top. I sat down too confidently. The pupils and the teacher started to laugh loudly. I got more confused and not realising the joke, I too started laughing. My style of laughing was so unique (tears roll out of my eyes when I actually laugh even to this day) that I fell off the chair. It was then that I noticed that everybody else had taken their chairs off the table and were sitting on them.'

From *Our Lives* – Young People's Autobiographies, The English Centre, ILEA

NAME

SWEET TRUTH!

'...A Bootlace, in case you haven't had the pleasure of handling one, is not round. It's like a flat black tape about half an inch wide. You buy it rolled up in a coil, and in those days it used to be so long that when you unrolled it and held one end at arm's length above your head, the other end touched the ground.

Sherbet Suckers were also two a penny. Each Sucker consisted of a yellow cardboard tube filled with sherbet powder, and there was a hollow liquorice straw sticking out of it. (Rat's blood again, young Thwaites would warn us, pointing at the liquorice straw.) You sucked the sherbet up through the straw and when it was finished you ate the liquorice. They were delicious, those Sherbet Suckers. The sherbet fizzed in your mouth, and if you knew how to do it, you could make white froth come out of your nostrils and pretend you were throwing a fit.

Gobstoppers, costing a penny each, were enormous hard round balls the size of small tomatoes. One Gobstopper would provide about an hour's worth of non-stop sucking and if you took it out of your mouth and inspected it every five minutes or so, you would find it had changed colour. There was something fascinating about the way it went from pink to blue to green to yellow. We used to wonder how in the world the Gobstopper Factory managed to achieve this magic.

Pear Drops were exciting because they had a dangerous taste. They smelled of nail-varnish and they froze the back of your throat. All of us were warned against eating them, and the result was that we ate them more than ever.

Then there was a hard brown lozenge called the Tonsil Tickler. The Tonsil Tickler tasted and smelled very strongly of chloroform. We had not the slightest doubt that these things were saturated in the dreaded anaesthetic which, as Thwaites had many times pointed out to us, could put you to sleep for hours at a stretch.

From *Boy* by Roald Dahl (Puffin)

◆ Look closely at your sweet, possibly using a magnifying glass, and describe the following:

Shape   Colour   Texture   Does it have a wrapper?

How do you prefer to open the wrapper?

Is it possible to describe: the smell?   the feel in your hand?

Place the sweet in your mouth. What does it feel like on the tongue?

Does the texture change in your mouth? If so, record the changes.

Is it possible to describe the taste? Does it taste like any other sweet or food?

Is it possible to eat this sweet in different ways?

Which method of eating do you favour?

Is there any place or any particular time when you love to eat these sweets?

How often do you eat them?

NAME

BEING ILL

My illness (or accident)

1 How old were you when this happened?

2 Describe the first symptoms of your illness or describe your accident.

3 Who was the first person you told about your illness or knew about your accident? What did that person say?

4 Describe what happened when you went to the hospital or saw the doctor. What was said?

5 If medicine was prescribed, describe the taste and appearance. How often did you take this.

6 Did you have to stay in hospital, go to bed at home or did you lie on the couch?

7 What did you think about – during the day? during the night?

8 What did you hear people saying – during the day? during the night?

9 Write about the people who came to visit and the gifts or cards you received.

10 When you were recovering, describe the first time you went out and what you said to yourself.

Waiting for morning

- Without opening the bedroom curtains, most of us know if it is light outside. What are the signs in your room that day has dawned?
- Depending on where you live, the sounds that tell you it is morning will be different. List the sounds that mean 'morning' for you.
- Describe the things about your bedroom that can seem alarming when you are ill and unable to sleep.
- Describe your bedroom as it looks in the comfort of morning light.
- Remember to describe the objects that you particularly like in your bedroom.
- Why do you think that being ill seems worse during the night?

NAME

CELEBRATION AND REVIEW

Dear Reviewer

I have pleasure in presenting the story of my life so far!
This is a recount of some of the hilariously funny, some of the terribly sad and some of the seemingly ordinary events of my life. Reading my autobiography may remind you of events and emotional experiences in your own life and it will tell you of the life of a child growing up in modern times. I hope that you enjoy reading this book, and I ask you to please fill in the review sheet provided, continuing on the back of the page if necessary. If you answer the questions on the sheet in sentences, then your finished writing will form a review, which will be presented in the back of my autobiography. This will make you an official reviewer for this publication. Please be kind and gentle with your comments!

Many thanks from the author of this book.

Signed ______________________________ (author)

Please comment in sentences.

Which part of this book did you find most interesting and why?

Name one event in the book that reminded you of an event in your own life.

Was this sad or happy?

Is there an opinion expressed in the book with which you strongly agree or disagree, for example favourite sweets?

Could you copy one or two sentences from the book that illustrate the good quality of the writing?

Do you feel proud to know the author of this book personally? Why?

If not, would you like to meet the author of this book? Why?

Would you like to read other publications written by this author?

Signed ______________________ Reviewer

Review

I do/do not recommend this book to other readers.

Chapter Nine

MAKING A CLASS NEWSPAPER

INTRODUCTION

Project description

This project provides the children with a wide range of opportunities for writing in different non-fiction genres. It also allows pupils to become more familiar with the types of newspaper they will encounter in real life, introducing them to their different emphases in content and the range of registers in which articles may be written. This exploratory angle, allowing children to familiarise themselves with the world of newspapers, should work in tandem with the production of the class newspaper. Many pupils will already know about newspapers but some will be learning about them for the first time. They should be allowed to experience the news medium and share their understandings of how it works at their own pace.

Children will also learn that newspapers contain much that is not news and that genres other than recount are represented. Although all newspaper articles tend to be called reports, teachers should note that most are in fact recounts. Persuasive writing is seen in editorials, 'letters to the editor', critical reviews and advertising, discursive features on fashion and current issues, procedural writing seen in recipes and DIY: all these will present pupils with a range of models for functional writing and for different forms of layout. Not only is each of these pieces written for a different purpose, but authors will use a range of appropriate registers. Developing writers often need most help with this aspect of writing and the activities in this project will help them to select appropriate registers and communicate information effectively.

Why this context?

This project offers a range of good models and a clear purpose for writing – both good reasons for producing a newspaper. The children will still require suitable content and it is suggested that personal and local concerns are used to provide this. Local issues of interest to parents and children will include:

- availability of play areas,
- volume of traffic;
- forthcoming events in the sporting and leisure life of the community;
- interviews with local dignitaries;
- prize puzzles and competitions.

Some of the activities have been left 'content-free' so the ideas can be adapted to a chosen focus.

A possible extension of a local focus is to find a school in another town that would be willing to take part in a 'twinned' newspaper challenge. Each class would have to produce a newspaper to inform the other about its own community, thus providing another audience for writing.

Project organisation

It will take about three to four weeks to produce the first edition of the class newspaper. After this you will have to decide how often the paper will be published and who will be allowed to contribute.

Before you begin the project set up a newspaper corner in your classroom. Arrange to have a selection of newspapers 'delivered' (perhaps by striking a deal with a local newsagent to take excess copies of yesterday's papers at a cut rate or by asking parents to supply yesterday's news). Set up a computer with a word-processing or desktop publishing package in the corner. (This is, however, not essential.)

Publication, celebration and review

Children should be involved in deciding on the actual content of their newspaper and how it should be put together. One possible suggestion is to set up a chart which shows the content of each page. This might be based on the activities in this project, but could easily be adapted to incorporate other sections.

Publication and presentation will be facilitated by using A3-size paper as it is easy to photocopy and provides an authentic tabloid-sized product. The illustrated example would require four sheets of A3, using both sides of the paper.

Once the children have decided on the sections to be included in their newspaper, divide them into groups, giving each one responsibility for the selection of copy for a particular section. Some groups might be responsible for more than one of the shorter sections, such as classified ads or reviews. The information on responsibilities should be added to the classroom display chart.

Other issues you should consider include:
- planning regular times for editorial groups to meet;
- how submitted copy should be organised (possibly in folders entitled 'Being considered', 'Selected' and 'Rejected' or on display boards);
- ensuring that final copy is read thoroughly.

A visit to a newspaper plant or a visit from a journalist would help pupils to understand the range of tasks which have to be completed and the scale of the operation involved in printing the news on a daily basis.

The first four activities help build up the children's knowledge of the various sections in a newspaper, before editorial committees are formed to take responsibility for the selection and organisation of specific sections. Pupils should be given opportunities to write in a number of different genres, rather than just the one for which they have editorial responsibility.

Books the children may find useful

Information books about newspapers will be useful additions to the classroom while the children are engaged in this project.

The Greek News by Anton Powell and Philip Steele (Walker Books, 1996)
The Roman News by Andrew Langley and Philip deSouza (Walker Books, 1996)
Newspapers by Brenda Mann (Wayland, 1987)
Newspapers by Philippa Perry (Wayland, 1994)
Newspapers by Lucy Williams (Wayland, 1993)

WHAT'S IN A NEWSPAPER?

Teaching content

Newspapers have different sections. This makes them easier to read.

What you need

A selection of newspapers (at least one per pair), large sheets of paper, writing materials.

What to do

Start by asking the children what newspapers they know of. Their response to this will depend on their backgrounds and the newspapers they encounter in their own homes. If this line of questioning throws up a very limited range you might want to give groups an opportunity to examine the selection you have provided. Try to build up a range, including:
- daily, weekly, monthly distributions;
- tabloids and broadsheets;
- local and national.

With the children organised into groups of six, give three different types of newspaper, perhaps a daily tabloid, a weekly broadsheet and a local free sheet. Ask them, in pairs, to focus on a particular newspaper and to list, on a large sheet of paper, all the different sections they can find. The group of six should then collate, on a separate sheet, the sections that are common to all three newspapers and the sections that are distinctive to each. They should use different colours to record these two categories.

This should produce a comprehensive list of contents, including:
- news reports;
- reviews (films, music, theatre, books, and so on);
- editorial comment;
- opinion column or 'letters to the editor';
- entertainment information;
- sports reports;
- classified advertisements;
- features pages (such as fashion, music, cooking, travel or lifestyle);
- weather reports, charts, forecasts;
- television and radio listings.

Display the sheets where the whole class can see them and discuss which sections they think would be most suitable for their class newspaper. Provide some guidance to ensure that their choices are:
- feasible in terms of their access to information;
- likely to engage them in writing in different genres;
- manageable in terms of classroom organisation.

If your school has teletext facilities these will provide access to much information on current weather, entertainment and travel which children will be able to reorganise into suitable formats. Weather data, for example, could be retrieved from teletext just before publication and set out in a format similar to those used in other newspapers.

The end of this activity would be an appropriate time to discuss a name for the class newspaper. Ask the children to collect as many different banner headlines as they can over the coming week and build up a collection of these for display in the class. This should produce a good list of common (and some uncommon) titles from which the children can generate further suggestions. Draw up a short list and use this as an opportunity to stimulate advance interest by involving parents, staff and pupils in a survey to find the most popular title.

WHO'S READING THE PAPERS?

Teaching content
Different types of writing serve different purposes and are read for different reasons.

What you need
One newspaper per pair, large sheets of paper, felt-tipped pens.

What to do
The main purpose of this activity is to establish the range of contents, purposes and audiences for different sections of newspapers.

The day before you engage in this activity ask each child to find out from two adults which parts of the newspaper they like to read most, and in what order they read the content. They should bring this information with them to school.

Explain to the children that people like to read newspapers for different reasons and that these might vary depending on their mood, interests, whether there is a story that has been running for a number of days and how much time they have available to read the newspaper. Establish with the children that these might be grouped under headings that show the different purposes for which various parts of the paper have been written:
- news reports and TV listings *inform*;
- cartoon strips, star signs and special interest features *entertain*;
- advertisements *persuade*;
- editorials *explain*;
- recipes *give instructions*.

These categories are not rigid and some time should be spent considering how, for example, an advert might both inform and persuade or an editorial might explain and persuade. Some readers might consider that star signs inform rather than entertain!

The children should discuss their findings about the readers they have surveyed within their groups of six. They should then, in pairs, work with one newspaper and identify four different sections in it. Next they should fold their large sheet into quarters, recording the title of each section in a separate quarter. Under each title they should state why this piece has been written – to inform, to entertain, to persuade, to explain, to give instructions or combinations of these. They should then try to match each person surveyed to the section of the newspaper that would most interest them.

Finally, the pairs should report back to the group of six on each of the adult readers in their survey stating what would be of interest in their newspaper. For example 'If Mrs Evans were to read the Daily Blurb she would enjoy the recipes and the news reports'.

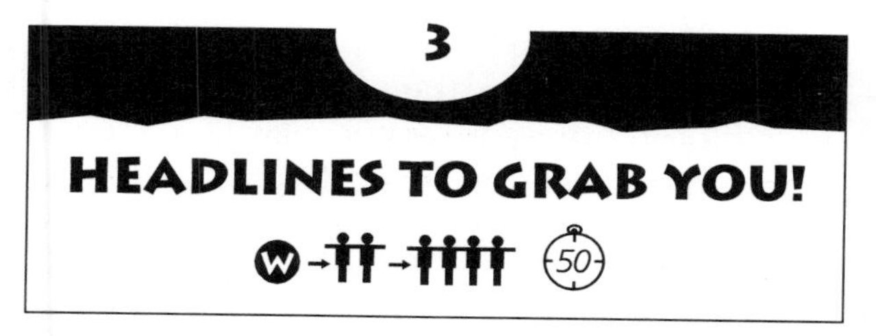

Teaching content

Effective headlines are short, vivid and capture the essence of the story.

What you need

One newspaper per pair, scissors, small strips of card, writing materials.

What to do

Use two current newspapers, one tabloid and one broadsheet, to start this activity. Read the children two or three headlines from reports in each of the newspapers and ask them to suggest what the stories are going to be about. Choose examples that best illustrate the relative sensationalism of tabloid headlines and the factual tone of broadsheets. Discuss which are more effective in introducing the content to the reader and which are more likely to make you want to read on. Opinions on this will differ but it will provide a good opportunity to consider the reasons why headlines are written in different ways.

Give each pair a newspaper and ask them to select four reports, cut out the headlines and reports and separate them from one another. Ask each pair to exchange their headlines and reports with another pair and to try to match up the set of headlines and reports they have been given. Discourage the children from using matching tricks (such as shape or typographical clues) and explain that the aim of the activity is to see if the headlines are effective in summarising the main idea in the report.

- What are the key words that give them clues?
- Why does the headline grab their attention?

Answering these questions should allow them to rate how effective the headlines are at summarising the contents of the report and how much they appeal to readers. Encourage them to justify their judgements on the headlines and to rate them from 1 to 5, on both of these criteria, giving reasons for their ratings.

Finally, ask each pair to write alternative headlines on the small strips of card for those they consider to be unsatisfactory. Headlines and reports should then be returned to the original pairs who should comment on the new headlines.

Teaching content

Exploring the relationship between headlines, text, pictures and captions.

What you need

One newspaper per pair, card for masking, scissors, Blu-Tack, writing materials.

What to do

Use the front page lead story from a current newspaper to begin this activity. Ask the children what gives them information about this particular story, apart from the report itself. They are likely to identify the headline, the picture and the caption. Continue the discussion by asking a number of questions:

- What are they likely to look at first? Why?
- What purpose does the caption serve?
- Does the caption match the picture? Does it tell you something more about the report?
- Does the headline attract your attention? Does it give you a clear sense of the likely content of the report?

Read the report to them and ask if they can suggest alternative, more appropriate headlines.
- Has the photograph been well chosen?
- Does it tell you about the characters or the setting? Is it informative or merely decorative?
- Are there other pictures that would have provided better support for the article?

Give each pair a newspaper and ask them to select a report. Then, using the card and Blu-Tack, they should mask the picture, headline and caption. Now ask each pair to exchange newspapers with another pair. Challenge them to read the report they have been given, then draw a suitable picture and supply new headlines and captions for it. When this has been completed they are allowed to reveal the masked items and, in fours, should compare their suggestions with the originals. Have they chosen the same or different aspects of the report to illustrate and summarise?

A simple variation on this theme would be to mask the text and ask the children to write the report. This would also introduce them to producing copy in columns. This could be tried in Activity 5 when children have been introduced to the structure of reports and have been provided with a strategy for writing.

Teaching content

There are key categories of information that make up reports.

What you need

One news report (taken from your class stock), chalkboard, writing materials.

What to do

This activity is devised to help children deconstruct news reports to see how they have been written. This should provide them with a better understanding of the essential ingredients and a model for reports for their own newspaper.

Explain to the children that you are going to read them a news report and as they listen you would like them to note down information under the headings:
- Who is this report about?
- Where did it happen?
- When did it happen?
- What happened?
- Why did it happen?

Allocate particular responsibility for one category to one person in each group. As you read, try to emphasise the key points, so that they glean as much information as possible. Allow the children to ask questions to check or clarify items of detail and to confer in their groups to confirm understanding and identify gaps in their knowledge. Read the report a second time to allow them to verify the accuracy of their notes.

Then build up on the board a complete set of responses from the groups to check for accuracy and reinforce the different categories of information. Discuss with the children:
- the tense in which the report is written;
- the sequence of events;
- the key events in the report.

Invite the children to suggest items of school or local news that would be worthy of inclusion in their newspaper. Write their suggestions as a list on the board and then choose one to show the children how you would plan your report by listing information under each of the categories. Go on to develop with them how you would use this to write the report.

Now ask them, in pairs, to prepare 'Who? Where? When? What? Why?' lists to ensure that they will include all the necessary details of school or local news issues when they come to write their reports.

6 LETTERS TO THE EDITOR

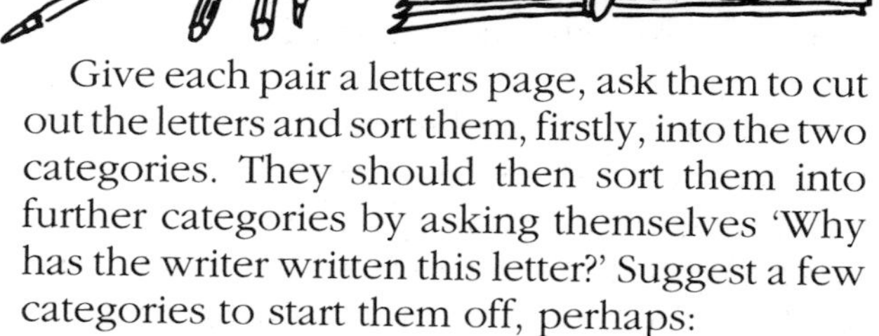

Teaching content

Each purpose requires a different structure and language.

What you need

Letters page(s) from newspapers, scissors, chalkboard, writing materials.

What to do

The letters that children will encounter in newspapers are likely to be of a different nature from those that they have written or received either in a school or a personal context. This activity is devised to help them survey a variety of purposes for writing and to familiarise them with the range of tones and registers employed by the writers.

Begin by asking the children to note down anyone they have written to in the last few months and to specify the reason for writing. After five to ten minutes collate examples on the board of people they have written to and what they have written about. This list might include:

- letters to friends met on holiday;
- thank-you letters to relatives for presents received;
- letters to comics or magazines to express opinions or take part in competitions;
- letters home (if they have been on trips to stay with friends or relatives).

Ask the children to help you divide these into letters that *give* and *seek* information.

Explain that you are going to invite pupils from other classes to write letters to the editor for your class newspaper. With the children draft a poster to send to other classes. This should include information about where to send their letters and suggestions on the type of topic they may wish to write about.

Explain to children that the editor of a newspaper has to make decisions about what to put into the newspaper and what to leave out. Suggest that people may write to the editor of a newspaper for many different reasons and that you should survey some letters pages to find out what these might be.

Give each pair a letters page, ask them to cut out the letters and sort them, firstly, into the two categories. They should then sort them into further categories by asking themselves 'Why has the writer written this letter?' Suggest a few categories to start them off, perhaps:

- to express an opinion;
- to entertain by telling a story.

This sorting activity should show that each letters page has different emphases and help the children to decide on the range of letters they would like to include in their letters page.

Provide starter frames for each type of letter and assign one to each pair. The following suggestions may be helpful:

Dear Editor,
I would like to tell you something funny that happened to me recently...

Dear Editor,
I feel I must write to you to tell you how I feel about __________. In my opinion...

These starter sentences are intended to set the tone of the piece and are likely to direct the writing towards either recount or persuasive genres. The writing which results from this activity should provide further material for the children to examine differences in structure and language. Use these to start a collection from which the committee responsible for the letters page will be able to make its final selection. They could be displayed on a 'Letters to the Editor' board so that children can add comments or responses over the coming weeks.

Teaching content

In the classified ads section of a newspaper people advertise to buy, sell and exchange goods and services. Persuasive writing requires clear, succinct details which emphasise the features that will appeal to the reader.

What you need

Writing materials.

What to do

Explain to the children that the classified advertisements section of the class newspaper will give them, and their parents, relatives and friends, a chance to advertise items and services that they might want to buy or sell. Elicit that each advertisement will have to include information about:

- the item for sale or wanted;
- how much it costs or how much will be paid;
- the name of the buyer or seller.

Ask the class to suggest examples of appropriate goods and services and build up a list that children can take home. This might include:

- toys;
- household utensils;
- car washing;
- gardening.

Explain that they are going to find out if anyone at home would like to use space in the newspaper to advertise something. Suggest they use a format such as the table below for recording the information from their home survey.

The class should compose a covering letter to explain the service to parents. Children should then be given two or three days to collect the details of interested parties.

When the children have collected this data organise them into groups of four to report on their potential customers. They should decide on layouts for their advertisements and check that all the necessary details have been included. They might well identify gaps that have to be remedied by further discussion with customers. Explain that newspapers often charge by the number of words or lines and that, although no charge is to be made, it is important to keep the ads brief, while ensuring that all necessary details are included. Children should then write their advertisements in pairs, edit them in groups of four, and display them on a 'Classified ads' board for final selection for the newspaper.

Person	Item/service	Buy/sell	Details
Mum	tea set	sell	18 pieces, willow pattern, good condition, £10 o.n.o.
Asif and brother	car-washing	sell	Service on weekly/monthly basis, £3 small cars, £5 big cars

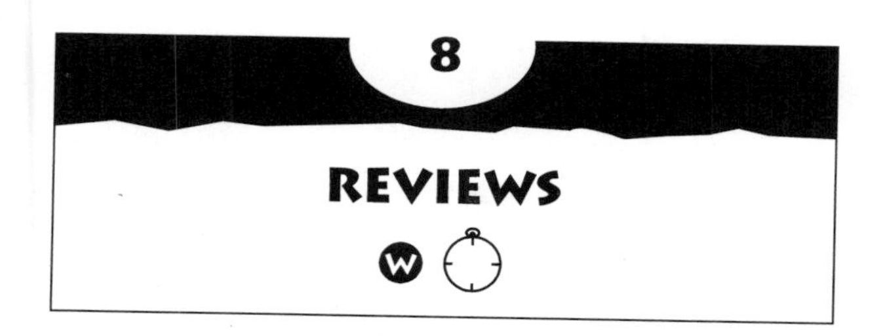

Teaching content

Reviews of books, films, videos and music can all have elements of report writing and persuasive writing.

What you need

An initial stimulus, such as a piece of music, a book shared with the class or a video or television broadcast; chalkboard, writing materials.

What to do

The specific review section selected for your newspaper will depend on the interests and recent experiences of the class. Many teachers will have encouraged children to share their book experiences with others through reviews and may wish to add variety to this activity by choosing a different focus, such as videos, films or television programmes. Whatever the specific focus, the key teaching point is that the reviewer must include two basic elements:

- a brief summative description (recount);
- a statement of opinion which usually contains an explicit or implicit recommendation (persuasive).

The activity works well when a short cartoon video is used. This has the advantage of having limited content, it will appeal to most children, and is a medium to which most will have ready access. It offers opportunities for them to extend their review skills by subsequent attempts based on further viewing at home or in class.

Let the children watch the video for the first time for enjoyment only. After watching it once, discuss with the children the characters and plot of the story and record these on the chalkboard. Explain that they are going to watch it a second time, and that you want them to look out for further details and to think about what makes this a good, bad or indifferent cartoon. Ask:

- Are the characters likeable, funny, heroic?
- Is the animation smooth, attractive, astounding?
- Do the voices match the characters, help create the mood of the piece and add to the fun and humour?
- Is the story-line interesting and easy to follow?

Pool the children's responses after the second viewing and then provide a frame that will encourage them to include in their reviews both the factual details in a recount of the story and their opinions of it.

Cartoon title
The cartoon begins with...
After that...
The producer has created characters who...
If you like funny cartoons...
In my opinion this cartoon...

Some children will want to break away from the constraints of this frame in subsequent reviews and should be encouraged to look at reviews of films and television programmes in the entertainment section of newspapers.

Once again, a display board should be started. Further writing can then be added to this as appropriate.

Teaching content

Any controversial issue will require discussion of different points of view. Discussions can be structured by listing points for and against. Discussion involves giving reasons or evidence for each viewpoint.

What you need

Photocopiable pages 119 and 120, chalkboard, writing materials.

What to do

Many newspapers make special features out of the results of mini opinion polls on issues of specific and current local interest. Constructing this type of page with your class will give them the opportunity to collect data and present arguments for both sides of a case. This is the most distinctive feature of the discussion genre, and is one of the most difficult to master.

The activity requires the construction of discursive text within a collaborative framework, which allows for optimum peer support. The photocopiable sheets are open-ended and can be adapted for use with any local issue.

Photocopiable page 119 is designed to help children to collect data systematically and draw conclusions from the data; photocopiable page 120 is designed to help them to present their findings systematically, construct arguments for and against, summarise the issue and state conclusions.

In order to model quickly the process in which the children are about to engage, ask the class a simple question that will evoke a yes/ no response. Try something like:

- Who likes wearing uniform?
- Who thinks that chewing gum should be banned in school?
- Who would like more room in the playground for organised games?
- Who would like litter monitors to patrol the playground at playtime?

Record the responses in a table similar to that on photocopiable page 119 on the chalkboard. Ask for and record some reasons for their responses. Construct with the children a conclusion that will summarise the results.

Explain that you have just undertaken the kind of mini-poll that newspapers conduct to monitor popular opinion and that now, in groups, they are going to conduct similar polls. These can be about issues connected with the class, the school or the community. Brainstorm for ideas that fit into each of these categories. These are likely to range from class rules and procedures, through tuck shop provision, school meals and the playground, to community concerns such as traffic, litter and vandalism. The topic chosen will need to be of interest to the sample population being polled and groups will have to suggest strategies as to how and when this will be done.

Distribute photocopiable page 119 and allow the groups to work on this for 10–15 minutes. Ask for feedback from each group and then, with the whole class, refine the questions and ensure that the suggested strategies are feasible. Explain that they will have two days to collect their data and that this should be done in out-of-class hours.

In the next session ask groups to report on their findings and focus this discussion on the reasons for their opinions given by those polled. Distribute photocopiable page 120 and, taking the original topic used as a stimulus in the first session, model how you might construct your feature page.

Groups should then allocate tasks to individuals to complete the various sections of the Special Features Page.

You may decide to run more than one special feature in the first edition of the newspaper, if not, it will always be possible to keep some in reserve for subsequent editions.

10 MEETING THE DEADLINE

Teaching content

Putting the newspaper together

What you need

All written work prepared so far, A3 sheets, adhesive, scissors.

What to do

It is best to put aside one whole day to assemble the newspaper. This gives a proper sense of occasion and an authentic feel of working to a deadline. The principal tasks to be dealt with are:

- proofreading of all possible content in pairs;
- selection of final copy by editorial groups;
- sequencing of content;
- layout of copy on pages;
- modifications (trimming and cropping) of headlines, articles and so on based on layout;
- inclusion of 'fillers' for awkward gaps (forthcoming events and newsflashes are good for this);
- photocopying;
- arrangements for distribution.

This will prove to be a fairly hectic, but very rewarding, day! Your pupils should gain a considerable sense of satisfaction from knowing that they have produced their own version of one of the most important adult media. Their knowledge of the different non-fiction genres will have been extended considerably and their competence in writing a range of texts will have grown.

NAME

JOURNALIST'S NOTEPAD

Topic under investigation

People to be surveyed ______________________________

____

Number to be surveyed ______________

Main question to be asked:

Do you or do you not think that ______________________________

______________________________? Why?

Results of survey

	Those in favour	Those against
Tally score		
Number		

Some reasons given

____

____

____

Conclusion –

From these results it would seem that ______________________________

____

NAME

SPECIAL FEATURES PAGE

Headline

The issue we have been investigating is ______________________

____

Our team thought this was an interesting issue because ______________

____

We asked ______________________________________

____

The case for
Some people thought that

____
____
____
____
____
____
____
____
____

The case for
Some people thought that

____
____
____
____
____
____
____
____
____

We publish the results of our mini-poll below.

These results show that ______________________________

____

____

Chapter Ten

THIS IS YOUR LIFE!

INTRODUCTION

Project description

In this project, children choose a person who works in, or has a strong association with, the school to be the celebrity in a 'This is your life' simulation. The focus of this is the celebrity's involvement with the school. The children interview people who have contact with the celebrity in school and record their comments in a 'This is your life' book before the actual celebration takes place. At the event, several invited guests speak about the celebrity, with one person speaking about the celebrity's life outside school. The children are responsible for organising the entire programme, including alerting the media by sending press releases to local newspapers and radio stations.

Why this context?

Many organisations recognise the hard work and commitment of staff by giving 'worker of the month' awards or bonus schemes. Within schools, many schemes exist for recognising children's commitment but, apart from end-of-term gifts, the staff's dedication is celebrated only when they retire!

This project gives children an opportunity to recognise the work of adults who care for them. Too often, the valuable contribution made by playground supervisors, caretakers or cooks is marginalised and overlooked.

This context offers children the chance to focus on the generous contribution made by one adult in the school, who is singled out for special thanks.

Children 'own' the project from the beginning; they make the choices and organise the event. Activities structured to drive the project forward harness children's enthusiasm and energy in a variety of purposeful writing tasks.

Project organisation

The whole class is involved in the project, brainstorming ideas, discussing and debating choices and making joint decisions. Writing pairs construct a piece of writing together and then share a practical task. Some individual writing is required, then pairs evaluate each other's writing and construct a joint piece. Self-evaluation and peer evaluation are built into the activities and are crucial for the success of the event.

Publication, celebration and review

The children's transcriptions of interviews for the 'This is your life' event are stuck into a 'This is your life' book. You will need a large, heavily-bound volume for this – an old wallpaper sample book is ideal. Cut the wallpaper samples out, leaving about 10cm of paper sticking out from the binding. Cut sheets of sugar paper to fit the book and stick them in, sandwiching each one between two of the 10cm strips of wallpaper. The number of pages required will vary and pages can easily be added. Trim any unused strips of wallpaper when the book is complete. Pad the cover with tissue paper and cover it with suitable material.

The first few pages should be made up of a title page and a list of people who attend the event – with space for them to sign and comment, of course.

PRE-SESSION

Decide the scope of the event in advance. It could be a small class or a whole-school event, it could take place at an assembly, or you could invite a guest audience of parents. You will need to use the school telephone for Activities 2 and 4 and you will need access to a quiet place, several tapes and tape recorders for Activities 6 and 7. Although children select the celebrity, you should have a short list in mind. Children can often be gently guided to make sensible decisions!

Teaching content

Selecting according to a list of criteria.

What you need

Photocopiable page 132, writing materials.

What to do

Explain to the children that they are going to organise a special 'This is your life' celebration for a person who is associated with the school. Their task is to choose the most appropriate person to receive this honour. Organise the children into groups of four and tell them that they will be writing out a list of deserving candidates.

Allow five minutes for this list to be drawn up and then ask a spokesperson to read out each group's list. Suggestions may include the caretaker, the headteacher, secretary, teacher, nurse, cook, dinner lady, road crossing attendant, playground supervisor or any other person who has a very direct and long-standing link with the school. Make a long list of class suggestions and then point out to the children how difficult it is to select one candidate from such a wide variety of people.

Tell them that when adults are making a selection of this sort, they generally produce a long list and from this choose a shorter list of people, each of whom can then be considered more carefully. This process is aptly called 'drawing up a short list'. Suggest that this might be a good way to go about choosing a candidate for 'This is your life'. If possible, let the class vote for candidates, or suggest a ready-made short list. Point out that one person must now be selected from this short list. Explain that this decision must be made in as fair a way as possible. One method would be to draw up a list of essential and desirable qualities against which every candidate could be compared in order to make the final selection. This sort of list is called a list of criteria.

Distribute photocopiable page 132 and discuss why the listed criteria would be useful in choosing a celebrity. Children should add criteria to customise this list for their individual school. In groups of four, children should discuss each short-listed candidate against the list of criteria and decide who is the best choice. The discussion should then be widened to the class as a whole, with groups expressing their observations. It may only be possible to shorten the list of candidates to two or three names. The final decision may have to go to a vote.

At the end of this activity, impress on the children that the celebration must be kept completely secret. If even one person mentions this event outside the classroom, then it will have to be abandoned.

Teaching content
Writing and using a telephone checklist.

What you need
Photocopiable page 133, access to a telephone, writing materials.

What to do
Explain to the children that most of the guests at their 'This is your life' event will be from the school but it will be fun to have one person who can shed a little light on the celebrity's life out of school.

Tell them that you have researched the life of the celebrity and decided who the contact person should be. It is now the children's responsibility to contact this person, explain about the 'This is your life' celebration and invite him or her to contribute. Every child will prepare to have a telephone conversation with this person but only two names will be pulled out of a hat and these people will do the actual talking.

Ask the children what type of information they will need to give the chosen liaison person at the beginning of, and during, this phone call. Organise children into pairs and ask them to make very brief, rough lists of the things that will need to be said on the telephone, including an introduction when the contact person answers the phone.

Distribute photocopiable page 133 and ask children to compare their lists with the checklist provided. Depending on the children, the personality of the contact person and local circumstances, there will probably be points that need to be inserted into or deleted from the photocopiable list. When the list is completed to everyone's satisfaction, compare ideas for the introduction when the phone is first answered and agree a class convention for the introduction when a phone call is made from school, perhaps:

'Hello. This is X speaking from X school. Could I speak to X please?'

Explain to the children that many adults, when they are making important telephone calls, write a list of things they must remember to say, similar to the lists produced by the children. It is particularly important to write a list if time is limited or if you are feeling nervous or if there is a great deal of information to be communicated. This is called a telephone checklist. It is a good idea to place every piece of information on a new line so that it can be ticked as the phone call progresses. It is also a good idea, when making an important call, to write down the opening and finishing phrases that you intend to use.

The liaison person will have to be informed that a list of questions will be sent by post, detailing the information on the celebrity's out-of-school life that the 'This is your life' team requires. A date and time for a follow-up phone call to answer these questions should also be agreed. The phone call will end with a promise to send a letter of confirmation and the question list of information required.

After writing the closing part of the phone call, remembering to include sincere thanks for co-operation, a promise to get in touch soon and, of course, a warning about secrecy, children should role play the phone call in pairs. The teacher should circulate to check that endings are appropriate and, if necessary, organise a conventional ending that will be used by all.

Finally, paired names from the role play should be drawn out of a hat to make the actual call. One of the pair will speak, while the other gives support. Items on the checklist should be ticked off as they are dealt with during the call, ensuring that all necessary information has been communicated. The pair will report back on how useful they found the checklist, and the practice role play, when making the call.

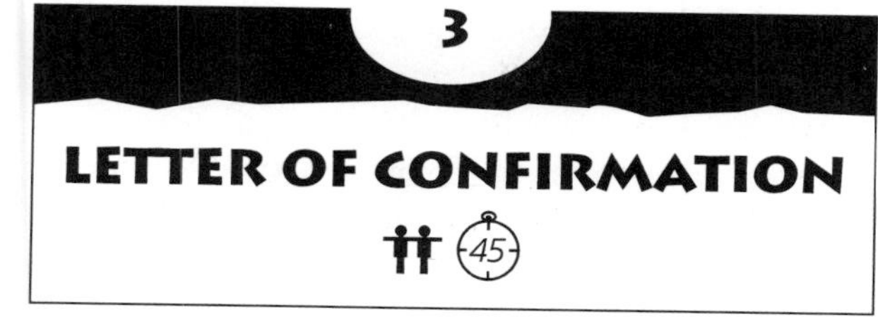

3 LETTER OF CONFIRMATION

Teaching content
Writing a letter of confirmation.

What you need
Photocopiable page 133 (from Activity 2), photocopiable page 134.

What to do
Distribute photocopiable page 133 (one for each pair), showing samples of letters confirming phone calls. Point out the conventional beginning that must be followed. Only the facts need to be confirmed. In pairs, ask the children to write a letter of confirmation to their outside contact, using the photocopiable sheet as a model and the telephone checklists for planning and information.

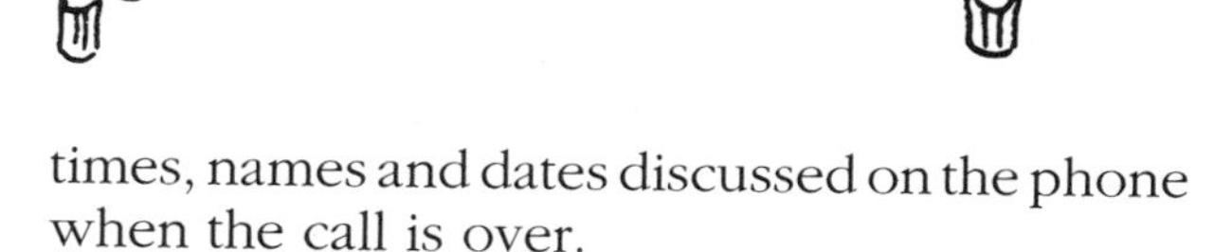

Rough drafts should be displayed and the pair who made the phone call should select the best letter from the class. This should be rewritten, signed by the writers and the pair who made the phone call, and posted to the liaison person, along with the list of questions.

4 TELEPHONE NOTES

Teaching content
Making brief notes while someone is speaking. Preparing key headings in order to take notes efficiently.

What you need
Access to the telephone, photocopiable page 133 from Activity 2, writing materials.

What to do
Explain that the children will now prepare a follow-up telephone conversation to the outside contact. A second pair pulled out of a hat will make the actual call. Ask the children to look at photocopiable page 133 and think about the information they asked their contact to supply. Enquire how they will remember the details of times, names and dates discussed on the phone when the call is over.

Point out that it is important that they jot down this information during the conversation. They can abbreviate words if they wish, but the notes will have to be taken quickly and then translated into proper writing as soon as possible after the conversation, before they forget what they mean! Remind them to be ready with a clean piece of paper and a pen that works.

Explain to the children that adults often prepare a list of key headings to organise their notes when they require a great deal of information over the phone. Suggest that the list of points sent to the outside contact will provide these key headings. They could cut up or copy these so they have more room under each key heading.

In pairs, ask the children to jot down their introductory statement and their concluding remarks, which should include a promise of a third phone call to confirm details of the actual 'This is your life' event. They should then rehearse the conversation. The person playing the part of the guest should invent information and, at the end, test the partner's notes to see if the information recorded is correct.

Children should be given time to practise this activity, as taking notes from a telephone conversation is an essential life skill. Stress that there is no need to record *every* word. At the end of this activity the names of one pair should be drawn from a hat to make the phone call. They should then report back to the class. Ask these children to evaluate and tell the rest of the class how useful they found the key headings and practice at note-taking.

The success of the activity will, of course, be evident from the amount of information gathered about the celebrity. Telephone notes will have to be kept safely and photocopied for the next task.

Further development

Games can be organised in which one person gives information on an imaginary phone and a second person makes notes. The children will enjoy comparing the facts gleaned during this exercise. Many schools now have phone systems linking different areas of the building and these could be used for this activity.

5 BEGINNING THE BOOK

Teaching content

Organising rough notes from a random order into a personal recount.

What you need

Copies of telephone notes from Activity 3, writing materials.

What to do

See 'Project organisation' (page 122) for suggestions for making the 'This is your life' book, which will contain stories and comments by the guests about the celebrity. The text is presented as though the writer addresses the celebrity directly, with each piece written in the following style:

'I remember when you first came to work in our school in 19xx. You had long hair in those days...'

Point out that this very direct style will speak in a personal way to the celebrity.

Explain to the children that every child in the class should now write up an account of the telephone conversation from Activity 3. This will allow them to practise the skill of transcribing and establish the style in which all interviews will have to be written for publication in the book.

Begin the session by explaining that transferring information from one type of writing into another is called transcribing. Discuss with the children how this task might be done. Suggest that the first thing they need to do with the telephone notes is to decide the best order in which to write the information given. This can be done by numbering the notes in the most logical sequence. It will depend on the ability of the particular class whether this part of the exercise is carried out as a whole class activity or done individually and then drawn together.

The numbered sequence will now serve as the base of a plan for writing. Model the style of presentation required for the book by writing the starting sentences on the chalkboard with the help of the children. It may be something like this:

'I first met you in 19xx when we were both out walking our dogs. I remember that my dog chased yours and you shouted...'

Children should now finish this writing task and the best version should be written out again for the book. Photographs will make a welcome illustration and addition to the writing if these can be provided by the guest.

6

INTERVIEW PROMPTS

Teaching content
Writing questions that will elicit particular information.

What you need
Access to a cassette recorder; writing materials.

What to do
Organise the class into pairs and explain that each pair is now going to prepare a taped interview with one person in the school who knows the celebrity well. Brainstorm a list of people who might be interviewed – remind children they may include anyone, from the youngest child to the most senior staff member – and then distribute these names around the pairs.

Explain that when professional reporters interview, they first make a list of the sort of information they are seeking from the interviewee. Brainstorm the sort of information that is being sought on the chalkboard. Work of a similar type covered earlier in the project with the outside contact should help with ideas and children will probably suggest:

- length of time the interviewee has known the celebrity;
- funny stories that the interviewee can tell;
- times when the celebrity has helped and been kind to the interviewee;
- the attributes of the celebrity most valued and admired by the interviewee.

Point out to the children that the information that can be given will depend both upon the age of the interviewees and the relationship they have with the celebrity. Children, in their pairs, should choose the person they'd like to interview and list the information they require from him or her. Give them about ten minutes for this and then invite some of the pairs to report back. Use this discussion session to reinforce the fact that different information will be sought from people of different ages and roles in the school. In the light of class discussion, these lists should be adjusted.

The next step is for questions to be written, in a logical sequence, that will generate the information required. Model this process on the chalkboard, using the points of information. The questions might be:

- How long have you known the celebrity?
- Can you tell us anything funny that you can remember happening when you were with the celebrity?

After ten minutes ask one person from each group to read their two best questions. Stress the fact that the questionnaire the children have produced is not to be gone through systematically with the interviewee. During the course of the interview discussion, it is likely that people will answer some questions before they are asked! This list is called an 'interview prompt', which means that it should be glanced at throughout the session in order to check that nothing has been left out, but it should not be followed slavishly. One of the things that professional reporters are skilled at doing is abandoning the interview prompt if interesting and unexpected information comes to light. If this happens then children will have to be ready to ask new questions that have not been written down!

At the beginning of their interview prompt, children should write how they intend to introduce the interview. A clear statement of who is being interviewed, who is interviewing, the date, time and place will be essential information. At the end of the prompt, it will be a good idea for children to write the words which they will use to thank the interviewee and complete the conversation. The pairs will next have to decide who will do the introduction and conclusion and who will conduct the actual interview.

Interviews should be practised in pairs, then scheduled, and carried out in a quiet place. When interviews are finished, children should check prompts to ensure that all information has been covered.

7

WRITING THE BOOK

45

Teaching content
Transcribing from a taped interview. Choosing a key sentence or phrase.

What you need
Access to several tape recorders, writing materials.

What to do
The next task for the children is to transcribe the interviews from the tapes for the 'This is your life' book. Tell the children that copying taped speech into writing will not be appropriate, but remind them that they have already practised the correct style of writing in Activity 4. Take a few minutes to remind the children of the writing style needed for the book.

Children will have to listen carefully to the interview in short sections and then summarise each piece of information, writing as though the person is talking to the celebrity. Take an example of the beginning of one tape in order to model this on the chalkboard, for example:

Tape recording:
'When did you first meet the celebrity?'
'When I first started school, two years ago, I wasn't very happy. I noticed that Mrs Brown walked around the playground and I used to walk with her. She used to talk to me.'
Writing for the book:
'When I first started school, two years ago, I wasn't very happy. I noticed that you walked around the playground and I walked with you. You used to talk to me.'

The interview prompt sheets written in Activity 6 will be useful for this activity, as well as the interview. Both partners must do each piece of writing (cassette and book) separately and then compare and rewrite in order to make each part perfect before moving on. Finally, partners should check that writing flows and is consistent in style throughout. The piece of writing should be split equally between partners, giving both the responsibility for producing a beautifully copied final version of half the interview. This writing must be displayed for use in the next activity and will later be stuck in the book, possibly with appropriate photographs.

Lastly, pairs must choose from their writing the most interesting phrase or sentence spoken by the interviewee. This will be the statement the person will speak if chosen to appear at 'This is your life'. Tell the children that an interesting, dramatic or controversial short statement is called a 'soundbite'.

Teaching content
Identifying and sequencing a list of guests in order of appearance.

What you need
Transcribed writing from the taped interviews, chalkboard, writing materials, poster paper.

What to do
Explain to the children that their next task is to choose which individuals should actually make an appearance as surprise guests at the 'This is your life' event. It will be important to have representatives of a variety of ages and roles in

the school. There should be no more than seven guests in all, including the liaison guest from outside the school.

Display copies of the writing produced for the 'This is your life' book as transcripts of taped interviews. Ask the children, in groups of four, to select seven pieces that they feel are particularly interesting. The people who gave the interviews that generated the most interesting pieces of writing will be the ones chosen as guests. Remind children that they must include a range of ages. They will be required also to justify their choices and must therefore make brief notes explaining their decisions. A spokesperson from each group should propose a guest list. The names of guests selected by most groups should be written on the chalkboard. There will probably be debate about other choices but this is where the need for a balanced list will help with selection. The children should also consider the clarity of people's speaking voices as this may also help in the final selection.

Having agreed on a list, children should next organise a 'Guest appearance list'. Point out that the order will be crucial to the success of the event. A balance of age and role must be achieved, and the importance of placing a very confident person in first and last place should be stressed.

Each group should then decide on an order and reasons for that order. Group lists should be written on large sheets of poster paper by a scribe, while a second group member writes reasons for the order of the list. A spokesperson should then read out and justify the proposed list for each group. A class consensus should be reached according to general feeling. Debate will be an important part of the decision-making process but a little guidance or a final vote may be needed from the teacher.

As soundbites have already been decided, invited guests should now be invited to the classroom, where they will be told of the part they have to play in the 'This is your life' celebration. It should be explained that they will be hidden in a secret room until it is time for them to appear. They will speak their soundbite from behind a screen, before making their entrance. After greeting the celebrity they will read out the transcript of their interview from the book. (If any of the guests are particularly young, their pieces of writing may be read by the presenter.) Guests will then take a seat beside the celebrity.

The actual ceremony may sound something like this:

PRESENTER: It was two years ago that you first met our next guest. Do you recognise this person?

VOICE OUTSIDE THE CURTAINED DOOR:
When I first started school, I hated playtimes and you used to talk to me while I walked around the playground with you.

CELEBRITY: Tom Black! Of course, I remember him clearly!

PRESENTER: Yes! The boy you helped at playtime when he first came to school. Come in, Tom Black!

TOM BLACK ENTERS AND SAYS HELLO TO THE CELEBRITY. THE PRESENTER PASSES HIM THE BOOK AND TOM READS OUT THE TRANSCRIBED INTERVIEW, THEN SITS DOWN WHILE THE PRESENTER INTRODUCES THE NEXT GUEST.

This ceremony will have to be practised several times before the actual event.

9 PRESS RELEASE

Teaching content
Writing a report for a press release.

What you need
Completed telephone checklist from Activity 2, writing materials, stamp and envelope for each group.

What to do
This activity can only be carried out once definite decisions about the time and date of the event have been made. Check that guests find these convenient, particularly the outside contact, who should again be phoned to check that the date and time are suitable. If time allows children could be encouraged to confirm arrangements in writing, using the sample letters on page 134 as models.

Explain to the children that if people want a local newspaper to write about an event they often issue a press release. On this they present the basic facts about the event to give the editor of the newspaper an opportunity to decide whether it is newsworthy or not.

Tell the children that they are going to issue a press release about 'This is your life'. In groups they should decide the main points that need to be made. Suggest that the telephone checklist will be useful in sequencing some (but not all) of the main ideas. They will certainly need to include the date and time of the ceremony and will need to check that the information given in the press release is accurate as it may be used by reporters from the local newspaper to write a report. Check that all groups have mentioned the main points, then encourage them to write up the release in neat writing to be posted to local newspapers and radio stations. The school will almost certainly get a mention and possibly a photograph, particularly if the teacher follows up the press release with a phone call.

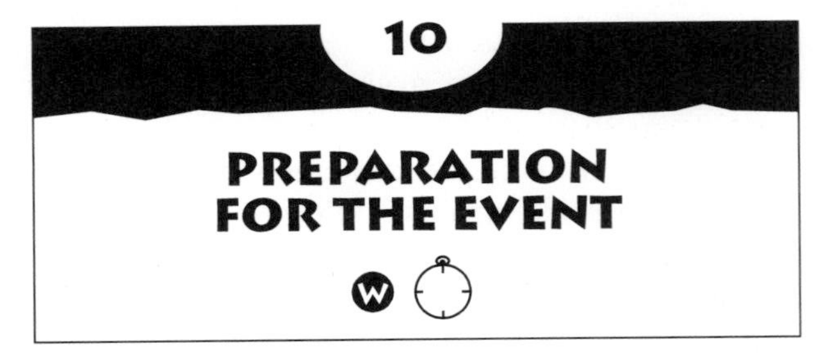

10 PREPARATION FOR THE EVENT

Teaching content
Checklists are useful in ensuring events run smoothly.

What you need
Writing materials.

What to do

A great deal of organisation is needed to prepare for 'This is your life'. This will involve the teacher and the children. Explain that people who organise important events always write lists detailing every single thing that needs to be done. In groups of four, ask children to produce a list of items which can then be ticked as they are carried out. Lists will probably include suggestions that pupils should:

- check that all guests are able to come;
- ensure that the celebrity is coming;
- organise refreshments for after the event;
- choose someone to spring the surprise and arrive with *the book*;
- make the book (see Introduction, page 122);
- practise their speeches;
- rehearse the entire ceremony from start to finish, with children playing the roles of celebrity and guests if necessary;
- ring the press to check whether they are coming in response to the press release;
- organise a camera or video recorder and appoint a photographer;
- find a place to hide the guests before and during the ceremony;
- appoint a person to prepare the guests to make their entrances;
- screen off a doorway so that guests may be heard speaking their soundbites;
- practise passing the book from one presenter to another.

Pupils who have heard the recorded interviews should help guests decide what they will say before they make their dramatic entrance. Collate checklists into one big class list and put this on the wall. Remember to tick each point as it is completed.

Teaching content

Writing a press notice.

What you need

Photocopiable page 134, writing materials.

What to do

Children know it is polite to say thank you to people who have helped with school projects and are accustomed to writing thank you letters. For this activity a press notice will be an interesting way to thank the many people involved in making 'This is your life' a success.

Distribute the second half of photocopiable page 134, which shows a variety of notices in this genre. Read through these with the children to check they understand that there is a clear conventional style associated with thank-you notices. Ask if they know why the wording is so brief and to the point. One child should ring the local press to ask details of the cost of publishing a notice. This will explain the need for brevity, if the children haven't already guessed!

Each child should now write a thank you notice in the style shown on the photocopiable sheet. Display the finished notices and let the class select some to send to the local newspaper and radio station. A covering letter from the teacher very often guarantees a free notice.

NAME

LIST OF CRITERIA FOR SELECTING A SCHOOL CELEBRITY

This person must:

- be known by the majority of pupils in the school;
- be well respected;
- have a sense of humour;
- have been involved with the school for long enough to have a series of interesting recollections;
- like children;
- have a friend or relation outside school who will supply a sense of the celebrity's 'outside' life;
- appreciate the amount of work involved in making the event a success;
- appreciate the fact that many people have managed to keep a *secret*!
-
-
-

NAME

TELEPHONE CHECKLIST

- Write your words of introduction first.
- Explain about the 'This is your life' idea.
- Explain that ________________ has been chosen to be the celebrity.
- Explain why this person has been chosen.
- Explain that one person from outside school is needed to come as a guest to the event and that he/she has been chosen. Explain the reason why!
- Explain that he or she will not be expected to say a great deal.
- Ask the person if they are willing to be a part of this celebration.
- Explain that he or she will be sent a letter to confirm the phone call and to list the questions which the 'This is your life' team needs to know answers to in order to organise the book and event.
- Explain that another phone call will be necessary to write down the information needed. Ask when it would be convenient to make this call.
- Write here how you intend to say goodbye and thank you.

LIST OF INFORMATION REQUIRED ABOUT CELEBRITY FROM GUEST

(to be posted with letter of confirmation)

How long have you known each other?

Do you remember how you first met?

Give one reason why you are glad that the celebrity has been chosen for this event.

What are the main qualities that make this person special, in your opinion?

Do you remember a time when the celebrity showed you special friendship?

Mention a time when you two had a good laugh together.

(Please miss out any points that you do not wish to answer or discuss.)

NAME

LETTERS OF CONFIRMATION

Dear Mrs Brown,

Further to your phone call on Tuesday 8th May, I would like to confirm that the following bookings have been made:

Dear Ken,

I would like to confirm the arrangements we made on Monday 4th December over the telephone. The children will be happy to sing carols at Sunnyside House on December 16th. We have arranged to leave the school at 1.00pm and will arrive at...

Dear Mr Smith,

Thank you for your telephone booking.
I would like to confirm these arrangements:

Party of 20 people
Finger buffet required
Tuesday 4th April.

THANK YOU PRESS NOTICES

Bridgette Atkinson would like to thank all those who made her surprise 80th birthday party such a success.

St Patrick's PTA would like to thank all those who made the Christmas Fair such a success. A grand total of £400 was raised for school funds.

FORBES

Congratulations Mum and Dad on your Diamond Wedding Anniversary. Thanks for being wonderful parents. From Gordon, Henry and Grace.

CARPENTER – Claire would like to thank all family, friends and neighbours for kind expressions of sympathy shown since the recent sad loss of her mum Evelyn, also thanks to the Rev. May for spiritual comfort and most uplifting service, and Jane at Co-operative Funeral Service for efficient arrangements.

THANK YOU

Jeremy and Elizabeth Allen would like to thank Peter and all the staff of The Mill Tavern for making their wedding day on 6th July a wonderful day to remember.

Scholastic WORKSHOP

Chapter Eleven

DIALECT DICTIONARY

INTRODUCTION

Project description

In this project, the children work in pairs to research and compile a local dialect dictionary. Photocopiable sheets help to prompt discussion of differences in language use that arise from geographical and social differences. Activities then help children to consider the purpose, function and layout of dictionaries, the variety of information they contain and the range of dictionaries available, as well as the problematic nature of word definition.

Children are then encouraged to research local dialect words which describe relationships, food and occupations and these provide a base for further work on housing, furniture, games, plants and wildlife terms. As part of the research process, the children write letters to local organisations and individuals, thus learning that such letters need to explain clearly what information is needed, by whom, and how it will be used. This information must be requested in a persuasive manner so that the recipient believes it is important to respond.

Finally, the children are taught how to structure and write a press release to launch the publication of their dictionaries. These are distributed to the various local organisations that helped in researching the dictionaries, along with a photocopy of the dictionary and a covering letter.

Why this context?

Awareness and knowledge of language are important parts of the school curriculum. While working on this project children will develop a better understanding of the nature of language and language change as well as some of the problematic aspects of word definition that face all lexicographers. This work will help them to become more sensitive to their own use of language and to the language they hear around them. They learn to appreciate the importance of using words in a precise and careful way.

The children also consider how and why different people use dictionaries, the range of functions and purposes that dictionaries serve, and how these issues are reflected in the content and layout of specific versions. The cumulative effect of the project is that the children develop an appreciation of the skill involved in planning, researching and writing what may initially have appeared a 'simple' reference book.

When writing press releases for their dictionaries, the children are required to reflect on and evaluate their work in a way that combines descriptive, explanatory and persuasive writing.

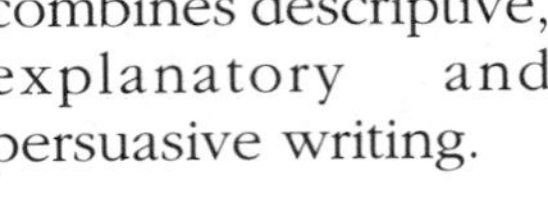

Project organisation

The children work in pairs throughout the project, keeping the same partner from one activity to the next. They combine their research efforts and make joint decisions about the content and approach of the dictionary. The paired nature of the work ensures that each child has one other person in the classroom who will offer informed support and with whom important decisions can be discussed. The common vision and shared responsibility for the work help to maintain involvement and momentum.

Publication, celebration and review

The dictionary is published on A4 paper and is presented to and discussed with another pair. The written part of the celebration and review takes the form of a press release, produced by the authors, which is sent, along with a photocopy of the dictionary, to any local organisations and individuals who helped in the research process.

Books the children may find useful

First One Hundred Words (Usborne)
Poetry or song books in the local dialect.

1

WE ALL KNOW DIALECT

Teaching content

Written and spoken language can both vary. Change in language may happen as a result of time or geographical location.

What you need

Photocopiable page 144, writing materials, a sheet of A3 paper.

What to do

Introduce the lesson by explaining that there are many varieties of both written and spoken English. Today the class will explore some of these and think about how they differ from the language they use.

Organise the children into pairs and give each pair a copy of photocopiable page 144. Ask the children to read it carefully. Explain that they may not recognise all the words or phrases on the sheet, but will probably be able to guess their meaning by using clues from the surrounding text and by thinking of words they know that sound similar. Ask the children to read the photocopiable sheet quietly to each other and to circle or underline all the unfamiliar words or phrases, writing their guess at the meaning in the margin of the sheet.

Stop the class once the children have worked through the first extract. Discuss the unfamiliar words and phrases they noticed and the possible meanings they have suggested. Explain that each of the extracts represents a different dialect and that dialects are varieties of the same language which use slightly different words and grammar. Do the children think the first extract is from the present or the past, and can they suggest who might speak (or have spoken) in this way?

You may want to tell the children about the history of the other dialects, or ask them to guess the area or period of each one and discuss their ideas at the end.

The examples of dialect are:

- Cockney (*Oliver Twist*)
- Middle English (*Canterbury Tales*)
- Missouri Negro (*Huckleberry Finn*)
- Yorkshire (*The Secret Garden*)

Tell the children to continue to read the photocopiable extracts, identifying unfamiliar words or phrases and their possible meanings. Once everyone has finished, hold a class discussion about each extract. Encourage the children to recognise how the dialects differ from each other, from standard English and from any local dialects with which they are familiar. Promote the view that the differences between dialects are interesting.

Ask the children if they can think of any benefits of speaking in dialect. They may suggest that:

- it gives the speaker a unique identity;
- it is part of their culture;
- language is enriched by dialect words;
- some of the words are particularly beautiful or satisfying to say aloud;
- the world would be boring if we all spoke the same way.

End the lesson by explaining that the children will be doing some work on local dialect variations. Explain that the number of dialect words used now is smaller than a generation ago. Television and films promote linguistic uniformity and ease of travel means that people moving from one area to another tend not to use the dialect of their home area. However, there are still local dialect words and phrases which are used. Ask them to listen carefully to the language – words, sayings and phrases – that they hear spoken around them.

Provide an A3-sized poster at a convenient place on the wall for children to record any examples of local dialect that they hear. Explain that children should add to this throughout the project. Try to refer to it at various points, encouraging the children by commenting on any particularly interesting words or sayings as they appear on the poster.

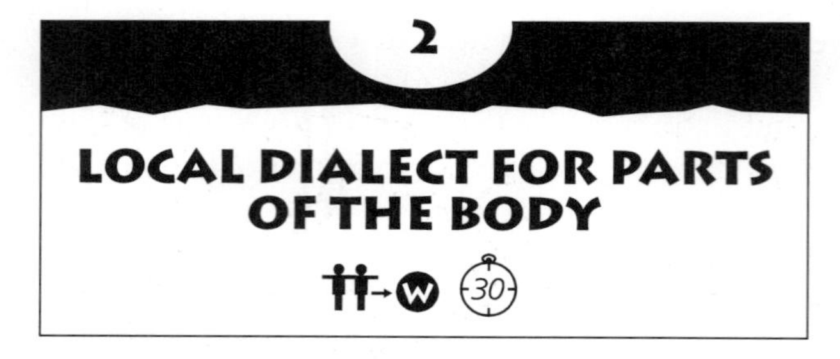

2 LOCAL DIALECT FOR PARTS OF THE BODY

Teaching content
Different dialects use different words.

What you need
A4 paper, chalkboard, writing materials.

What to do
Organise the children into pairs. Remind them of the dialect variations discussed in the previous activity and, if appropriate, discuss the words or phrases recorded on the A3 sheet. Then list on the board some different parts of the body (see illustration below).

Give each child a sheet of paper, and ask them, working in pairs, to list as many different names as they can think of for each of the body parts listed on the board. Encourage them to list any words at all – slang and 'informal' words as well as the more mainstream ones – perhaps 'noddle', 'noodle' or 'brainbox' for brain.

Allow about five minutes, then ask the children to share their ideas with the class. Advise them to use this class discussion as a source of further ideas, adding new words to their sheets. Take opportunities to discuss the words with the class.

- Do some sound more descriptive than others?
- Do they sound natural to all the children?
- When would they choose to use some words rather than others?

End the session by asking the children to take the sheets home and see if they can add more words by asking parents, grandparents, friends and neighbours. Suggest that older people may be able to provide examples of words that were used when they were younger but have now been dropped from common use. All these words should be recorded.

Tell the children to take care of their lists because they will be used in future lessons.

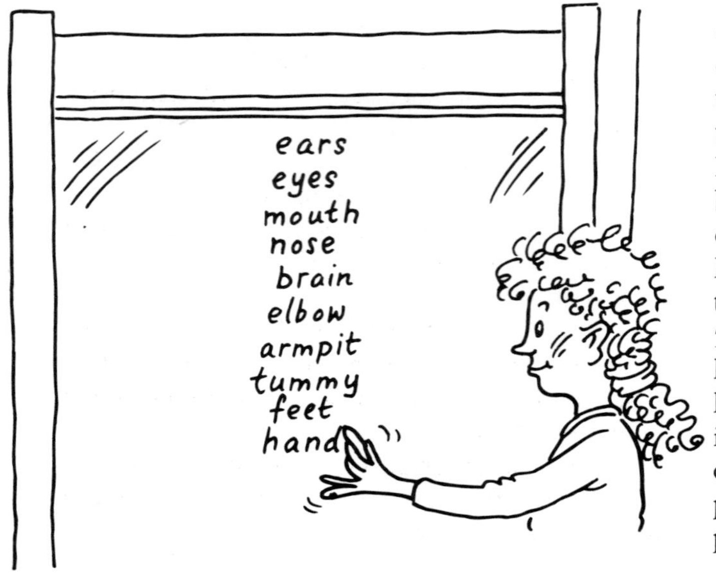

3 INTRODUCING THE DIALECT DICTIONARY

Teaching content
Structure, content and purpose of a dialect dictionary.

What you need
Photocopiable page 145, writing materials, completed lists of words from Activity 2, notebooks (one per pair) with an envelope stuck to the last page of each one, dictionaries (one per pair if available).

What to do
Arrange the children in pairs. Explain that these are the pairs in which they will be working for the rest of the project.

Give out photocopiable page 145 and the class dictionaries. Explain that the photocopiable sheet shows extracts from two different dictionaries: one is from an illustrated children's dictionary while the other is from a dictionary of the Scots dialect.

Point out that many of the words listed in the dialect dictionary will not be given in a dictionary of standard English, then prove this by asking the children to look up some of the words from the Scots dictionary in their own dictionaries. Explain that a dialect dictionary is important because all languages change over the years. A dialect dictionary gives a snapshot of how language is used in one area at one point in time. Tell the children that by the time they are 50 years old, the local dialect will probably have changed – some familiar words will no longer be used and new words will have been introduced. The children may be able to provide examples of this from their discussions with parents and grandparents on names for different parts of the body.

Tell the children that they are going to work in pairs to make dialect dictionaries. Each pair may decide whether to illustrate their dictionary or not, but all must follow the basic dictionary format. Pick a few entries, either from the photocopiable sheet or from class dictionaries and read them out to the class. Then list important features of the dictionary entries on the board. This might include the following:

- The words are listed in bold, in alphabetical order.
- Each word is followed by a definition of its meaning in standard English.
- An example of the use of the word is given.
- The pronunciation is given.
- The locality or origin of the word is given, if known.
- The word class (n., v., adj. or ad.) is given.

Explain that the dictionaries the children are going to make may not include all these features. In particular, because the words will be entered as they are discovered, the entries under each letter of the alphabet will not be in strict alphabetical order. They may also choose to distinguish the word entries by using a different colour rather than a thicker pen. Tell each pair to discuss which other features will and will not be included in their own dictionary and to record this decision, along with a sample entry, on a piece of paper which should be stored in the envelope stuck to the last page of their book.

Tell the children to leave the first two pages of the notebook blank, then to write capital letters at the top of each page thereafter. Show them how each letter can be customised to their own design – they could even make illuminated letters. Demonstrate how to divide the pages into two columns so that each word can be written with its meaning alongside.

If any children plan to make an illustrated dictionary, you will probably need to specify a reasonable limit on the size and number of illustrations. It is often a good idea if children cut a number of appropriately sized squares, circles or ovals at the start of the project to use for illustration space. Point out that each pair may also need to discuss the location of these on the page. Tell the children to look carefully at the illustrated dictionary excerpt on photocopiable page 145 to note the type of words illustrated and how these illustrations aid understanding. Explain that drawings should be in fine black pen and should be detailed and accurate with appropriate labels.

Let the children make a start on their dictionaries. Once the alphabet is in place, and the 'parts of the body' lists from Activity 2 have been checked to ensure that appropriate words have been included and obvious ones not missed out, the children can use these for their initial entries.

Teaching content

Writing simple sentences to help with definitions of words.

What you need

Notebooks, writing materials, chalkboard, a class dictionary for each group.

What to do

This activity may be introduced to the class now, or carried out at some point between activities 6 and 9.

Before starting, find a few suitable definitions in a dictionary which uses a context to explain the meaning of a word.

Ask the children if they can think of any way to explain the meaning of a word apart from defining it or drawing a picture of it. Suggest the word 'knack' and ask someone to define it. They will almost certainly put it into a context such as 'He's got an uncanny knack of knowing how to get under my skin'. Explain that dictionaries often give words in context to help to explain their meanings.

Organise the original pairs of children into groups of four and ask them to look up three words which you know are defined in context in the dictionaries provided. When they have read these, explain that different context sentences have to be used for different parts of speech. Write the following sentences on the chalkboard and explain to the children that the word 'visit' is a verb in one context, and a noun in the other:

This year our school visit was to Warwick.

When I visit my neighbour, she usually gives me a biscuit.

Give each group a sheet of paper and explain that they are to suggest contexts for a number of words you will now write on the board.

history
finished
number
visit
stubborn
score
add
opposite

Ask the groups to suggest a context for the first word – a spokesperson from each group should read these out while you write them on the chalkboard. Discuss the suggestions with the class and, when you are sure that everyone understands fully what using a word in context means, give the groups time to list and find a context for each word. Any groups who finish quickly could go through their notebooks looking for words which need to be put in context to help with their definition. This may need extra time, so plan accordingly.

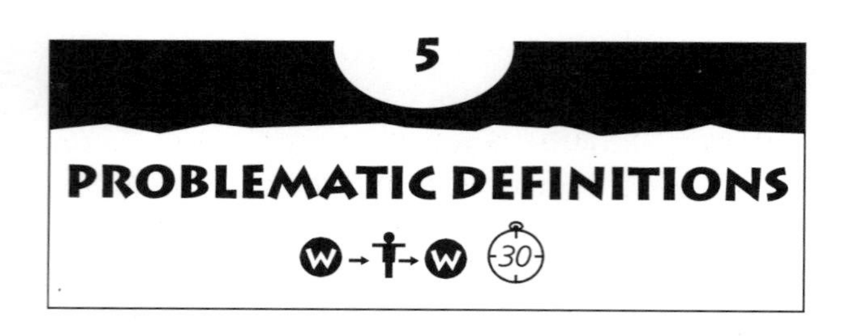

Teaching content

Words draw their meanings from their use. People often work to different definitions of a word. Writing definitions requires thought and discussion.

What you need

Paint colour charts showing shades of colours (such as red, blending to orange, blending to yellow), photocopiable page 146, writing materials, scrap paper.

What to do

Begin by giving a paint colour chart to each table or group of children. Explain that the chart shows several colours. Choose the two or three basic colours that the chart represents and write these on the board (for example, the sheet may have shades of red-orange-yellow or blue-green).

Ask the children to look carefully at the chart and decide at which point they would call the colour by a different name. Where do they judge that the orange ends and red begins, for example? Ask them to record their answers quickly, on pieces of scrap paper. They should avoid any discussion and should not indicate their decision to other children.

When everyone has completed this task, ask them to report their decisions to the class.

- Did everyone divide the chart at exactly the same point?
- Did some people identify a colour as red, while others still had it on the orange side of their line? Explore how we all may picture slightly different things when we talk of particular colours. Ask if the children think that this may also happen for words.

Give out the photocopiable sheet and read the question at the top of the first section 'Is it a plant?' Explain that the children must consider each of the items listed in turn. If they think it definitely *is* a plant, they should tick the 'yes' column; if it is definitely *not*, they should tick the 'no' column; if they are not sure, they should tick the column marked 'not sure'. Tell the children to work individually and in silence. They should not show their decisions to anyone at this stage.

When the children have made decisions about all the items on the list, ask them to share their answers with the person sitting next to them. If both partners agree on the classification of an item, ask them to discuss why this is so; if they disagree, or have ticked the 'don't know' column, ask them to put forward their different reasons and try to come to a common decision.

Then, call the class together and discuss each item on the list in turn.

- Did everyone classify things in the same way?
- What different reasons did they give?
- Are the children surprised by the decisions made by others in the class? Why?
- Now ask them to define the word 'plant'.

Explain that the process of discussion and negotiation has enabled the children to form a more precise and detailed definition. Determining accurate definitions of words can be difficult and is a skill that all lexicographers (people who investigate words and make dictionaries) have to learn. The definitions have to be clear, concise and exact. Now work through sections 2 and 3 (on toys and work) in the same way. Ask the children to make individual decisions, discuss these in pairs and then with the class before writing a definition for each. Try to formulate class definitions of toy, plant and work that satisfy everyone.

If you are short of class time, set one or both of the remaining sections of the photocopiable sheet as a homework task, with children enlisting the help of parents and siblings to help them clarify the range of meanings and definitions of the words.

Explain that writing definitions for words in their dialect dictionaries may not be easy but that with thought and discussion they should be able to arrive at precise, and concise, definitions. Remind the children that dictionaries often give examples of words and phrases in context to help explain the meaning of a word. Illustrate this with an example from the dictionaries that children use in class, or from Activity 4. Ask the class for quick examples of the words they have just defined, used in context.

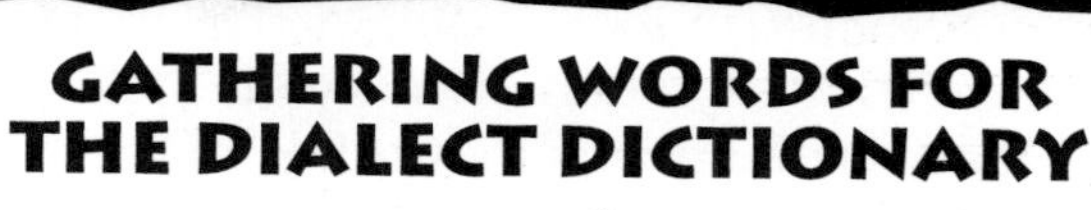

6

GATHERING WORDS FOR THE DIALECT DICTIONARY

Teaching content

A range of dialect words is used in the local community.

What you need

Photocopiable page 147, dialect dictionaries.

What to do

Begin the session by sharing some of the good work done on the dictionary entries so far. Remind the children of the format and specific features they may or may not have chosen to include by commenting on the work of individual pairs.

Explain that now they need to think of gathering more dialect words for their dictionaries. Some children may already have begun to note words that they would like to include. Explain that, as they come across such words, they should jot them down with a quick definition. These can be stored in the envelope stuck to the last page until they are ready to enter them on the appropriate page.

Distribute photocopiable page 147 to each child. Ask them, working in pairs, to list on a separate sheet of paper as many different names as possible for each of the items shown. Remind them to write neatly, as these lists will be used later. As before, encourage the children to list slang and 'informal' words as well as the more accepted versions.

Allow about ten minutes before asking the children to share their ideas with the class. Tell them to use this class discussion as a source of further ideas, adding any new words to their lists. Finally, suggest that the children take the sheets home to ask parents, grandparents, friends and neighbours for new words to add. Remind them that it is often worthwhile asking people for words they can remember being used when they were younger or lived in a different place. These words should all be written down carefully, along with their definitions, which should be sought from the interviewee at the time.

This process (which could be carried out over a number of sessions) should generate a substantial range of words for each pair to include in their dialect dictionary.

The sheets can also be used as a blueprint for how to structure further inquiries. The children may wish to design their own sheets to list and investigate other words they think might show strong dialect variations. Some ideas might be:

- types of housing;
- rooms in the house (how many different words can they find for toilet?!);
- family relationships/members;
- games and toys;
- plants, minibeasts and wildlife.

7 LOOKING FURTHER AFIELD

Teaching content

The format and structure of a formal letter. Using persuasive reasoning to encourage a response.

What you need

Scrap paper, headed paper, writing materials, envelopes, stamps.

What to do

Explain to the children that they now have a great many words in their collections, but will be able to extend their list further, and also involve the school community, by asking local people and organisations for help.

Ask the children who they think they might approach. Suggestions might include:

- senior citizens' groups;
- the local library;
- the literary society;
- the local gardening or allotment society (good for old or local names of flowers and plants);
- local historians;
- the local newspaper;
- museums;
- even grandparents who live some distance away!

List all these suggestions on a large sheet of paper to display on the wall. Arrange the class into groups so that there is one group for each organisation listed. Explain that the children are going to write letters asking for help with their dialect dictionaries. Allocate, or ask each group to choose, one person or organisation to whom they will write. Revise the format of a letter. Explain that the first paragraph should explain who the writer is and why he or she is writing. Tell the children that some local societies will get many letters

requesting help, so to encourage a positive response, the opening paragraphs of their letters should explain why this *particular* society has been chosen and the unique contribution it can make. With the children, list key ideas that the letters should include, along with helpful advice and reminders about the tone, and the importance of explaining what is needed and why.

Tell each group to draft an appropriate letter, appointing one person per group to act as scribe and another to ensure that everyone participates.

Once finished, ask each group to read out their first draft and discuss it with the rest of the class. Give the groups time to alter their drafts before distributing headed school paper and asking each group to appoint one person who will write the letter out neatly.

Explain that the letters will be checked and then photocopied so that any replies that are received can be filed with the appropriate letter. Once you are satisfied with the letters, provide each group with a stamped envelope to address and post.

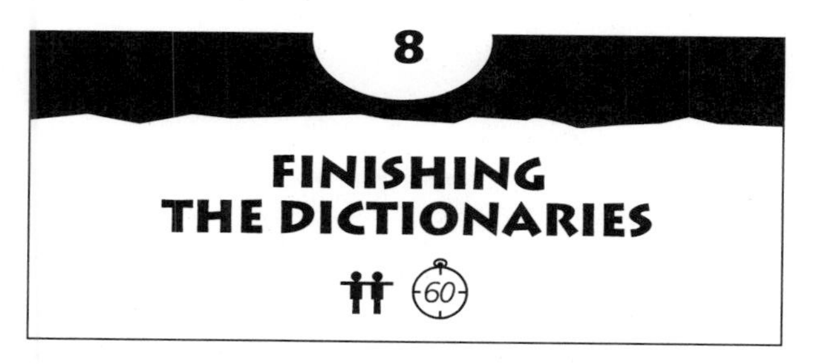

8 FINISHING THE DICTIONARIES

Teaching content

Publishers and authors are able to choose some of the details included on the cover and initial pages.

What you need

A variety of professionally published dictionaries, the children's own dialect dictionaries.

What to do

Show the children the selection of dictionaries. Ask them, in their pairs, to look at the first and the last few pages of the dictionaries and discuss what other pages they would like to include. Suggestions might include:

- a page explaining what the dictionary is, why it was written and what it means to the authors;
- a dedication;
- a thank-you section or page listing those who have helped.

The children may like to have an optional section to include the 'local sayings' they have collected and written on the A3 wall poster in the classroom. These could be written in a section of their own at the back of the dictionary.

Tell the children to look carefully at the front covers of the dictionaries to determine the information these contain. They should then design front covers for their own dictionaries.

9 THE PRESS RELEASE

Teaching content

A press release must describe the product clearly and succinctly. It uses the explanation of why the product is important and its unique qualities to persuade.

What you need

Photocopiable page 148, writing materials, headed writing paper.

What to do

Combine the pairs into groups of four and ask them to present their dictionaries to each other. Distribute a copy of the photocopiable sheet to each group. Explain that this is a real press release that was sent out to newspapers to promote the publication of a new dictionary. Read through it with the children.

With the class, analyse the press release to determine the purpose and rough content of each paragraph. Explain that it has been written to describe the product, explain why it has been made, and how it is different from other dictionaries. It aims to persuade people to use and write about it. Outline this structure on the board and highlight some key language features of the tone and structure.

Ask the children, in their groups, to draft and publish a press release for their own dictionary. This should explain why and how the dictionary was made, and highlight interesting words, sayings and debates that arose during the making of their own dictionary.

Once finished, the press releases can be sent, along with a covering letter and a photocopy of the final dictionary, to all the local people and organisations who helped by providing dialect words, as well as to local newspapers and radio stations.

NAME

MAKING A DIALECT DICTIONARY

"Never mind wot it is! I want a boy, and he musn't be a big un. Lord! if I'd only got that young boy of Ned, the chimbley-sweeper's! He kept him small on purpose, and let him out by the job. But the father gets lagged; and then the Juvenule Delinquent Society comes, and takes the boy away from a trade where he was arning money, teaches him to read and write, and in time makes a 'prentice of him.

For him was lever have at his beddes heed / Twenty bokes, clad in blak or reed, / Of Aristotle and his philosophye, / Than robes riche, or fithele, or gay sautrye. / But al be that he was a philosophre, / Yet haddle he but litel gold in cofre.

'Laws bless you, chile, I'uz right down sho' you's dead agin. Jack's been heah, he say he reck'n you's ben shot, kase you didn' come home no mo'; so I's jes' dis minute a-startin' de raf' down towards de mouf er de crick, so's to be all ready for to shove out en leave soon as Jack comes agin en tells me for certain you *is* dead. Lawsy, I's mighty glad to git you back agin, honey.'

'Tha'll see him often enow after a bit,' answered Dickon. 'When th' eggs hatches out th' little chap he'll be kep' so busy it'll make his head swim. Tha'll see him flyin' backward an' for'ard carryin' worms nigh as big as himsel' an' that much noise goin' on in th' nest when he gets there as fair flusters him so as he scarce knows which big mouth to drop th' first piece in. An' gapin' beaks an' squawks on every side. Mother says as when she sees th'work a robin has to keep them gapin' beaks filled, she feels like she was a lady with nothin' to do. She says she's seen th' little chaps when it seemed like th' sweat must be droppin' off 'em, though folk can't see it.'

NAME

INTRODUCING THE DIALECT DICTIONARY

prize – something you are given when you win, or do well.

pudding – a sweet dish you eat at the end of a meal.

puppet – a doll that is moved by strings or with your hand.

puppy – a young dog.

purse – a small bag to keep money.

puzzle – a question you have to think hard about – sometimes a game.

pyjamas – trousers and a top that you wear in bed.

swage [swadge] *v* **1** subside, settle down, shrink. 2 relax after a good meal.
swall [rhymes with 'pal'] *n, v* swell.
swalla [-a- as in 'cat'], **swallow** *n* 1 a swallow, the bird. 2 *a* martin.
swallae *see* **swallie.**
swallie, swallae [rhymes with 'pally'] *v* swallow.
n 1 a swallow. 2 a drink, especially an alcoholic one: *'D'ye fancy gaun fur a wee swallie?'*.
swallow *see* **swalla.**
swalt *past tense* swollen.
swang *see* **swing.**
swank *adj* agile, strong; (*especially of a young man*) smart, well set-up.
swankie *adj* = swank.
n a smart, active, strapping young man.
swap [rhymes with 'cap'] *v* 1 strike, hit. 2 fold or wind a rope, strip of cloth etc) over on itself, criss-cross.
sware *see* **sweer.**
swaree *n* a social gathering, especially one organized by a church, Sunday school etc.
swarf *v* faint.
swarrach [-ch as in 'loch'] *n* a crowd, swarm (especially of young children in a family) NE.
swat *see* **sweit.**
swatch [rhymes with 'match'] *n* **1** a typical piece, example, selection etc. 2 a glimpse.
tak (a) swatch o take a critical look at: *'Tak a swatch o his new computer'.*
tak the swatch o take the measure of, be a match for NE.
swats [rhymes with 'cats'] *npl (in past times)* newly-brewed weak beer.
swatten *see* **sweit.**
swatter [rhymes with 'batter'] *n* a large collection or crowd, especially of small creatures NE.

NAME

PROBLEMATIC DEFINITIONS

Is it a plant?

	Yes	No	Not sure
A daisy			
A tree			
Seaweed			
Mould			
Grass			
Moss			
A toadstool			

My definition of 'plant':

Is it a toy?

	Yes	No	Not sure
A computer			
A board game			
A skipping rope			
A trainer			
A doll			
A ball			

My definition of 'toy':

Is it work?

	Yes	No	Not sure
Washing up			
Digging the garden			
Doing sums			
Baby-sitting			
Watching a video for a topic			
Practising a musical instrument			
Doing a paper round			
Writing a story			
Going to football practice			

My definition of 'work':

NAME

GATHERING WORDS FOR DICTIONARIES

Relationships

mother
father
friend
wife
husband
child
older brother or sister
younger brother or sister
neighbour
work colleague
baby

Food

chips
potatoes
cake
bread
biscuits
sweets
pie
sausages

Occupations

teacher
baker
shopkeeper
church leader
solicitor

Weather

cloudy
sunny and hot
snow
slush
light rain
sleet

NAME

PUBLICATION, CELEBRATION AND REVIEW: THE PRESS RELEASE

COLLINS
DICTIONARIES

POLES APART?

As commercial links between Eastern and Western Europe grow ever stronger, the ability to communicate in each other's language becomes ever more important. Collins has the answer for the Polish market.

Collins Polish Dictionary - the first new Polish-English English-Polish dictionary to be published since before the end of the Second World War - is the essential reference tool for anyone learning or working in Polish. It gives unparalleled coverage of all the vocabulary of current issues and treats business, computing and financial terminology in-depth.

Clearly and attractively presented for maximum ease of use, the dictionary also gives detailed help with the most frequently-used words in both languages.

The dictionary has already been launched to wide acclaim in Poland, where the huge economic and cultural changes that have taken place since the first strikes in the Gdansk shipyards and the founding of Solidarnosc have had an enormous impact on the Polish language. Collins Polish Dictionary covers the old and the new.

With over 80,000 references and 120,000 translations, Collins Polish Dictionary also offers a supplement on Polish grammar, help with Polish irregular verbs and a full guide to Polish pronunciation. And at just £25.00 for the two-volume set, it truly is worth every zloty!

Chapter Twelve

HEALTHY BITE

INTRODUCTION

Project description

In this project, children plan and organise a school business. The activities could be applied to any business context but the subject suggested here is to open a healthy tuck shop. In the first activity, children decide the aims for their venture and these become the first page in a business plan, similar to those developed by many small businesses. The end result of the project is the actual opening of the tuck shop, backed by a professional business plan. This will contain evidence of the careful planning and continuous evaluation that sponsors, advisors and customers will wish to see.

Why this context?

More and more teachers are using the context of a class or school business enterprise to give children purposeful experience in functional writing.

Opening a healthy eating tuck shop has the added advantage of raising awareness of health issues as the children research to choose appropriate produce. The existence of the tuck shop enables them to educate their peers.

Going through the process of starting a business offers senior pupils in primary school a genuine insight into the adult world. The real responsibilities that children agree to shoulder in order to ensure the success of the business allow them the opportunity to develop, express and demonstrate abilities which often go unexplored in the primary curriculum.

Project organisation

This project requires some advance preparation by the teacher. Tasks that should be carried out before the project is mentioned to the children are detailed on page 151.

The project entails children working individually, in pairs and in groups to set up a business enterprise that involves the whole class. Key ideas or decisions are often generated and discussed in small groups before consideration by the class as a whole.

Although the teacher will have made many decisions about the school business in advance, it is an important part of the learning process that children should also collaborate in decision-making. Pupils often arrive at conclusions and come up with ideas that adults have not thought of, and many of their decisions, sometimes guided with a light touch, can be woven into the loose plan made by the teacher.

Publication, celebration and review

All writing about the business venture is kept in the business plan folder – a large ring binder. This accommodates the individual pages of the business plan that are published at the end of every activity, and the appendices, which consist of packages of children's notes, ideas and evaluations, relating to the business plan. At the end of the project, the business plan folder will demonstrate exactly how the business has been organised.

PRE SESSION

If this project is to be successful, the following preparation should be carried out before the venture is mentioned to the children.

- Senior school management must approve the idea and may be able to suggest names of people who might help with health advice and funding.
- Alert health advisors that the children will be asking for their help. If possible, arrange for dates for them to give short talks and provide practical advice to help the children choose which produce to sell.
- Look into any opportunities for funding. It is useful to have some cash to pay for the first order. There are often enterprise grants available for projects such as this and health-promoting organisations and shops may wish to contribute. Local business people may also be prepared to give a small donation to encourage children, and some banks run schemes for funding school business ventures.
- Arrange all the dates for meetings in advance. Once the project begins it needs to move forward swiftly, otherwise the children will lose interest.
- Choose a number of possible locations for the tuck shop in consultation with other staff members who may be affected, such as the caretaker.
- Decide on times when the tuck shop will be open. It will be easier to control if it opens only once a day. You may decide to open on only three or four days a week.
- Set provisional dates for the four promotional assemblies, which will target four different age groups in the school. Allow the four children in each team to take a turn at presenting the talk on the produce.
- Make a provisional date for the grand opening.
- Be sure that you have all the materials needed for the project in advance. These will include a ring binder for the business plan, A4 plastic pockets with punched holes to hold the material for the business plan appendix, access to the phone for children to place orders, access to the photocopier, a supply of poster paper and board writers.
- Find a company that sells a range of healthy snacks and will deliver to the school.
- If you plan to sell fruit, only buy stock once a week and be sure to buy less than demand, otherwise the fruit will perish, along with the profits.
- Decide what sort of profits the tuck shop aims to make. If the healthy snacks are to be competitive and attractive, they will probably have to be sold with a low profit margin. Some schools use tuck shop profits to buy playground toys and play equipment. These are not expensive, so do not demand a high level of profit. They also benefit the customer (particularly if they promote fitness).

1 BUSINESS PLAN

Teaching content
Writing aims for a business; prioritising aims.

What you need
Photocopiable page 161, writing materials, scissors.

What to do
Introduce the idea of setting up a tuck shop that promotes healthy eating. This project would follow on naturally from any recent health study carried out either with the class or the whole school. This would ensure that children had built up some understanding of, and commitment to, the importance of good health. Alternatively, it could be the starting point for a focus on general health awareness in the school.

Explain to the children that when adults plan to set up a business, they first think about drawing up a business plan. This sets out, on paper, the details of how the business is going to be made to work successfully. Tell children that there are a number of reasons why beginning with a business plan is a good idea.

- It is a clear and organised way to pull ideas together and check that they work as a whole.
- If money needs to be borrowed or grants applied for in order to set up the business, then a well-presented plan of action will inspire confidence in the lender.
- Once the business is up and running, a business plan will provide a framework against which the ongoing success of the venture may be judged.
- At any time, the business plan may be

produced to show interested parties the work, to date, of the business. Other children in school, parents, teachers and business advisors should be given access to this plan, which could be kept in the library or another accessible place. People from other schools may want to seek advice on setting up a similar business and the business plan will detail the steps taken. Advisors who have given help and financial backers also have a right to scrutinise the books.

The business plan will be written and developed, a little at a time, during the process of setting up the business and then throughout its working life. Appendices will contain evidence of collective planning and evaluation.

The first part of the plan will be a brief description of the aims and nature of the business. Ask the children, in groups of five, to brainstorm statements about the aims they might have in setting up a healthy tuck shop. Tell them to begin each sentence with the words 'We aim to _______', as this will lead them into the manner in which aims are often expressed.

Allow five minutes for this and then distribute photocopiable page 161, one per group, which shows the brainstorm written by a group of primary school children who set up a very successful tuck shop. Tell the children that eventually a few of these aims were rejected by the rest of the class but that the remaining ones were included in the business plan, after being placed in order of priority. Ask each group to do just this, cutting up the aims, throwing some into the bin and organising the remaining ones into a prioritised list.

Ask the groups to read out their lists and compare and discuss results. This exercise will raise many issues as there is no correct order for the aims. Next, ask groups to read out any aims they had written earlier that were not part of the list on the photocopiable sheet. Decide as a class whether these extra aims are important to your business and add them at the appropriate point on the list.

The definitive list of business aims should be rewritten in a large poster format, and this should be displayed on the wall as the aims will be used later in the project when writing letters and when children draw up their final 'business charter'.

A beautifully handwritten or word-processed copy of the aims should also be made and filed as the first page of the business plan. The list may change, as it is very likely that new aims will emerge as the children reach a greater understanding about running a business.

2 EVALUATING OUR BUSINESS CHANCES

Teaching content

Filling in a self-evaluation sheet.

What you need

Photocopiable page 161, writing materials.

What to do

Having raised awareness of some aspects of running a business, the next task is to evaluate the chances of success. Explain that this is a business venture that will be set up and run by the class with the teacher acting as advisor. Read out the following list, which contains a sample of the type of decisions that will have to be taken by the children over the coming weeks. This list will give them some idea of the responsibilities that they will be taking on if the business venture goes ahead. It should also inspire those who enjoy challenge, independence, responsibility and those who have entrepreneurial spirit! Point out that during the course of several meetings in the future, children will have to decide on:

- a business name and logo;
- design for stationery;
- advice needed and people to ask for help;
- exactly what products to sell;
- how to order and where to buy the stock;
- where to obtain the money to pay for the initial stock;
- how to keep records;
- where to set up shop;
- how to convince other children that healthy snacks are a good idea;
- which children will do the ordering, the book keeping, the selling, the daily counting of the cash and the advertising.

Tell the children that, before setting up in business, adults evaluate their realistic chances of success and this is the next step that they must take. The main question they must asking themselves is: 'Do we stand a chance?'

Distribute photocopiable page 162 to each child and read through the questions. Explain that if they answer these dishonestly they will only cheat themselves and it might even lead to financial disaster. Reassure the children that there will be time laid aside in school for setting up the business and business meetings will always be held in class time. However, selling the healthy tuck is something that will have to be done at playtime, so children should consider the implications for losing free time!

Allow children to fill in the evaluation sheet alone, stressing that straightforward 'Yes' or 'No' answers are sometimes appropriate but there will be times when some explanation on a separate sheet of paper will be necessary, such as 'I will *sometimes* be willing to give up my playtime to help in the shop.'

Explain that these sheets may be useful when it comes to deciding which jobs people will take on. However, if the business goes ahead people will be allowed to change their minds in the light of new information.

3 CHOOSING A NAME

60

Teaching content

Examining the conventions using in choosing the name for a shop.

What you need

Photocopiable page 163 (three per group), A4 paper ruled into eight columns, writing materials, scissors, adhesive.

What to do

Having evaluated their chances of success, the children next have to decide on a name for the tuck shop. Distribute photocopiable page 163 to groups of five. Explain to children that the headings on this sheet show several different ways in which business names are chosen. Discuss the meaning of these headings, perhaps asking for one example of each from local shop names or from those on the sheet.

After discussion, ask groups to give responsibility for one of the following jobs to each child in the group:

- reader;
- cutter;
- sticker;
- scribe;
- reporter.

'Cutters' should now cut out the headings while 'stickers' attach these along the top of the eight columns on a sheet of A4 paper. 'Readers' then say aloud the name of each business on the photocopiable sheet, and the group will discuss and decide in which column it belongs.

'Cutters' will then cut out the name and 'Stickers' will place the name in the appropriate column. Ensure that every group has at least three sets of names, as some will fit under more than one column. The group should try to reach a consensus on difficult decisions, and 'scribes' should add at least two local shop names to each column.

Next, 'reporters' from each group should read out the columns one at a time and the opinions of groups that differed should be voiced and discussed. There will often be no absolutely correct decisions, a fact which highlights the complexity and wit of the wordplays found in shop names. A discussion of favourite names will further focus attention on clever puns and the interesting language involved in the creation of shop names.

Tell the children it is now time to invent a name for their new business. In the light of their work on the photocopiable sheet, individuals should be given the opportunity to think quietly by themselves and write down any good ideas they wish to bring to a group discussion. At this point stress that ideas from different people often merge well to produce an even better idea. Ask each group to select their best three names, write these on separate pieces of paper and pin them on the wall. After discussion of the strengths of all proposals, a vote should be taken to decide the name of the new business. Groups, of course, are not allowed to vote for their own names. Leave proposals on display as they will probably provide good soundbites for use in advertising.

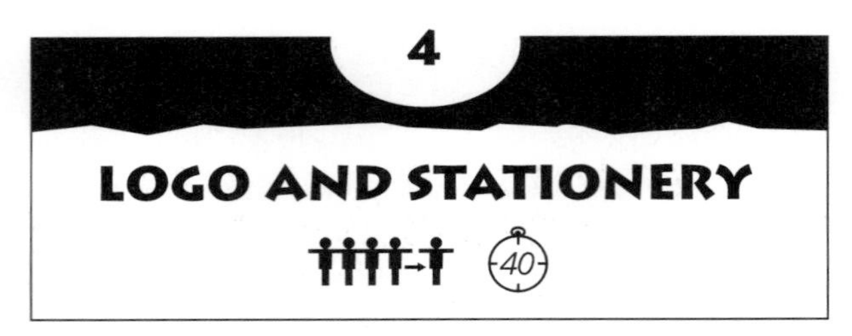

4 LOGO AND STATIONERY

Teaching content

Examination of symbols that can sometimes replace words in conveying a message or an idea.

What you need

Collection of business logos, drawing materials.

What to do

Point out to the children that many businesses have a logo which symbolises the spirit of the enterprise. Ask for examples of such logos and then show the class the logos you have collected. Discuss the style and symbolism of these.

Organise the children into groups of five and ask them to discuss possible logos for the tuck shop. Remind them of the way in which the discussion of ideas can often lead to better and richer ideas. When most groups have thought through a number of ideas for the logo, ask the children, individually, to draw a sketch of the idea they like best. All the finished logos should be displayed and a trusted judge invited to choose the best, which will then be adopted for the business.

The next step is to incorporate the logo and company name into the business address (the school address). Children should examine the collection of logos to see the way in which the addresses can be integrated before thinking of their own design ideas. The word processor or a typewriter may be used for a cut-and-stick design and some schools may have the technology to produce a computerised heading. Either way, attractive photocopied stationery for the new business should be produced.

Further development

A business slogan could also be created. It can be interesting to have this translated into Latin to be used on stationery, business cards and advertising.

5 SEEKING ADVICE AND SPONSORSHIP

Teaching content

Writing a business letter.

What you need

Names and addresses to which children can write in order to seek advice on healthy snacks, names and addresses of business and private individuals who may provide sponsorship, local telephone directory, business stationery from Activity 4, poster of business aims from Activity 1, chalkboard, photocopiable page 164, stamps, envelopes, poster paper, marker pens.

What to do

Before this session, the teacher should have contacted people involved in promoting healthy living and asked if they are willing to speak with the children about the subject of healthy snacks. Most regions have experts in nutrition and dental health who are delighted to help with a project like this. Doctors, dentists and nurses are also pleased to help, but it is always best for an adult to prearrange this type of visit to avoid children being disappointed. Explain to the experts that the children must feel involved. Warn them to expect letters and ask if they would be willing to reply to these. Starting this lesson with a list of people to write to will move the project along quickly.

A number of possible sources of funding for the initial order of stock should also be considered before this lesson, though it is also worth contacting any local businesses that the children suggest. These people are not being invited into school, so it is unnecessary to contact them first, however it *is* important to enclose a covering letter from the school, explaining that this is an authorised project being supervised by adults!

Point out to the children that now the tuck shop has its own stationery, it will be possible for them to write business letters requesting the following help:

- advice about healthy snacks;
- finance to buy the first order of stock.

Organise the class into groups of five. Give some groups responsibility for finance and other groups responsibility for advice. Tell the advice groups that their first task is to brainstorm lists of people they might write to, requesting advice on healthy snacks. The finance groups must list all the businesses or individuals who might be prepared to donate a small amount of money to buy the initial stock. Lists should be written on large sheets of poster paper.

Allow ten minutes for this task, then ask the finance groups to display and read their lists. Children who were not part of this group, and the teacher, should add any ideas they may have to offer. This process should be repeated for the advice group.

Guide the children to the names of people you know will be helpful, then organise the groups into writing pairs, giving each pair one name to write to. It doesn't matter if some names are duplicated as two, or even three, letters can go to the same person.

Discuss the sort of information that writers should include in their letters and jot down the children's ideas on the chalkboard. Distribute photocopiable page 164 and read it through with the class, comparing the ideas it contains with those on the chalkboard. The sheet also offers suggestions on how to organise the business letter. These may be useful for children who need support in this difficult activity.

Explain that a business letter must be written in a particular style, obeying certain rules that are observed by most business people. Suggest that, because these people are very busy, they write and read only facts that are expressed as concisely as possible. Read through the list of rules on the photocopiable sheet and ask the children to keep these rules in mind as they write.

Each pair should now draft the letter for which they are responsible. The poster from Activity 1, showing business aims, should be referred to and used as a plan to explain the purpose of the business venture. After careful correction, both children should write a final draft. One copy should be posted and the other kept as part of the appendix for the business plan.

A list of the names of people approached for finance and advice will become page 4 of the business plan.

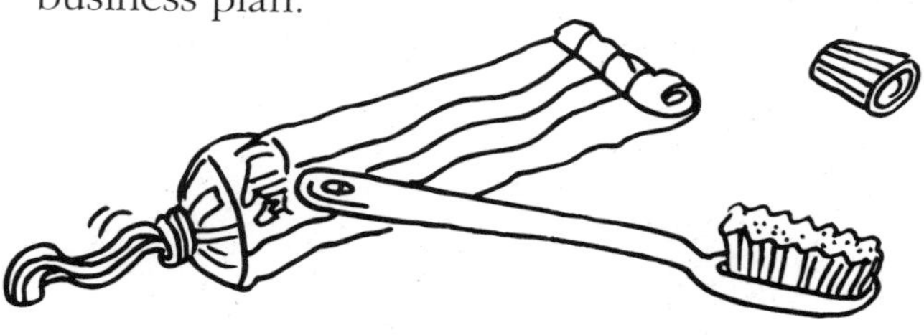

6

KEEPING RECORDS OF BUSINESS MEETINGS

Teaching content

Taking notes when people are speaking.

What you need

Writing materials.

What to do

Explain to the children that when running any business it is essential to keep records of official meetings. There will always be information that needs to be referred to in the future, so keeping records of discussions and consultancy sessions is vital.

Discuss with children the various ways of keeping verbal records of meetings offered by modern technology. They may mention the following:

- tape recording;
- video recording;
- taking minutes or shorthand.

All of these ways of recording meetings can pose problems. Children will probably know that some people object to being recorded on tape and that it can take a great deal of time to find a particular reference on tape. Taking notes of important facts as people speak and summarising main points at the end is probably the best way to record meetings.

Check to see if children know about shorthand, which is an accepted form of note-taking used by secretaries when recording the minutes of meetings. Explain that this is a difficult skill to learn and is possibly an interesting area of language study that children might be given the opportunity to learn in secondary school. Children will be familiar with some accepted abbreviations and should be able to recognise eg, etc and ie.

Discuss with the children the difficulty of noting main points as people speak but also point out how important this skill might be in later life when noting main points in lessons at secondary school, in further education and at meetings (if children join committees which run sports teams, clubs and business ventures).

Explain that when the invited health experts arrive in school to offer advice on healthy food, children will have to note the main points of information they give as these will be used:

- to decide on the products to be sold;
- to educate customers on the value of these products;
- for general advertising.

Shortly before a visitor is due to speak to the class, organise the children into groups of four. Explain that each group will take notes for five minutes only. This will mean a short concentrated writing session and then freedom to relax and enjoy the rest of the talk. Emphasise the fact that only memory-jogging notes are necessary. Before the session begins, explain to the guest that groups will be taking notes and apologise in advance for the fact that you will be indicating changeover times.

Before the guest leaves, ask children to glance briefly at their notes and check whether there are any points that need to be clarified. Immediately after the guest has left, groups should compare notes and a scribe should write a list of main points that were made. Listing points will cut out the need for connecting language and highlight the importance of skeleton facts. Ask each group, in turn, to report back to the class on the main points covered during their five minutes. This will give you an opportunity to check for accuracy and the inclusion of main points only. Irrelevant detail should be crossed out and any information omitted should be inserted, after comments from the class. Finally, one person from each group should list points neatly, and papers should be collated for inclusion in the appendix of the business plan. Word-processing these notes will give a truly professional finish.

Teaching content
Writing explanations.

What you need
Copies of notes from Activity 6, chalkboard.

What to do
Tell the children that decisions must be made on exactly what items will be sold in the new tuck shop. Organise the class into groups of five and distribute the notes made at the visits of the health advisors. The groups should refer to these notes and make a list of the products that they think should be sold.

Allow 15 minutes for this activity and then ask a spokesperson from each group to read the lists to the class. Make a list on the chalkboard showing items that they all agree upon. Share the items equally between the groups and ask each group to explain the reason why the product they have been given should be sold as a healthy snack. Remind children that an explanation needs an orientating phrase at the beginning, which in this case could be modelled on the chalkboard:

'We think that (name of product here) is a good thing to sell in our healthy tuck shop because...'

Ask groups to read their explanations and ask for comments from the class. Explanations should then be amended in the light of comments.

The list of products, with the explanations, should be placed in the business plan.

Tell the children that some products may be borderline cases, perhaps because they contain too much sugar but are otherwise nutritious. Suggest that these might be sold on one day of the week only.

Rules should be made on how many of each item an individual may buy. Ask every group to consider these issues and then, as a class, discuss the ideas generated by each group.

To complete the activity, give each group part of the writing task, explaining the rules which govern the sale of slightly unhealthy snacks, and those for ensuring that the healthy tuck shop does not allow gluttony! These should be added to the business plan.

When children hold their promotional assemblies, the explanations and rules for the sale of the produce will be used.

Teaching content
Explanation and persuasion.

What you need
Writing materials, overhead transparencies with suitable pens, or poster paper and felt-tipped pens, list of products to be sold and the explanations from Activity 7, A4 paper.

What to do
It will be necessary, a few weeks before the tuck shop is opened, to hold a promotional assembly or business launch, introducing the idea of the healthy tuck shop, promoting the products, introducing the personnel and explaining practical points such as where, and when, the shop will be open. This event should be held once the tuck shop has a firm opening date but needs to be organised well in advance so that presentations may be carefully practised over the coming weeks.

Groups should be allocated one type of produce or product to promote. The explanation sheets backing the sale of particular products (written in Activity 7) should be copied and distributed, as children will find these useful in writing promotional material. Write the following headings on the board:

Name of product
Points that make this product healthy
Words and phrases that sum up the task sensation of this product
Eat this product and you will save yourself from...
Good slogans for healthy eating generally, or for this product in particular.

Give each child a sheet of paper and ask them, using the information gained from the health consultants, to list, under the first heading, relevant healthy points about their product. Under the next heading, they should list words and phrases that conjure up the taste. Before doing this children should, of course, be given a taste of their particular product and should then be encouraged, while eating, to record the taste sensations!

Under the heading 'Eat this product and you will save yourself from...' children should record the adverse effects of eating unhealthy snacks, such as lack of vitality, rotting teeth, obesity, sugar dependency, and so on. Finally, they should think of one or more good slogans for their particular product or for healthy eating generally.

Remind the children of what they learned in the shop-naming session (Activity 3) about crisp and concise language using alliteration, rhyme and repetition. Suggest a few slogans to focus their minds on the style of writing required, for example:

Be happy – Be healthy
In health lies wealth

Now, using the notes they have made on the planning sheet, every group should design an overhead transparency or a large poster to be used at the presentation. The name of the product should figure prominently and other vital information should fit around this. Four different promotional assemblies should be organised, to give every child in the group the opportunity to talk through the visual aid. Children should practise the delivery of these promotional talks regularly until the actual healthy tuck shop launch. If they are using the overhead projector, children should be reminded to:

- face the audience at all times, reading from the transparency rather than the screen;
- point to the transparency, *not* the screen, when emphasising words.

One A4 copy of each presentation should be made and filed in the appendix of the business plan.

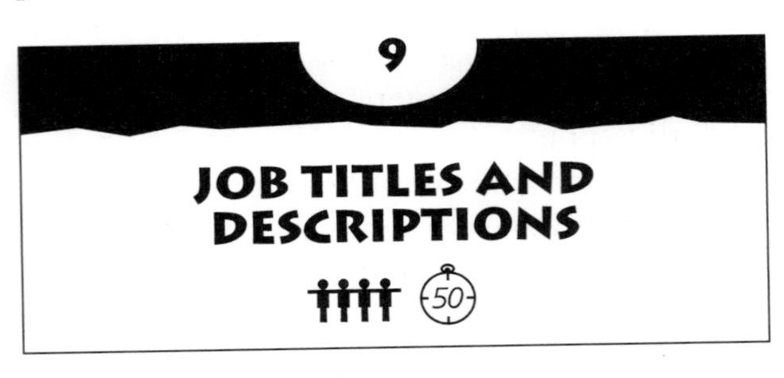

9 JOB TITLES AND DESCRIPTIONS

Teaching content

Deciding the duties involved in a job of work.

What you need

Writing materials, photocopiable page 165, chalkboard, scissors, adhesive.

What to do

The next sensible step in setting up a business is to decide what jobs need to be done. Ask children, in groups of five, to write a list of every task they can think of that will need to be done to run the tuck shop. Explain that this does not mean writing titles like 'secretary' or 'managing director'. Give a few examples from photocopiable page 165 as illustrations of what is required.

After ten minutes, ask a reporter from each group to read out their list of tasks. Write these on the chalkboard. Distribute photocopiable page 165 and check that all tasks identified on this sheet are also on the chalkboard. Add any extra tasks the class consider important to the blanks on the photocopiable sheet. It will become clear that some small tasks can be grouped together as one job and that some tasks might be carried out by the same person. Point out that adults working full time often carry out several tasks as part of their job. Remind children that the tuck shop business will be run by people who already have very busy lives (as young students) and warn them to be sure not to overload jobs when they come to creating posts.

In groups, children must now cut out the tasks from the photocopiable sheet and organise these into sets with a job heading for each. Give the example of 'Shop assistant' as a heading, so that children understand. Stress the fact that this is *their* business and they are allowed to invent any job titles they wish.

If this task is too open for the class, then issue a list of job titles and ask children to organise tasks under these headings. Titles will probably include: managing director, secretary, shop assistant, advertiser, customer relations, stock controller, banker.

Give children 15 minutes to carry out this task, but tell them not to stick anything down until complete agreement has been reached by all participants.

The next step is to draw together all group decisions. Some jobs within the business will be obvious and straightforward, while others will involve a great deal of discussion and debate. The teacher should take a vote on stalemates and, as chief advisor, has the right to make the final decision. When the final list has been agreed on the chalkboard, tell the children that they have just drawn up 'job descriptions' so it will now be possible to advertise the jobs.

One child in the class should be made responsible for writing the final agreed list of job titles with the tasks to be carried out by each one. This sheet will go into the business plan under the title 'Job description'. Completed photocopiable sheets may go into the appendix.

Teaching content

Specifying the qualities and previous experience required to carry out a particular job of work.

What you need

Job descriptions from Activity 9, writing materials.

What to do

Before advertising the jobs decided upon in the last task, explain to the children that they must also consider the qualities they would expect in a person who would carry out the job successfully.

Organise the class into groups and give each group responsibility for one job. Ask them to write a list of the qualities they think would be required to do the job well. Ask children to consider the following areas:

- the school subjects that the person should be good at;
- the character qualities that the person needs to have;
- any previous experience that might prove helpful in the job.

Point out that the children will need to look very carefully at the tasks involved in the job for which they are responsible.

After 12 to 15 minutes, ask a spokesperson from each group to read out the list. Seek agreement upon each list in turn, and alter them according to the comments of the class. Next, each child should draw up a final list of the qualities sought for their allocated job. Suggest the heading 'Specification for shop assistant' (or other job title, as appropriate).

Choose the best person specification for each job and file these in the appendix of the business plan. These can then be used when jobs are advertised.

Teaching content

Persuasive personal writing; revision and practice of the business letter format.

What you need

Photocopiable page 166, job descriptions and person specifications drawn up in Activities 9 and 10.

What to do

Tell the children that today they are going to apply for the jobs they would like to do in the new business. Distribute job descriptions and person specifications. Ask the children to look at these and then decide which jobs they feel they are best qualified to apply for.

Explain to the children that a letter applying for a job follows a standard pattern. Distribute photocopiable page 166, one per child, and talk through this with them. Encourage the children to jot down the notes and then re-write the letter, in sentences, on the back of the photocopiable sheet. If necessary, remind them of the conventions of business letter writing by looking again at Activity 5.

Now ask the children to write and submit their final drafts. Tell them that they will hear within three or four days if they have been successful in their applications.

Read the letters carefully and give the jobs to the pupils you know will do them best. If possible, give an alternative job to those who are not successful, or share out the jobs over the course of the predicted business life, so that each child has an opportunity to contribute to their business venture. Write a sensitive refusal to unsuccessful candidates, adding a personal note on the bottom. It is best if these letters can be posted to children's homes, so they can experience the whole process of applying for a job. The one experience children must *not* have at this stage is that of being disappointed!

Teaching content

Organising for a celebration.

What you need

Poster paper, card, business stationery from Activity 4, chalkboard, names and addresses of people who have helped with sponsorship and advice, business plan with appendices, overhead transparencies prepared in Activity 8.

What to do

Decisions about the breadth and scope of the launch of the new business will depend upon the priority set by the school on the venture. The launch provides an excellent opportunity to share the learning about both the business aspects of the project, and good health issues, with children, parents and the wider community.

Gather the children together and choose a day to launch the new business. (The four short assemblies prepared in Activity 8 should be held during the two weeks before the opening. These will allow the children to promote some of the products they will be selling.) Organise children into groups of five and ask them to brainstorm other publicity ventures. These may include:

- inviting a celebrity interested in good health to open the shop;

- displaying posters which persuade people of the benefits of good health;
- displaying posters which advertise the healthy (and tasty) produce;
- displaying banners announcing the date of the grand opening;
- writing jingles (which can be sung in assembly or around the school) advertising the shop;
- inviting children and parents to inspect the business plan;
- writing a letter explaining the aims of the business to parents and asking them to support it by encouraging their children to buy healthy snacks at school;
- sending an invitation card to every child or every class in the school and to all sponsors and advisors;
- organising a ceremony of cutting the ribbon tied around the counter, before opening for business on the first day;
- writing speeches about good health and the business aims of the new tuck shop for the grand opening;
- proposing thanks to everyone who helped and welcoming all customers;
- giving a free balloon to all new customers;
- offering a prize for specific customers, perhaps the first and the fifty-second. Numbers will have to be kept secret, one child will have to keep count of the customers, and winners should be announced at the end of the first day.

Allow ten minutes for discussion and brainstorming, then ask every group to contribute ideas to a list on the chalkboard. Add any points from the above list that are appropriate and then, with the children, select launch ideas for your school.

Organise children into groups to carry out tasks in preparation for the grand opening. Whatever the size of the launch, the business plan, which includes all the writing activities carried out in this project, should be prominently and permanently displayed for public viewing.

NAME

BUSINESS AIMS

- We aim to run a service for the children and adults in our school by selling healthy snacks.
- We aim to learn about how to run a successful business.
- We aim to stop children's teeth from rotting by selling sugar-free food and drinks.
- We aim to enjoy ourselves by bossing the children around who come to our shop.
- We aim to make a profit so that we can buy things for the children in the school.
- We aim to run this business with as little help as possible from the adults.
- We aim to educate the children and adults in our school about healthy eating.
- We aim to ask the customers which snacks they like best.
- We aim to seek the help and advice of people who are experts about healthy food.
- We aim to give ourselves free snacks (after all, we are running the tuck shop).
- We aim to show that children can be very responsible.
- We aim to swap the jobs around so that everyone in the class gets experience of different types of business responsibility.

NAME

DO WE STAND A CHANCE?

- Are you healthy and strong?
- Do you have the support of your school friends?
- Are you willing to give up some of your free time in order to run the business?
- Do you think that these products will sell?
- Do you believe that these are good products?
- Are you totally committed to the success of this business?

Are you willing to learn:

- How to sell?
- How to do the paperwork?
- How to order the produce or products?
- How to run a business meeting?
- How to apply for a grant of money to set up the business?
- How to borrow and pay back money in order to set up the business?
- How to do several jobs at once?
- Are you willing to try convincing other people that healthy tuck is a good idea?

◆ Write a list here of any previous experience you have had that will be useful in the new business – you may have served in another shop, or ordered from a catalogue, or helped at a school sale.

NAME

CONVENTIONS FOR CHOOSING SHOP NAMES

Column headings

Play on words

Name of owner

Rhyme

Promise of high quality

Exotic place name

Alliteration

Bold statement of produce

Names of businesses

Pizza Palace

Top Spot

Pizza Planet

Swift Fix

Mum's the Word

The Perfect Body

Light Bite

Costcutter Supermarket

Rimini Restaurant

Smith's

Riviera Restaurant

Oasis

Kids Stuff

Good Start

Speedy Shoe

Athlete's Foot

Save-a-lot

All Tied Up

Fabric Factory

Sunnyside Stores

Walk Inn

Taj Mahal

The Caring Chemist

Invitation Inn

Toy Box

Honest and Trusty

Premium Pizza

Photo Quick

The Medicine Cabinet

Reject Shop

Run-A-Way Sport

Skin Style (leather goods)

Best Burgers

Spuds 'n' Things

Pete's

NAME

WRITING A BUSINESS LETTER

Explain who you are

We are writing to you on behalf of ...

We are writing to you as representatives of ...

We are pupils at (name of school) and we are hoping to set up a ...

Explain why you are writing

We are writing to ask you if ...

We would like to invite you to become a part of this exciting venture by ...

Say what you have done so far

Up to now we have written our aims and ...

Already we have thought carefully about our aims. These are ...

Summarise in what way this person's help will fit into the plan

With your help we hope to ...

If you can help us, then we will be able to ...

Rules to remember when writing a business letter

- Be as brief and to the point as possible.
- Make sure that you have included all the essential information.
- Use language that is simple and uncomplicated.
- Sign off with 'Yours faithfully' if it is someone you have never met and 'Yours sincerely' if you know the person.
- It is *extremely important* to spell every word correctly! If the reader is distracted by bad spelling, then he or she will not be concentrating on the message! People will not take you seriously if they think you can't be bothered to check spelling.
- The final draft must be beautifully presented if the letter is to be taken seriously in the world of business.

When you have finished writing, tick the items on the list above after you have checked each one.

NAME

TASKS TO BE DONE IN THE NEW BUSINESS

- Deciding what needs to be ordered, and how much.
- Checking that all stock ordered has been delivered.
- Selling.
- Dealing with customer complaints.
- Ensuring that customers line up in orderly queues.
- Advertising.
- Deciding upon special promotions.
- Checking upon customer satisfaction.
- Checking on the good behaviour of customers.
- Checking which items are most/least popular.
- Deciding rules for how many packets of each item children are allowed to buy.
- Chairing the business meetings.
- Phoning in the orders.
- Counting the money.
- Putting the money into bags for the bank.
- Taking money to the bank.
- Setting up the shop every day.
- Clearing away at the end of each session.

NAME

PLANNING A JOB APPLICATION

First paragraph for this job

- You are letting people know that you are keen on applying.
- Introduction. Why are you writing this letter?
- What interests you about this job?

Second paragraph

- You must let people know that you have read the advertisement carefully and have understood what it says.
- What do you think are the requirements of the job from what you have read?
- What qualities do you have that make you a good person for this job?
- What qualifications do you have for the job?
- Do you have previous experience in this sort of work?

Third paragraph

- Make it clear when you will be able to start work and how many sessions you are prepared to work.
- When will you be able to start work?
- How many sessions are you prepared to work?

Fourth paragraph

- Let people know finally that you are sincere about wanting this job.
- Why do you want the company to consider you for this job?

Go back through the notes you have made checking that you have only written each point once. Decide where important information fits best and don't keep repeating yourself. Check all spelling and write neatly!

Chapter Thirteen

BULLYING

INTRODUCTION

Project description

This project develops through a series of structured tasks which provide opportunities for children to discuss concerns that are central to the issue of bullying. Discussion activities focusing on themes such as 'Am I a bully', 'Is bullying a new phenomenon?' and 'Is it always easy to spot bullying?' result in an interesting mixture of writing outcomes. These are organised at the end of the project into an interactive pack on bullying which can be used in other classes or displayed in the school library. Children are then involved in organising an assembly to launch this new learning resource.

Why this context?

Bullying is an issue of great concern to children and adults, so it is important to offer children every opportunity to reflect, discuss and write about this subject. Through a dynamic, personal involvement in thoughtful oral and written activity, victims and bullies among the children may become able to examine their own motivation and find solutions to their personal problems. Role play allows children to confront their fears and guilt, and they are then given an opportunity to offer general solutions to the problems of bullying. It is possible that, as a result of this project, children's perceptions of bullying may be changed. Children's genuine interest in this subject means that the quality of their involvement is heightened and a lively curiosity and commitment are maintained throughout the project.

Project organisation

Initially, groups brainstorm questions they would like to explore and to which they would like to find solutions by the end of the project. Posters featuring these questions are displayed on the wall in order to focus ideas for the project. Eventually some of these questions will form the sections of a *Big Bullying Book* that the children will publish.

Deciding upon a definition for bullying generates debate as children seek to identify the central concerns that define the issue. Following this, children produce short dramas on the subject of bullying and performances are evaluated with the help of photocopiable sheets. These taped dramas and evaluations become part of the interactive bullying pack.

Children are next given an imaginary scenario in which a character has been excluded from a game. They are asked to generate the counter-arguments in the discussion. In order to investigate the question of whether or not bullying is a new phenomenon, children interview parents about their youthful experiences and then write recounts which are included in the bullying pack.

Children design personal search questionnaires for distribution throughout the school. Private and honest completion of this questionnaire should reveal whether or not the respondent is a bully! A set of blank questionnaires will also be supplied in the bullying pack. Finally, advice is produced to help both bullies and victims in the form of large posters.

Apart from the activity in which children interview and write recounts of their parents' experience, all the activities in this project are carried out by groups. The dynamic discussion orchestrated and structured by this gives children the opportunity to reflect upon and express their feelings.

Teachers should read through the activities and then select the ones that they feel will be most useful for their class. Most of the activities are discrete and may be used in any order. Children should be advised to retain all written work until the end of the project.

Publication, celebration and review

The final activity in this project details the way in which materials should be assembled for including in an interactive bullying pack to be used in classes and housed in the library. A school assembly is used to present the new school resource, where children present some of their short dramas and then tell about the contents of the package. This would be an excellent awareness-raising exercise to launch a whole school project on bullying.

1 BULLYING QUESTIONS

Teaching content
Writing a list of investigative questions.

What you need
Strips of paper, large markers.

What to do
Discuss with the children the fact that bullying is an issue of serious concern in schools. Advice to bullies and to victims can be found in many places, but most of this is written by adults. Tell the children that they are going to create a pack on bullying for the school library. This will reflect the views of children on the subject, and will be read by both children and adults in the school.

Ask the children if they have ever noticed that books that discuss issues, and try to explain the reasons why people behave in certain ways, are often organised under question headings. Encourage the children, individually, to write down three or four questions about the subject of bullying they would like to have answered. If they cannot think of anything, then write on the chalkboard the first, central, question – 'What is bullying?'.

Allow five minutes for children to carry out this part of the activity and then organise the class into groups of five or six. Distribute large strips of paper to each group and ask them to take turns to read out their individual questions. To avoid duplication, a scribe from each group should write each question on a long strip of paper. Encourage them to add any other questions that come to mind during discussion.

Next, a reporter from each group should read out their questions and a complete set of class questions should be collated and arranged on the classroom wall, with the heading 'What is bullying?'. The questions should be displayed for reference until the project is completed.

Explain to the children that all these questions must be considered during the writing project and that, by the end, answers to a great many of them should have been found. Eventually, the questions will form the section headings in the book that they will publish to help other children come to terms with their own feelings about bullying.

2 DEFINING THE WORD 'BULLYING'

Teaching content
Defining the essential meaning of a word. Introducing the idea of a glossary. Comparing the definition of a word from several different dictionaries.

What you need
Several different dictionaries, writing materials, large sheets of paper, large felt-tipped pens.

What to do
Explain to the children that it is always a good idea, before considering an issue, to agree a general definition, so they should write a definition of the word 'bullying'.

Point out that dictionaries, when they are defining words, have to reach the heart of the meaning and sometimes several meanings of a word. Ask the children to imagine that they are attempting to describe the meaning of the word 'bullying' to someone who has never heard it express the essence of the meaning.

Ask individuals to write their definitions of what bullying means. This should ensure that every child has done some thinking and has ideas to take to a group discussion. A high level of teacher involvement will probably be involved during the activity as defining a word is very difficult.

Allow three minutes for the individuals to reflect upon their definitions then organise children into their original groups and ask them, in turn, to put forward their idea of the meaning of the word. After adequate discussion, a scribe should write out a group definition on a large sheet of paper. Ask a reporter from every group to read out definitions and then display the definitions under the heading 'Our definition of the word "bullying"'.

Next, distribute different dictionaries around the class and ask one person in each group to find and read the definition of 'bullying' to the class. It is probable that children will have written equally sound definitions. Remind children that many good information books have glossaries, and suggest that the word 'bullying', along with their group definitions, would obviously feature in the glossary of their book on bullying. Finally, display definitions under the heading 'Dictionary definitions'.

Teaching content

Producing a short drama. Completing an evaluation sheet.

What you need

Photocopiable page 176, a cassette recorder and blank cassette.

What to do

Organise the children into groups of three and tell them that they are going to produce a drama on the subject of bullying. The following points should be written on the chalkboard.

- The drama must have a strong, short title.
- It must last only three minutes.
- There will be three characters.
- The drama will begin with the joint announcement of the title.
- After the title, one person will state where the action is taking place.
- The drama will end with all characters standing in a row and bowing.
- There will be no props and no costumes.
- There will be no physical contact between characters.
- Any violence must be mimed.

Be sure that the rules of the drama are clear before children begin to practise. Explain that the characters may be:

- two victims and one bully;
- one victim and two bullies;
- one victim, one bully and one other character who intervenes.

Discuss the fact that bullying is not always physical in nature. Verbal abuse and exclusion are typical forms of bullying and the children may wish to portray these.

Tell the children the time they will have for planning before they begin, as the best drama work is generally produced under strict time pressure! Allow five minutes for initial planning and five for rehearsal. The teacher should check to ensure that all dramas are completed before stopping the rehearsal time. Tell the children that they can have a final, timed, run-through and, having allowed this, begin the actual performances. Record each performance from the announcement of the title to the applause at the end.

After each performance, ask the audience to give positive, oral evaluation of the drama. Use the headings on photocopiable page 176 to focus comment and insist that all observations are positive.

Finally, distribute the photocopiable evaluation sheet, one to each group with one drama title, ensuring that no group is evaluating its own play. Explain to the children that evaluation sheets have become a part of everyday life. The information gained from them helps companies and individuals to assess the success of their products and performance. Remind them to read the instructions carefully before they begin filling them in and point out that honesty is essential. Negative comment is encouraged under the positive heading of 'Give one piece of advice to the drama group...'.

Explain to the children that the cassette of their dramas is going to be included in the bullying pack and that the evaluations accompanying the tape will help listeners to decide which dramas will be most interesting for their personal use.

When completed, evaluations should be given to the appropriate performing groups to reassure them of the good quality of their drama. They should then be filed for inclusion in the final pack.

IS IT BULLYING?

Teaching content

How to compose a piece of discussion writing.

What you need

Photocopiable page 177, writing materials, scissors, adhesive.

What to do

Explain to the children that it is sometimes difficult to decide whether bullying is taking place or not.

Read through the scenario described on photocopiable page 177 and ask children if they feel that this counts as bullying. Allow a few minutes for the debate to heat up in the class, then organise groups of four and give each one a copy of photocopiable page 177. Ask each group to elect a spokesperson and a scribe.

Read through the arguments put forward by Bill and Ambreen for not including Gary in the activity. Tell the children that Marianne and Pete argued that Gary should be allowed to join the team. Ask the groups to take the part of Marianne and Pete to find counter-arguments to weigh against each point. An opposing viewpoint should be sought for each bulleted statement and a group scribe should write this on the photocopiable sheet. Allow ten minutes for this activity and then ask every group to put forward their counter-arguments. Discuss these and point out that both sets of arguments do not seem unreasonable.

Next ask children to imagine what they would feel like if they were Gary and ask them to consider which would be the better outcome of this discussion for him.

Finally, ask them to make a group decision as to how Gary's request should be answered and write this down at the foot of the sheet, followed by their reasons for the decision.

Explain to the children that they have written the notes for a discussion in which two sides of an argument are carefully weighed and a final decision is reached.

Now ask two children from each group to take the arguments and write a paragraph explaining the case for excluding Gary, while the other two write a paragraph from the arguments for including him in the building project. They should then cut out the scenario from photocopiable page 177 and place this at the top of a sheet, followed by the two paragraphs underneath. Finally, the group should write their conclusions and the reasons for this as the last paragraph.

These sheets should be included in the *Big Bullying Book* possibly under the question heading 'Is it always clear when bullying is happening?' Children may come up with a better heading, or there may even be a question from the original brainstorm which suits the section better.

Finally, draw the session to a close by pointing out that much bullying is carried out in a subtle way that is difficult to pin down. It is this aspect of bullying that makes it so difficult to deal with, both for the victim and the authorities. Often, for children and adults, the worst bullying is the careless variety that simply excludes people from the main group. It becomes important therefore for people to be constantly aware of those who appear to be left out and try to include them. Point out to the children that the next person to be excluded may be one of them!

Teaching content

Recount writing is the re-telling of an event that has happened. Description of emotions can make the recount more vivid.

What you need

Photocopiable page 178.

What to do

Explain to the children that it is often difficult to obtain true accounts of bullying. Victims may be reluctant to describe their experiences because they often feel that it is their own fault that they are bullied or they may worry that the bullying will get worse if they tell anyone about it. Bullies themselves are unlikely to own up in case they are punished; sometimes they may even feel ashamed.

When people are older, and look back over the years, they may be more willing to talk about bullying experiences. Suggest that it

would be interesting to find out whether parents, or other adults in the children's lives, have ever bullied or been bullied.

Distribute the bullying questionnaire on photocopiable page 178. Read this through with the class, then ask the children to take it home and either fill it in for an adult at home or ask an adult to complete it alone. The experience of being bullied is so painful that some adults will be unwilling to record memories, while others will have no experience of bullying. Children who are unable to complete the questionnaire at home could ask the teacher, or another adult member of staff, to fill it in. This school-produced sheet could then be photocopied and given to other pupils who have not completed one at home.

Ask a few children to share their findings with the rest of the class. Discuss similarities they notice between bullying over 25 years ago and in the present day. They will notice that the stories are remarkably similar.

Children should now write a recount of the experiences they have researched. Remind them that a recount is the re-telling of things that have really happened, and stress the need for events to be in chronological order. Point out that supporting the story with emotions that adults have described feeling at the time will help the reader to empathise.

Stories should be filed for later inclusion in the *Big Bullying Book* under a section entitled 'Has bullying always happened or is it a new phenomenon?'

Teaching content
How to devise and design a questionnaire.

What you need
Use of a photocopier, writing materials, large sheets of paper.

What to do
Tell the children that before bullies can change their behaviour, they must first recognise the fact that they are bullies! People often do not realise that their behaviour is threatening to others. Explain to the children that they are going to devise a questionnaire that will be photocopied and distributed to school pupils, helping them to establish whether or not they are bullies. Posters will then be designed to advise people what they should do if they have discovered they *are* bullies.

Arrange the children in groups of five and ask them to brainstorm the way that bullies behave towards other people, starting with the basic physical bully and moving on to the more subtle type. Allow five minutes for this, with group scribes writing on large sheets of paper. Display the brainstorms and ask a spokesperson for each group to read their list. The points covered may include:

- unprovoked punching, kicking, slapping, pinching, pushing;
- unprovoked swearing, name calling, insults;
- making fun of other people's colour, race, gender, religion, accent, size, features, family, clothing, intelligence and so on;
- excluding other people because they are different in any way at all.

In order to allow pupils in the school to reflect upon their own bullying behaviour, it will be important to include this list on the questionnaire, along with other relevant examples from children's own lists.

The first part of the questionnaire may read:

'Have you ever been involved in any of these types of behaviour?'
If the answer is 'yes' please tick the box next to the behaviour type.
Leave it blank if the answer is 'no'.

Next, groups should brainstorm the reasons why they think bullies behave in the way they do. Allow five minutes for this activity then display the posters produced and ask a spokesperson to report. They may have generated some of these ideas:

- to make themselves feel important, powerful, strong, popular, part of a gang;
- because they gain pleasure from hurting people or from ignoring them, calling them names or making fun of them.
- to take someone else's money, lunch, sweets.

The next section of the questionnaire might ask:

Have you ever bullied or threatened another person because it made you feel important...?

The complete questionnaire will have to fit on to one side of A4 and must allow space for tick boxes because at the end, it must say:

If you have ticked any of these boxes then you are a bully. Look out for advice on posters around the school showing you what you must do in order to change your behaviour.

Each group should now design a questionnaire based upon their brainstorms and discussion. Photocopy every group's questionnaire several times and distribute these around the school. It would also be a good idea to enlarge some of these and display them on the walls around the school under eye-catching headings, such as 'Are you a bully?'

Finally, children will have to brainstorm advice that could be offered to bullies. This could be written up on posters for the school walls, following up on the questionnaires. Advice could include ideas such as:

- Next time you feel the urge to bully someone try imagining what it feels like to experience this behaviour. Some day the victim might be you!
- It is easy to get a laugh by making fun of someone. Really funny people don't get laughs in this cheap way.
- Some day you may be the one who is different. Would you want to be treated like this?
- If you enjoy hurting another person then there may be something wrong with you. Tell an adult that you feel this way and ask for help.
- If you have hurt someone recently then say you're sorry. That would be the really brave thing to do. Are you brave enough?

7 STOPPING THE BULLIES

Teaching content
Instruction writing is not always procedural.

What you need
Writing materials, poster paper, marker pens.

What to do
Tell the children that they are going to produce a poster advising children what to do if they are being bullied. The poster will be written as a set of clear instructions.

Organise the class into groups of four and ask each to brainstorm the advice that they would give to a person who is being bullied. Tell the children that there is no one answer to the problem, so they should produce as many good pieces of advice as possible.

Allow ten minutes for this discussion, then ask each group to display their brainstorm of ideas. A spokesperson from each group could read them to the class. Ask the children if they can see a way to arrange the advice in any order of priority. Discussion should lead to the conclusion that, apart from telling an adult (which will probably come top of the list), the rest of the advice would depend upon the actual circumstances and people involved. It is vital to make the point that sometimes the order of instructions is of great significance but with others it is relatively unimportant. If order matters, then this is called procedural writing.

Ask the children how their advice to victims of bullying could be displayed in a way that prevents the reader from thinking that the list is prioritised. Children will probably come up with the idea of displaying the ideas in a circle, possibly radiating from a central photograph or statement, or they may have alternative, better design ideas.

Distribute large poster paper and markers and ask the children to design a suitable poster. Tasks should be organised among group members, with one responsible for making a border, one for the central picture or statement and two for writing the radiating ideas, which could be written on strips and then stuck on to the large poster. Obviously agreement about size and style of writing should be reached first to achieve a consistent effect.

Finally, when posters are completed, they should be displayed in the school and other public places – the local police station, hospital or clinic may be keen to display them.

8 PUBLISHING AND LAUNCHING THE PACK

Teaching content
How to organise a class publication and how to prepare an assembly publication launch.

What you need
All written or taped work completed throughout the project, plastic wallets, writing materials, A2 sugar paper.

What to do
Ask the children to take out all the written work which they have filed. Suggest that they look again at the original set of questions. Many of these will have been answered during the course of the discussion, writing, drama, research and evaluation exercises. Questions that *have* been answered should be cut out from the poster lists and displayed separately from those that remain unanswered. List any unanswered questions on A4 paper and include these on the last page of the *Big Bullying Book* under the heading 'Questions for which we are still seeking answers'.

Explain to the children that if all the questions could be answered then there would be no bullying in the world. We are only at the beginning of a quest towards this end.

Headings for questions that have already been answered should be placed, side by side, along a set of tables. Written and taped work filed during the project should now be organised in sets along the tables under the appropriate question headings. These headings will include:

What does the word bullying mean?
Is it always easy to identify bullying?
Has bullying always happened?
Are you a bully?

Apart from the writing that answers these questions, and the questionnaires, you should also have:

- a tape of bullying drama;
- a set of evaluations of the dramas;
- posters offering advice to victims;
- posters offering advice to bullies;
- posters about how to stop bullying.

The tape and evaluations should be placed in an A4 plastic wallet ready to be put in the bullying box.

Posters should be prepared for display around the school after the assembly launch. After a few weeks, they should be taken down, folded or rolled, and included in the box.

Questions from the original brainstorm that have been answered but do not have a specific piece of writing should be distributed to groups, who should then write the answers that have been discovered on a sheet of A4.

Sheets of A2 sugar paper should next be folded into a large book. The cover and first two pages should be left blank. One of the questions about bullying should be displayed on the top of the fourth page with a few selected pieces of appropriate writing stuck on the page. In this way all the questions and answers should be stuck into the big book.

It is crucial that every child should have at least one piece of writing included in the *Big Bullying Book* and a glossary at the end should show the definition of the word 'bullying' decided in Activity 2 and any other vocabulary chosen by the children from the language involved in bullying, perhaps victim, exclude, gang, aggression and so on.

Teachers and children may decide that several pages of writing should be used to answer questions, so this may become a very large publication. Extra copies of the children's recounts of parents being bullied should be bound together with a cover and included as a separate publication in the box. Children should next gather their own remaining pieces of work and staple them with a cover to keep as a personal record of the project.

It will be important to design or customise a box or folder to contain:

- the *Big Bullying Book;*
- recounts of parents' bullying experiences;
- the tape and evaluations of drama;
- posters.

Finally, an assembly should be organised by the teacher and children in which the school is informed about the project. The following ideas may be used:

- an overhead transparency defining the word 'bullying';
- a selection of dramas;
- one example of parents' stories;
- a display of posters;
- a demonstration of the contents of the bullying box and information as to where this may be found for further study;
- names of staff who should be approached if help is required by either bullies or victims;
- the national telephone number helpline for those in trouble because of bullying.

NAME

DRAMA EVALUATION

Title of drama

Was this an appropriate title for this particular drama?

Name of producer and actors

Was this a realistic bullying situation? Why?

Were the characters realistic? Why?

Which was the most outstanding moment in the drama? Why?

If you could speak to the bully character(s) what advice would you give?

If you could speak to the victim(s) of this drama what advice would you give?

What sort of person do you think should listen to this drama?

Give one piece of advice to the drama group who produced
this piece to help them improve their composition or performance.

NAME

BULLYING OR NOT?

Ambreen, Bill, Marianne, Pete and Gary are a group of close friends. They usually do things together. One week there was heavy snow, Gary was unable to come to school for three days because his farm house was cut off by deep snow drifts.

At school, the older children were allowed to play in the snow at playtime and the group of friends had planned and begun to build an igloo. By Wednesday afternoon it was half built and the other children were watching the building progress with interest and a little envy. This group of friends always seemed to be able to find really interesting games!

On Thursday, Gary was able to come to school and at playtime he asked to join in with the igloo building. Bill and Ambreen said he couldn't, because:

Bill and Ambreen's arguments	Marianne and Pete's arguments
• They have planned this and Gary doesn't know what is to happen next.	•
• They have worked hard on this and by tomorrow it will be finished and Gary will get to share the glory for their hard work.	•
• This brilliant idea belongs to them and Gary can't just come along and join in at this late date.	•
• This can't be Gary's igloo in any way because he didn't help to plan it.	•
• Gary will probably have all sorts of ideas to change what they have started and that will spoil things for the rest of the group.	•
• Gary can't expect to be off school for three days and then just come back and join in as if he'd never been away.	•

We think Gary should ______________________________

because ______________________________

____

____

NAME

BULLYING QUESTIONNAIRE

1 Was a member of your family ever a victim of a bully? ______

2 How long ago did this take place? ______

3 What age was the member of your family at the time? ______

4 For how long was he or she bullied? ______

5 Was he or she bullied by one person or by a group of people?

______

6 Were the bullies older or younger? ______

7 What form did the bullying take? ______

8 Was the member of your family upset at the time? ______

9 Did he or she tell anyone about being bullied?

______

10 If so, who? ______

11 Why did he or she choose to tell that person?

______

12 Looking back, did they think that they should have told somebody sooner?

______

13 What was the result of telling someone?

______

14 What advice could they give to somebody who is being bullied?

______

15 Any other information that you feel is important.

______

Scholastic WORKSHOP

Chapter Fourteen

SPORT

INTRODUCTION

Project description

In this project, the children work individually, or in pairs, to write about a sport of their choosing. The initial planning and writing is structured to provide the class teacher with clear opportunities to emphasise the importance of asking key questions, structuring the project, identifying suitable research resources and planning the sequence of work. Thereafter, the project activities teach what are essentially generic techniques to help the children use resources, particularly reference books, in a way that reflects their own understanding and purposes.

Each activity is structured so that the children must start with their own ideas and questions. This helps to ensure that they cannot simply copy information from books. The activities involve children in writing:

- a recount of the historical development of a piece of equipment;
- a report on an important individual or organisation;
- a description and explanation of sportswear using annotated diagrams;
- a description and explanation of equipment, using key headings.

The activities are structured so that they may be taught as class lessons with the children applying their individual content issues. They can be tackled in any sequence that best suits the teacher and the class.

The children should obviously be encouraged to apply the same approaches in any subsequent work. The final reviews encourage the children to reflect on what they have learned about both the sport and about how to research and write a personal project.

Why this context?

Writing a personal project is a common school activity and is invaluable for teaching children to pursue individual interests and to work independently. However, left to their own devices, many children resort to copying chunks from books and often do this with minimal understanding. This project offers a structure that will teach children to make clear decisions about the content and purpose of their writing, as well as teaching them strategies to tackle the practicalities of planning, sequencing, structuring, researching and writing different aspects of the project. Sport is a topic of interest to many children. As a generic context it provides a unifying theme for class lessons but allows a degree of individual choice for pupils, enabling them to build on enthusiasms, knowledge and expertise gained outside school.

Project organisation

The personal projects can be planned and written by individuals or by pairs of children working together. The teaching activities have been designed to be carried out with a whole class working individually. Each lesson allows sufficient scope for children who are producing a joint project to work individually on different, but complementary, content issues.

Publication, celebration and review

The projects are published in an A4 book format and are reviewed in groups of four. The celebration and review focuses on both the content and presentation of the project and the processes used to plan and write it. The writers present a short talk on their own project before discussing how helpful or unhelpful they found the planning and writing techniques to which they were introduced.

Teaching content

Research questions must be neither too general nor too specific.

What you need

Writing materials, blank paper on the classroom wall for children to record their chosen sport, and working partner (if appropriate).

What to do

Before beginning the project, decide whether the children are to write their personal projects in pairs, as individuals, or be allowed to choose how to work. Tell the class that they will be doing projects on sport and ask each child or pair to choose the sport on which they will focus. Their choices should be recorded on a list on the classroom wall.

Introduce the lesson by reminding the children that they are going to produce personal research projects about a sport of their choice. Explain that during the project you will be teaching them some new methods and techniques to help them plan, research and write about their chosen sport in a way that is individual and interesting. Explain that many of these methods will prove useful on other occasions, when they will need to produce personal research projects on different topics.

Ask the class if they know what research is and what it may involve. From this discussion, try to build an understanding that research:
- may be carried out on any topic area;
- involves book-based or practical investigations which may take various forms (interviews, surveys, experiments or trials);
- must always be written up because the writing process helps to clarify issues for the researcher and produces a publication to tell others about the topic;
- is always driven by key questions which focus the researchers' efforts.

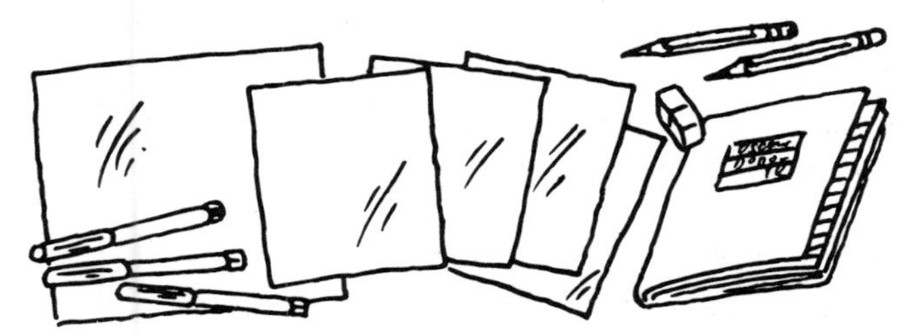

Explain that determining the key questions is one of the hardest aspects of doing research. Some questions are too general or too specific to provide a useful focus and so researchers must learn how to adapt questions that are too specific or too broad.

Take as an example a sport you have just invented called 'Bellyhopping'. Ask the class to suggest some key questions to research about this sport.

Write each question they suggest on the board and discuss it. Point out that a question such as 'What is it?' could involve describing the history, current practice, equipment required, rules, personalities and significance of the sport and so is too general. When children suggest very specific questions, such as 'Do you need a ball to play?' or 'On what date was it first played?', point out that these questions are too small to generate much research as the answers will be short and not terribly interesting on their own.

Use the children's questions to demonstrate how to broaden a narrow question to make a better research focus. So, 'Do you need a ball to play?' might become 'What equipment do you need?' and 'On what date was it first played?' would be 'What is the history of this sport?' If appropriate, explain that smaller questions can sometimes provide a useful checklist later in the research process to ensure that important aspects have been covered.

Recognising appropriate questions is the key to structuring any personal research topic. Children find this one of the hardest aspects of doing a personal project and so it requires solid teaching, with lots of worked examples, explanation and discussion.

When you feel the children have understood the level of question required, and have plenty of examples on the board, ask them to consider which of the questions about 'Bellyhopping' might be adapted to apply to the sports topic they have chosen. They should now choose about six key questions to research, and list these on the paper provided.

If appropriate, ask the children to take the questions home and think up some more specific questions to list under each key question. Tell them that, in doing this, they may explain the task and get help from one other person who lives in their household. If this is not appropriate, allocate about 15 minutes of class time and ask children to brainstorm between six and eight specific questions for each key question.

Teaching content

To learn one strategy for thinking about what the reader may need to know.

What you need

Illustrated books relating to the chosen sports, writing materials, photocopiable page 189 enlarged to A3 size, key questions from Activity 1.

What to do

Organise the class into groups of four and give out one A3 photocopiable sheet per group. Explain that the picture illustrates a sport with which they may not be familiar (lacrosse). Ask the children to look carefully at the picture, think of questions they would like to ask about this sport and write these in the space around the edge. Draw the children's attention to the question words across the top of the picture and explain that these may also help them to think of questions to jot down. Tell the children that they will have about eight to ten minutes for this task and that each group should try to write at least ten questions in this time.

Once they have finished this, call the class together and go around the groups asking each to suggest *one* question.

Explain that this is often a useful way to generate specific questions about a topic which can then be categorised under the appropriate key questions.

Distribute the books to the children as appropriate. Ensure that each child or topic pair has at least one book about their own chosen sport.

Write the seven question words on the board. Explain that they are going to apply exactly the same technique to their own sports topic. Give the children a short time to look through the pictures in the sports book they have been allocated. Explain that they should not attempt to read it, but simply identify two or three pictures that they find interesting. Suggest that they select pictures showing different aspects.

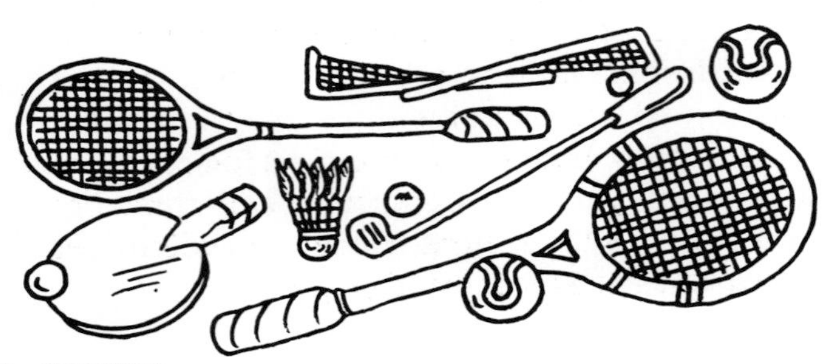

Give out paper to each individual or topic pair. Ask the children to examine the first picture they have chosen carefully and, using the seven question words, generate as many questions as possible, listing these on paper provided. They should then do the same for the second and third pictures they have chosen. If the children are working individually and have found it difficult to generate a range of questions, they could be given time to consult with a friend to increase the number of questions.

Call the class together. Explain that there are many different sorts of questions and ways to find answers to them. List some possible resources and methods of inquiry on the board:

Ways of finding out:
Books in school
Books at home
Books at the public library
Interviewing someone
Writing to experts
Using your personal knowledge
Videos, CD-ROM, Internet
Consulting local experts
Consulting local organisations, interest groups or societies
Consulting national experts, interest groups or societies.

Read through the suggestions with the class. Explain any that you think the children may not understand and briefly discuss the advantages and disadvantages of each. Ask a few children to provide a question from their personal lists and ask the class to suggest the most suitable way to research it. Do this until you are sure the children understand the different inquiry methods and the questions to which they might be applied.

Now ask the children to work on their own lists. Show them how to categorise their specific questions using the six key questions they identified in Activity 1. Each key question should have a list of more specific questions beneath it. Then, ask the children to indicate the most suitable method of inquiry for each question. Once finished, ensure that these sheets are stored in a safe place as they will be needed for the next activity.

Teaching content

Careful planning can make the organisation of a project much more straightforward.

What you need

Blank paper, writing materials,

What to do

Explain that each researcher, or research pair, now needs to make a plan of action to show the sequence in which they will work. Give out the blank paper and ask the children to write the heading 'Jobs to be done'.

Point out that if the children have any questions that require them to write to organisations or people – requesting information, an interview or a meeting – that these letters should be written and sent at an early stage to give the recipient time to respond.

Ask the children to scan their questions and identify any that require such action. Writing these letters should then be listed as the first job under the heading 'Jobs to be done'. Reassure them that you will give them some help in drafting appropriate letters. Then, tell the children that the class will be doing five more short lessons on the following aspects and questions that concern these should constitute the next 'Jobs to be done':

- choice and care of equipment and apparatus;
- historical development of one piece of equipment;
- appropriate clothing;
- spotlight on a hero or key person;
- spotlight on a team or club (local or national).

Explain that these parts of the project will be 'taught' and that the children should tackle the remaining jobs after these lessons. To determine a sensible sequence, tell the children to think carefully about the other aspects they intend to cover and the resources and inquiry methods likely to be involved. Stress that there is no right or wrong order – some people like to tackle either the routine or the difficult sections first, others like to write the sections in sequence, while others prefer to mix book-based research with interviews or with sections that can be written directly from personal knowledge.

End the lesson by explaining that the advantage of creating a plan of action at the start is that it helps to provide direction and add momentum to the work. The children may decide to change their plan of action during the project, and this too is perfectly acceptable.

Tell the children to keep both their plan of action and the A4 sheet of key questions in a safe place. Remind them that they will need to refer to both sheets during the project.

Teaching content

A formal letter needs to introduce the writer and the reason for writing. It needs to ask specific questions, explain why they are important and how the information provided will be used.

What you need

Photocopiable page 190, writing materials, sheet of poster-sized paper, marker pen.

What to do

Begin the activity by asking various children to explain who they need to write to for their personal project, and why. Explain that any sportsperson or organisation (local or international) will receive many letters requesting help and information. These people are usually busy and have many more important demands on their time than answering letters from interested individuals, even if they would love to do so.

Organise the children into pairs and give out the photocopiable sheet. Explain that it was taken from an interview with the Information Officer of a large company, who makes several important points about what makes written inquiries easy to deal with, and therefore more likely to be answered promptly.

Read the photocopiable sheet through with the class. Then, ask them to re-read it in their pairs, this time underlining important points that they should bear in mind when writing their own letters.

After ten minutes call the class together and construct a class list of important things to remember when writing a letter, recording their ideas on the poster-sized paper.

They will probably mention points such as:

- Say who you are and how old you are.
- Explain what you are doing and why you want the information.
- Be polite.
- Check you are writing to the correct person or organisation.
- Ask specific questions, but not too many.
- Make the questions clear.
- Ask the most important questions first.
- Ask them to suggest any other organisations or individuals who might be able to help you.
- Be realistic about how quickly you would like a reply.
- If possible, enclose a stamped addressed envelope.

Explain that this is a useful checklist and they should consider these points when they draft their letters. However, once they have finished their draft, they should again refer to the checklist, taking each point in turn and checking that what they have written meets the requirements of the reader. They should then write it out in a suitable letter format.

Finally, explain that most researchers keep a copy of their letter (either a photocopy or a rough draft) noting at the top when it was sent. This enables them to follow up unanswered letters and to make sense of a response which refers to paragraphs or questions but assumes the writer has a record of the actual content.

Teaching content

It is important to recollect what you know before reading; this helps to structure the writing, ensure it is fresh and original and that the information is linked in a way that represents the understanding and perspective of the writer. Reports are written in an impersonal style and draw on a variety of sources of information.

What you need

'Key questions' sheets from Activity 3, A3 paper, writing materials, adhesive and adhesive tape, a range of information books on the appropriate sport.

What to do

Introduce the activity by explaining that before conducting any research it is important to recollect what the researcher already knows. This will help ensure the children read for meaning and structure their writing.

Give out the A3 paper to each child or pair. Tell the children to write their key questions as a list down the middle of the A3 sheet, leaving space between the questions and a broad border around the edge. Ask them to take each question in turn, read the specific questions and issues associated with it, draw an arrow to a space on the A3 sheet and, in this space, jot down any information they may already know about that particular issue. Emphasise that they are only writing notes to jog their memories at a later date so they do not need to worry too much about grammar or spelling.

Now ask the children to consider the sports reference books they have in front of them. Ask them to take one book and use the index and contents page to look up the sections that may be relevant to the questions in their own project. Next they should skim through the information given in these sections and, if they think the book will be a useful source in dealing with any particular questions, they should record the title and relevant page number(s) beside the appropriate arrow. They might also record the key ideas mentioned. Additional paper could be stuck to the A3 border with adhesive or adhesive tape, if anyone runs out of space.

The children should do this for several reference books, so that, by the end of the activity, they have consulted a good range. At the end of the lesson, explain that this is part of the research process and can be helpful in several ways.

• It allows them to recollect what they know about the various issues. This is always a good start for any project.

• It gives them an opportunity to browse through and skim-read several different sources without the pressure of having to produce a coherent written piece. This gives them a feel for the key facts, for the range and variety of book resources at their disposal and allows them some thinking time to gain an overview and to mull over specific issues before they begin to write.

• The information they gain will inform their future inquiries and ensure that, when they re-read the relevant books to write any particular section, they start from a coherent and comprehensive understanding.

• The sheet provides an at-a-glance record of useful sources to access as they come to each section.

Teaching content

Recounts are written in sequence of time. Speculation helps to ensure the researcher is really reading for meaning by clarifying what is not known.

What you need

A4 paper, writing materials.

What to do

Start the lesson by explaining that, as technology has developed and society has changed, much sporting equipment and clothing has also changed over the years. With the class quickly list examples of equipment or clothing used in the various sports they are studying – perhaps footwear, clothes, balls, rackets or other hand-held implements, flooring, mats or larger floor-based equipment. Ask the children to each select one item connected with their sport that they think may have undergone some modification or change over time.

Explain that you are going to introduce one technique for raising questions and structuring a report. Give out the A4 paper to each child and ask the children to fold it into three sections. In the bottom section ask them to sketch the item in its most modern form and to jot down a short description beside the sketch. Then, ask them to think about what that item could have been like some years ago, and to sketch this in the middle section, again jotting down a brief description to highlight the changes. Finally, ask them to think what the item may have been like when the sport first started and to draw this in the top section, along with a brief description. Do not allow a lot of time for this. Emphasise that speculation rather than accuracy is the object of this activity and stress that the work can be very rough – at this stage, the drawings and written notes are thinking tools rather than finished products.

Many of the children will be unsure of the accuracy of what they have drawn and written and may have left blank spaces. Explain that their job now is to check exactly what changes did happen and the sequence in which they occurred. Ask the class to suggest how they might research this. Depending on the subject matter, they may suggest using reference books, examining old pictures, writing to manufacturers or museums, or telephoning local experts or societies. Agree that these things should be done (possibly as homework tasks) and discuss with the children how best to present the results of their completed research in drawings and writing. Remind them that the finished work will need a short explanatory title.

Explain that, once the facts are known, the children will be able to look back at their first rough sketches and assess the accuracy of their original ideas and what they have learned.

Teaching content

Key questions can help to structure a report and ensure that the information gained from reading is used to serve the writer's purpose.

What you need

Writing materials, sports magazines and books.

What to do

Introduce the lesson by explaining that all sports have famous teams, people and heroes. Many of the children will wish to include details of these key people in their projects.

Point out that, although it is interesting to read about sports people, teams and organisations who are nationally or internationally famous, it can also be interesting to spotlight local sporting heroes, organisers and supporters who are vital in ensuring that their sport or team continues to be successful and enthusiastically supported. It is even possible that tomorrow's famous international player is at this moment playing for a local club.

The children will probably have read articles in magazines which profile influential individuals or teams in the fields of music, sport and fashion. Ask them to describe the different ways in which these articles organise and present the relevant details. The class will also be familiar with the ways in which profiles are reported in the sports reference books they have been using in class and the fan magazines they read at home. If appropriate, suggest making a small display in class illustrating the different ways a profile report on an individual or organisation can be written.

The children are likely to suggest the idea of using questions to structure the report. Explain that many reports, even those which do not explicitly mention questions, may well have used this technique to plan and structure the information-gathering and writing stages.

Ask the children to think of a key person, team or organisation – it may be someone local or internationally famous – and to ask themselves 'What do I really want to know about this person?' Tell them to jot down between five and seven questions they would like to have answered.

Explain that any report should begin by orientating the reader. The opening paragraph needs to explain who or what the report is about and why it is important or interesting. After this, the different issues or topics are dealt with in whatever sequence the writer thinks appropriate. Tell the children to begin by roughly drafting their introductory paragraph, deciding on the best sequence for their questions and leaving a suitable space under each for notes or a first draft of the answer. They should then write, under each question, any facts or information they know that could answer, or partially answer it. Suggest that they use books, magazines, interviews and telephone inquiries to add more details until each question is answered as fully as possible. It may be sensible to suggest they use both home and school time to do this – the fact-finding and note-taking tasks could possibly be set as homework.

Finally, show the children how their notes in response to each question can be reordered and written up to make a coherent piece of text. Explain that they may choose to begin each paragraph with their original question, turn the question into a section heading or simply use it as the basis for the first line of each paragraph.

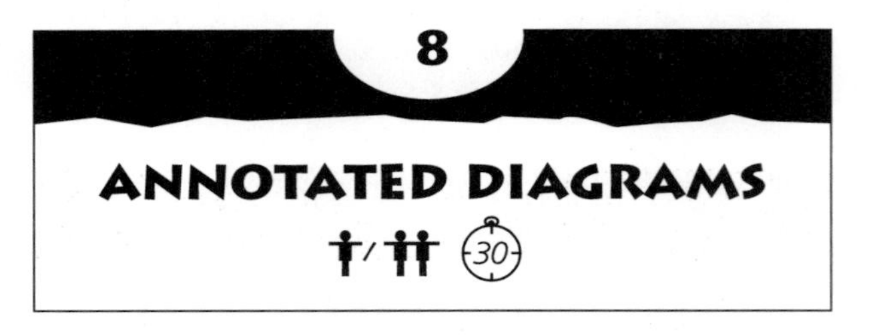

Teaching content

Information can often be presented succinctly in the form of an annotated diagram. The annotations must be short and contain only a few function words; these can be explained and expanded in an accompanying text.

What you need

A4 paper, writing materials, adhesive, reference books.

What to do

Introduce the activity by saying that a key part of many sports is that the players, particularly professional players, wear specific types of clothing. This is often for practical reasons – the sport may require players to move around quickly and easily, keep cool, identify those on the same side or to protect themselves in particular ways.

Explain that one good way to present information about what to wear (and why and how) is in the form of an annotated diagram. A picture of the clothing will provide a clear, image while the annotations can be used to add details about the function of particular items, important aspects of the materials from which they are made and key details concerning their colour or construction.

Give out one sheet of A4 paper to each child or pair. Ask the children to draw a person suitably attired to play their sport in the middle of the sheet, leaving a border at least 6cm wide around the edge. Tell them to make the drawing clear and detailed, using a book if necessary to ensure accuracy. They should then take each item of clothing in turn and name it, writing under the name a short description of the item, why it is worn, what it is made of and why it has been designed in this way. Explain that the writing should be direct and clear, with short sentences, and that any technical terms should be defined.

This can be done directly on to the A4 sheet, but it may be safer to write, initially, on smaller pieces of paper which can be stuck into place and linked to the appropriate item with an arrow. This allows children the opportunity to consider the layout of the annotations and ensures that any mistakes can be reworked.

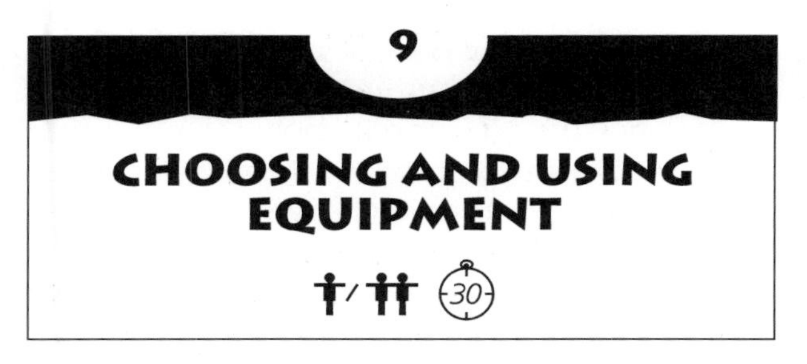

Teaching content

The use of headings and illustrations enables a writer to convey information in a systematic, succinct and clear manner. Any report requires a clear introduction which orientates the reader, explains what it is about and why it is important.

What you need

A4 paper, smaller rectangular and circular pieces of paper, writing materials, adhesive, reference books.

What to do

Introduce the activity by explaining that special equipment is required for most sports. Beginners will therefore need some information and advice about suitable equipment.

Brainstorm with the class the sort of questions that beginners might ask about equipment and list these on the board.

From the questions, ask the children to suggest possible headings, or questions that might be asked by beginners in any sport. For example, although there will be some variation between sports, anyone setting out to buy sports equipment for a sport they have taken up will have concerns about:

- what equipment a beginner will need;
- how to choose this equipment – things to look out for;
- how much it is likely to cost;
- how to take care of the equipment to ensure it lasts and remains in good working order;
- things that should not be bought until a level of proficiency has been reached.

Give out the A4 paper and rectangular and circular pieces of paper. Tell the children to draw one piece of basic equipment for their sport in each of the circles. Then tell them to choose three or four appropriate headings or questions and write these on another appropriately-shaped piece of paper, and then write short explanations or answers to inform a beginner about choosing, using and maintaining each piece of equipment on the rectangular paper provided. Show them how to make the headings even more effective by using capitals or bold lettering, a different typeface, size of print, colour or underlining.

Once this has been done, explain that the entire section will need an appropriate heading, as well as a short introduction of three to four sentences to explain what the section is about and why it is important. Suggest that the children also write this on a separate piece of paper. They can then decide the best sequence for their circular illustrations and written advice about individual items of equipment. These should be stuck in place once the layout on the page looks satisfactory.

Teaching content

Continuing useful planning techniques and advice on using them.

What you need

Photocopiable page 191, writing materials, completed projects, A5 paper.

What to do

Organise the children into groups of four, keeping project pairs together. Explain that, within each group, the children will initially work in pairs to evaluate the project(s) of the other two in the group. Each child should briefly present her project to the rest of the group, introducing the topic and talking through the headings in sequence, but not actually reading the project. Allow about three or four minutes per person for this.

Give out the first half of the photocopiable sheet and a sheet of A5 paper to each child or pair and ask them to consider the list of steps for writing a personal project. Remind them that these describe, broadly, the process they all followed. Tell them to discuss each step in turn and, on the A5 paper, to state:

- how useful, essential or difficult this step is and what it does (or doesn't) contribute to the successful organisation of a personal project;
- any helpful advice or comments they might offer about each step.

Briefly discuss the different experiences and opinions of the children in the class. Finish by suggesting that their written comments should be collated into a booklet of useful advice.

Finally, give out the second half of the photocopiable sheet. Ask each pair to answer the set of questions, writing brief comments on the project(s) produced by the other pair. These should be shared with both the teacher and the authors and then attached to the final page of the project. All the completed projects should be displayed in the class.

Teaching content

Reviewing research techniques.

What you need

Photocopiable page 192, writing materials.

What to do

Remind the children that, during the project, they were introduced to several different strategies for recollecting, planning, organising and writing about different aspects of their chosen sport. Explain that these techniques are generic; they can be applied to a range of topics and could be used in any future projects the children do. It is therefore important that they should reflect on the strategies they found useful in this context, and why.

Organise the children into groups of four and give out one photocopiable sheet to each group. Tell the children to take each technique in turn, describe the context in which they used it and discuss how helpful it was. Finally, ask them to tick the appropriate box. If they cannot agree, as a group, on which box to tick, then individuals should tick and write their name beside the box they consider most appropriate.

Finally, hold a brief class discussion to draw out the different opinions and experiences of the children in the class. Conclude the discussion by suggesting that the usefulness (or otherwise) of any particular strategy may vary – it may depend on the personal knowledge of the writer, the nature of the question or subject matter under consideration or the time available. A technique that has proven particularly useful this time may not always be so. Caution the children against ruling out future use of a particular planning strategy that they found ineffective for this project. Suggest that they will only come to understand the potential of each when they have used them several times in a number of different contexts.

NAME

QUESTIONS ABOUT THIS SPORT

WHO?

WHY?

WHAT?

WHEN?

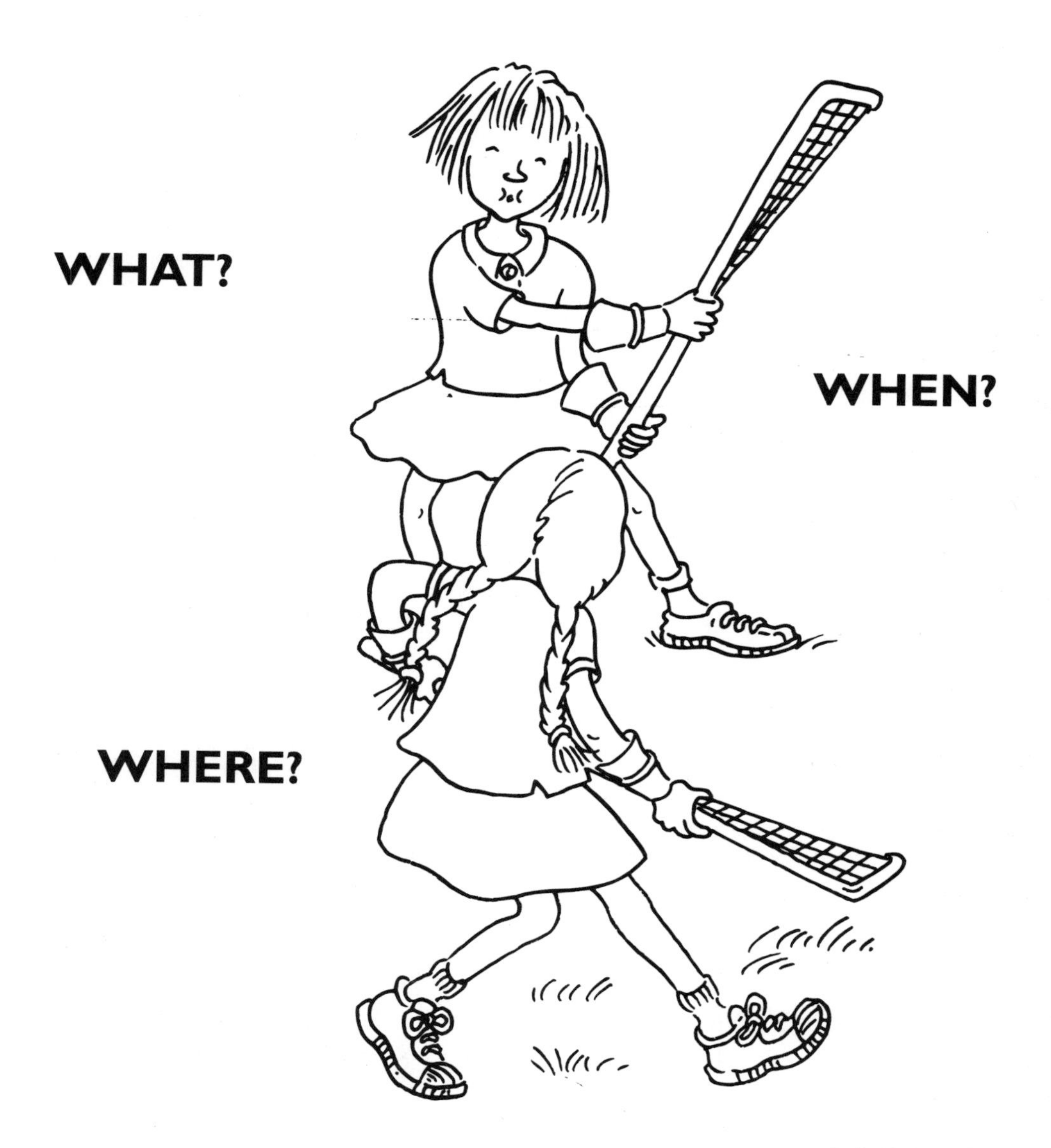

WHERE?

HOW?

WHICH?

NAME

WRITING LETTERS

As an Information Officer, I get lots of letters from children doing projects. Some of them ask a list of simple and clear questions that I can answer quickly, so I do those first. Unless, of course, the list is too long. If it's more than about four questions I think the writer hasn't done enough research so I answer the first four and recommend a book for the rest.

Of course, some people write wanting general information. I can usually help, unless the topic is so wide or vague that I don't know what to focus on. For example, if they say they want to 'know about the woods', well that's no good. I think 'Do they want to know about visiting the woods, about wildlife, about working in forestry...?'

Some children don't bother to tell me who or how old they are or why they want the information. I might have several leaflets on a topic but can't tell which would be most useful. Also, if they explain a bit more about what they're doing and why it sets me thinking and I can often give a bit of additional information they may not have thought of asking for. Of course, you don't want the letters to be too long – I'm a busy person – but I must admit, I try harder if the writer is obviously enthusiastic and genuinely interested in our work.

One thing that makes me quite cross is when they seem to expect a reply almost by return of post. I have lots of other things to do. I don't mind if they set a reasonable date by which they'd like to know. Also, you wouldn't believe how many letters are quite rude and don't bother to say please and thank you. Of course, we do appreciate it if they enclose a stamped addressed envelope for the reply – I hear some organisations now demand this. I do get some letters which I can't answer. The writer hasn't really bothered to check what we do. If they've enclosed a stamped addressed envelope, I usually write back and suggest someone who might be more appropriate to ask. Of course, some letters ask me which other organisations or books might be helpful to them.

NAME

EVALUATING THE PROJECTS

Steps for writing a personal project

Step 1

Brainstorm interesting questions.

Step 2

Organise the questions into categories.

Step 3

Consider the nature of the tasks involved and how long the different aspects will take. Make a plan of action.

Step 4

Start any writing by recalling what you know.

Evaluation questions for projects:

The most interesting part of this project is ______________________

because ______________________

The most effective part of the layout and presentation is ______________________

____

One thing we/I learned from this project was ______________________

____

One other thing we would like to know about this topic is ______________________

____

NAME

EVALUATING THE PLANNING AND WRITING TECHNIQUES

Annotated diagram

Definitely use again ☐

Perhaps use again ☐

Never use again ☐

Backtrack boxes

Definitely use again ☐

Perhaps use again ☐

Never use again ☐

'What I know about' sheet

Definitely use again ☐

Perhaps use again ☐

Never use again ☐

Letter plan

Definitely use again ☐

Perhaps use again ☐

Never use again ☐

Key questions sheet

Definitely use again ☐

Perhaps use again ☐

Never use again ☐

Headings

Definitely use again ☐

Perhaps use again ☐

Never use again ☐